MAY 1940 - WAR OVER HOLLAND

MAY 1940 - WAR OVER HOLLAND

- WINKELMAN'S WITZKRIEG -

Allert M.A. Goossens

ASPEKT PUBLISHERS

MAY 1940 - WAR OVER HOLLAND
© Allert M.A. Goossens
© 2023 Publishing House ASPEKT
Amersfoortsestraat 27, 3769 AD Soesterberg, the Netherlands
info@uitgeverijaspekt.nl-http://www.uitgeverijaspekt.nl

Cover: Lisa Dijkhuizen
Interlining: Aspekt Graphics

ISBN: 9789464629637
NUR: 680

All rights reserved. No part of these pages, either text or image may be used for any purpose other than personal use. Therefore, reproduction, modification, storage in a retrieval system or retransmission, in any form or by any means, electronic, mechanical or otherwise, for reasons other than personal use, is strictly prohibited without prior written permission.

INHOUDSOPGAVE

FOREWORD	7
GLOSSARY	11
PRELUDE TO A STRATEGY	31
THE COLD STRATEGY	57
THE HOT STRATEGY	87
CONCLUSION	119
ENDNOTES	129

FOREWORD

In 2019, the collection "Blitzkrieg under Fire - analysis and facets of a historical debate" (original title: "*Blitzkrieg onder vuur – analyse en facetten van een historisch debat*") was released in Dutch. Included in it were four treatises by as many authors. One of them was "*Winkelmans Witzkrieg*" in which the Netherlands' defence strategy in May 1940 was analysed on the basis of the formation of military plans and preparations as well as the strategy actually pursued during the battle in the May Days of 1940. The publisher and author came to the understanding in the summer of 2022 to publish this particular article as a single title in English. That book has now become a reality and differs from the original 2019 Dutch-language version in that a number of endnotes have been expanded to include international sources of repute, certain matters have been given broader explanations, necessary map material has been added and, in addition, photographs from the author's own collection have been added. For foreign readers, it is important to realise that almost all primary sources logically exist only in Dutch. However, the same also applies to the bulk of the secondary sources, for the simple reason that foreign governments, armed forces, agencies and individuals never saw any use or necessity in carefully studying the formation of Dutch strategy or its implementation during the short war in the Netherlands in May 1940. All attention went south where French and British formations in Belgium and northern France were trying to halt the German war machine. The Netherlands was a side-show that, moreover, laid down its arms very quickly. As a result, the reader searching for scholarly justification of what happened often finds exclusively Dutch sources, mostly to be found in the Hague at the National Archives (NA) or in the archives of the Netherlands Institute for Military History (NIMH). These sources are included with their archive names in endnotes. The same applies to the Parliamentary Enquiry Commission (in Dutch referred to as PEC), which, especially in 1948, conducted numerous interrogations of key players in order to establish the truth about government policy before and during World War II. The narratives of those interrogations are well documented, but only available in Dutch. This language barrier is high for foreign researchers to conduct detailed research on Dutch military policy in May 1940. The aim of this English-language book on this episode is to offer a nuanced but also sharp analysis of this subject to a foreign audience.

The German campaign against France and the Low Countries in May/June 1940 is probably one of the most studied and described episodes of World War II. The same is not true of the strategic choices made by the Netherlands. Hardly any proper detailed study has become known about these, other than the often dutiful tracking and interpretation of original assessments by the post-war general staff. However, there is much reason to look with a critical eye at the political, but especially the military-strategic choices of the Dutch army leadership in the period 1935-1940. The Netherlands turned its self-proclaimed neutral status into a complex of attitudes, behaviours and derivative positioning which, as a doctrine, is best termed 'neutralism'. That neutralism ensured that the military leadership had even less to say than in a democratic country that did not opt for neutrality. Democracy and neutralism together secured a mix of political-administrative policies that severely hampered military personnel and forced them to cope with countless compromises to the detriment of defence. The optimum, the military ultimate, can only be aspired to and achieved with a remote national government. This is the reason par excellence why dictatorships take great military leaps ahead of democracies. Democracy is therefore pre-eminently a peacetime regime, which, however, can be seriously objectionable in times of crisis. This is not a plea for abolishing democracy, but the notion remains a warning from the past that democracy requires quick and decisive adjustment in times of crisis. Countries with wartime experience, such as the UK and France in particular, understood this in the late 1930s and established war cabinets so that parliamentary and administrative rigidity could be reduced. This reality did not materialise in the Netherlands. On the contrary, with Prime Minister

De Geer, a pacifist took office shortly before the mobilisation. This government's meddling in defence was extreme, prompted partly by the fact that the predominantly pacifist government wanted a military man as defence minister to compensate for the otherwise lacking field of military knowledge. It chose the vain and ambitious general staff officer Lieutenant-Colonel Adriaan Dijxhoorn. The latter would subsequently operate in such a dominant and meddlesome manner that he effectively came to function as a shadow commander of the armed forces. His interventions created an unnecessary personal conflict with General Reijnders, who had been in charge of the army for over four years and had been appointed Commander-in-Chief at mobilisation. However, the minister wished to dominate the strategy himself and, through his own actions and manipulation, ensured that Reijnders had to step down so that he could appoint a pawn of his own. That became the dutiful and long-retired General Winkelman, who had previously been known for many qualities but was not highly regarded by anyone as a tactician. Winkelman would work out a curious strategy, divorced from realism and the logistical limitations of the armed forces. In doing so, he would lead the Netherlands into an a priori lost battle on 10 May 1940. He steered completely towards isolation and would turn his back on the allies from the first moment with his operational decisions. Meanwhile, he believed he could expect large-scale support from them and based his strategy on that, while a thorough preliminary reconnaissance in Paris and London could have saved him from this utopia. His strategy thus resembled a macabre joke that, however, no one but the German commanders could laugh at. This book provides an analysis of Winkelman's cold and hot strategy in a concise but justified framework with endnotes. It analyses the lack of logic and rational consideration of strategic decision-making in anticipation of a German invasion and, further on, how the 'hot' strategy was applied during the May Days of 1940.

My thanks go to the expert advisor Lieutenant-Colonel (ret.) Erik Jellema, until recently still actively serving in the Royal Netherlands Army and himself active in military history with a specialty in airborne troops and operations. I would also like to thank former member of parliament and university history lecturer Tobias van Gent, who kindly showed me study material from his library that he had compiled in preparation for his then still-to-be-published book on Minister Dijxhoorn (original title "*De Minister en de Majesteit*", 2022). Thanks also to historian Ruud Bruijns for his graphic support. He designed all general overview and situational maps. Special thanks are due to my historical friend, Jeffery A. Gunsburg. He is an US Army veteran, retired military history university lecturer in the US and Israel, and a specialist on the German conquest of western Europe in May-June 1940, especially from the French perspective. Jeff has published a book and several articles on the subject of value, such as 1979's "*Divided and Conquered: the French High Command and the defeat of the West, 1940*" and 2014's "*La Grande Illusion: Belgian and Dutch strategy facing Germany, 1919-1940*", which is frequently cited in the present book. Jeff and I have many exchanges on this episode and he follows my work critically and constructively. In this, he is irreplaceable and without equal, for which I am very grateful.

Allert M.A. Goossens
December 2022

The author is a Dutch military historian. He has many publications, websites and Dutch-language books to his name relating to the May Days of 1940, in the context of the larger German Westfeldzug of May-June 1940.

GLOSSARY

Dutch key commanders

OLZ   *Opperbevelhebber Land- en Zeestrijdkrachten* (Supreme-Commander of Land- and Sea-Forces). Until the end of January 1940 this had been General I.H. Reijnders, who applied for resignation of his position on January 31st. He was succeeded by General H.G. Winkelman who formally took office on 6 February 1940. The GHQ of the Dutch armed forces was situated in the Hague, Lange Voorhout, close to the seat of the Dutch Government and the Dutch Sovereign, Queen Wilhelmina.

C-of-S   *Chef-staf landmacht* (Chief-of-Staff army). Until the end of January 1940 this had been Maj-Gen N.T. Carstens. He resigned when General Reijnders resigned as the OLZ. He was succeeded by Maj-Gen H.F.M. Baron van Voorst tot Voorst.

CV   *Commandant Veldleger* (Commander Field-Army). Lt-Gen J.J.G. Baron van Voorst tot Voorst, with his HQ in Zeist.

C-VH   *Commandant Vesting-Holland* (Commander Fortress Holland). Lt-Gen J. van Andel, with his HQ in the Hague.

C-Lvd   *Commandant Luchtverdediging* (Commander Air Defences). Lt-Gen. P.W. Best. This branch included the ground-to-air defences, army air force and the aerial observation corps. His HQ was in the Hague.

Dutch defence-lines

Afsluitdijk
Afsluitdijk - Enclosure dike – the 32 km long dam and causeway between the northeast of the Netherlands and the northwest, that connected the land-extremities on either side (Noord-Holland on the west side, Friesland on the east side) but also turning the Zuiderzee – a salt water inlet of the North Sea – into a fresh water lake called IJsselmeer. On the extremities of the Afsluitdijk the Dutch constructed modern and extensive fortifications that not only faced the land-sides but also the sea-side. These fortifications were self-sustaining, contained hundreds of men, numerous light anti-tank and machine-guns and light anti-air defences.

Fortress Holland
Vesting Holland – the outwards defence around the capital north-western part of the Netherlands (provinces Noord- and South-Holland, large part of Utrecht) including the major cities Amsterdam, Utrecht, Rotterdam and the Hague. Its east- and south-front ran roughly from Amsterdam over Utrecht to the south and behind the Meuse-estuary to the coast. Its most forward north-front was on both the extremities of the Afsluitdijk (fortifications at east- and west-extremity) and further inland behind the Noordzeekanaal (North Sea canal between Amsterdam and IJmuiden). The defence of Fortress Holland was led by its own commander and staff, C-VH. He would become subordinate to the CV once the Field Army would have withdrawn onto the east-front of the Fortress. The defence of the Fortress was intended as a last but firm stand to keep the aggressor out and in anticipation of allied assistance.

Grebbe-line	*Grebbelinie* – the main defence-line in the heart of the Netherlands running from the shore of the IJsselmeer via the city of Amersfoort to the river Rhine near Rhenen. The defences strongly leaned on the natural strength of the Gelderse Vallei (Gelder Valley) and the small river Grebbe after which the line was called. It was also referred to as the *Valleistelling* (Valley-line) but that name fell out of use.
IJssel-line	*IJssellinie* – the forward defence-line in the north-eastern part of the Netherlands, north of the Rhine behind the river IJssel until the point where this river flows into the IJsselmeer near Kampen. It was a thin screen of linear defences behind the river with heavy concrete bunkers near bridges and small machine gun casemates in the intermediate sectors.
Maas-line	*Maaslinie* – the forward defence-line in the south-eastern part of the Netherlands, south of the river Rhine, behind the Maas-Waalkanaal (Meuse-and-Waal connecting canal) and the river Maas (Meuse), reaching to the most southern Dutch territory near Maastricht, where it neighboured the strategic Belgian position Eben-Emael. It was a thin screen of linear defences behind the river with heavy concrete bunkers near bridges and small machine gun casemates in the intermediate sectors.
Peel-Raam-line	*Peel-Raamstelling* – the main defence in the south-east of the Netherlands as an extension of the Grebbe-line, extending to the Belgian border near the Dutch city of Weert. It was situated behind a defended anti-tank canal and the southern extremity of the Zuid-Willemsvaart (Zuid-Willems Canal). It was a layered defence with casemates along the forward line and trenches in the deeper layers of the defences. Its

	construction was stopped in April 1940 when Winkelman's strategy was issued.
Orange-line	*Oranjestelling* – a theoretical defensive position between the cities Den Bosch and Tilburg. Also shorter variants straight up from Tilburg to the Meuse river were studied.
Fortification of Amsterdam	*Stelling van Amsterdam* – a 135 km long defensive line of 45 individual fortifications and redoubts around the capital of the Netherlands, constructed during the time-frame 1880-1920. It also incorporated two air-bases, the extended *Artillerie Inrichtingen* complex (Artillery Works – the national defence production and test complex) and large food and resources storages. The entire system was enhanced by water-works that could inundate the front-side of the fortifications as in a scaled Waterline.
Dutch Waterline	*Hollandse Waterlinie* – a system of extended water-based defences (inundations and fortifications) protecting the capital western part of the Netherlands. It was a defensive system first designed and used in extension to the large Dutch rivers, flooding large parts of the country in order to deny an enemy terrain or manoeuvre-space and forcing the enemy into easily defensible corridors. This Dutch Waterline was designed in the 17th century. A new version, the New Dutch Waterline, was developed during the 19th century, shifting the inundations and the arc of defences more to the east, thus including the major city of Utrecht and adding many modern water-works (sluices, pumping stations) and structural improvements. This New Dutch Waterline ran from the IJsselmeer at Muiden in front of Utrecht and Culemborg, east of Gorcum following the Biesbosch area and incorporating

the Meuse estuary (Hollandsch Diep), where it connected to the Haringvliet until its merged with the sea-arms of the North Sea. Its 19th Century east- and south-front would become the east- and south-front of Fortress Holland. The east-front saw only marginal improvements – because construction was halted during the winter of 1939/1940. The south-front was improved by the construction of many small concrete and steel casemates by May 1940. Further improvements were foreseen in the second half of 1940 and 1941.

Dutch armed forces in general

Armed forces

The Dutch armed forces in the Netherlands comprised around 280,000 activated men in uniform in the army (including training depots, coastal- and ground-to-air-defences and the army air force) and an additional few thousand in the navy units stationed in the homeland. There was no independent air force. The army and fleet both incorporated an aviation component. The Commander-in-Chief (OLZ) commanded the entire army, air-component and navy forces in the home waters. The Dutch armed forces were of mediocre quality, small in comparison to the territorial demands and its armament was a mix of modern and older weapons and equipment. Its organisation was quite comparable to German units. The army had no tanks and was short of an adequate number of modern armoured cars. The artillery was relatively modest in number but technically capable. The Dutch engineers were traditionally well educated and equipped and very capable in the water-rich country. Ground-to-air defences were quite modern and adequate in number, though lacking an ample ammunition supply. The army was under strength when it came to command & control facilities and skills, staff officers, professional field officers and modern tactics and practises. The Dutch army was still very much an officer army; the NCO-role was poorly developed and modest, not to the scale and importance of its German peers. Its GHQ was in the centre of the Hague, but its most important HQ were of the Commander of the Fortress-Holland in the east of the Hague and the HQ of the Commander of the Field Army (CV) in Zeist. The Dutch also had considerable armed forces in the Dutch East-Indies (current Indonesia), known as the *Koninklijk Nederlandsch-Indisch Leger* or KNIL (Royal Dutch East-Indies Army) and a large navy component, which mainly operated from the best equipped navy base of entire south-eastern Asia in those days, Surabaya – on the island of Java. The armed forces representation in the Western colonies of the Netherlands (the Dutch Antilles and Surinam) was no more than a couple of hundreds soldiers and marines. All these colonial elements resorted under their own commands and jurisdiction and remain out of the scope of this book.

Casemate	*Kazemat* – Dutch equivalent for constructions similar to those addressed with terms like 'bunker', 'blockhouse' or 'pillbox'.
7-Veld	The Dutch armed forces coded their weapon-systems with practical abbreviations. Field-artillery was available in field-guns (*Veld*) and preceded by the calibre in cm. The same was applicable to fortress guns of steel (*Lang Staal*) and howitzers. A 5,7 cm field gun was referred to as a

Field Army

'6-Veld', a 7,5 cm field gun as a '7-Veld'. The 12,5 cm steel fortification guns were designated as 12-*Lang-Staal*, and so forth. *Vickers, Krupp* and *Bofors* were the original suppliers of Dutch artillery equipment for the army.

Veldleger – the Netherlands had divided its armed forces in a number of subsidiary commands. The most formidable of those was the Field Army, which contained the bulk of the fighting elements (and support formations) of the armed forces and accounted for more than half of the able formations. Its formations mainly contained active soldiers and younger reserve personnel. The Field Army was organised in brigades (each comprising two regiments and an artillery component), divisions (each comprising three infantry regiments and one artillery regiment) and army corps (each comprising two infantry divisions and support troops) as the biggest tactical units. Its main forces formed four army corps, the *Lichte Divisie*, the *Peel Divisie*, three Brigades (A, B en G) and six regiments of hussar cavalry. It was commanded by the CV (*Commandant Veldleger*). It also had a dedicated Field Army component of the Military Aviation, which would, however, be detached from the CV's command on 10 May 1940 and be attached to the C-VH. Most of the remainder of the formations of the armed forces were concentrated in the *Vestingleger*, the Fortress Army. Other significant subsidiary commands of the armed forces besides the *Veldleger* and *Vestingleger* were the *Kustartillerie* (Coastal Artillery Corps), *Korps Luchtdoelartillerie* (Air-Artillery Corps), the *Militaire Luchtvaartafdeling* (Military Aviation Department) and the quite extended training and intendant depots.

Fortress Army	*Vestingleger* – the Fortress Army was concentrated in Fortress Holland and commanded by the C-VH. It was organized in battalions (each comprising three riflemen companies and a heavy machinegun company) and regiments (each comprising three infantry or artillery battalions) as its biggest tactical units. The formations of the Fortress Army were mostly filled with reservists, slightly lesser armed and had an absent or poor motorisation. It comprised mostly infantry and possessed mostly relatively old and largely fixed or horse-drawn artillery. Most units were attached to fortifications and permanent field-positions along the outer defences of Fortress Holland. Others occupied coastal defences or air-base security forces.
GS-III	*Generale Staf Sectie III* – the general staff, section III. This bureau was the military intelligence section of the armed forces, sub-divided in specialised trades such as IIIA (foreign intelligence), IIIB (homeland security) and IIIC (counter-intelligence). The Dutch military intelligence services were modest in size and ambition and highly dependant on foreign services, military attaches and procured services from individuals or private services such as the mighty Philips corporate intelligence service that was reputed for owning the largest databank of communists in western Europe of the pre-war period. GS-III was housed in a building on the Lange Voorhout, near the GHQ, and it was commanded by Lt-Gen H.A.C. Fabius. Section-IIIA was commanded by Major J.G. van de Plassche.
Light Division	*Lichte Divisie* – the (only) Dutch manoeuvre division. It was entirely composed of mobile formations and operationally self-sufficient by attachment of support-formations, pioneers and

engineers. It was intended as an interdiction and manoeuvre unit. The division was structured to be able to form two mature sub-manoeuvre formations (battle-groups), each composed of a full regiment with three battalions of mobile infantry, a small regiment of motor-hussars, motorized MG's and mortars, a motorized anti-tank company, an artillery battalion, an armoured car squadron of 12 off *Landsverk* L180/L181 wheeled AFV's and technical support troops. The division had an operational staff that could be split up in two full-scale battle-staff components to command each of the two battle groups independently.

Peel Division

Peeldivisie – this formation was not a genuine division in organisation and structure but in name, yet it was much more than that in force quantity. It was considered to be part of the Field Army. In initial stages of the mobilisation (April 1939) it had been composed of only the activated formations that pre-occupied the Peel region in the southeast of the Netherlands (hence the 'Peel Division'). Its duties were secretly expanded under General Winkelman so that on May 10th 1940 its formations had more than doubled and the division-command comprised no less than 23 individual battalions of infantry and one battalion of older 8 cm field-artillery for stationary support in the Peel-Raam-line. It had a fixed position in the south-east of the country's defences and its territory was sub-divided in five sectors (from north to south), each containing roughly one-and-a-half regiment of infantry and some support and each stretching from the border with Germany until a designated sector in the Peel-Raam-line. It lacked a genuine division structure, a regular division staff and much of

	the division support formations. This voluminous formation was commanded by Colonel L.J. Schmidt.
Border battalion	In 1936 the army had created so called '*Grensbataljons*' (GB; border battalions); infantry battalions intended for border securing duties. Every infantry regiment of the peace-army formation (22 numbered regiments and two named Guards regiments '*Jagers*' and '*Grenadiers*') delivered one such a GB, hence 24 battalions in total. They usually were formed from younger draftees and professional officers and NCO's, were well equipped, often reinforced with a battery of modern antitank guns and envisaged to be used for deployment along the borders and outer defences (IJssel-line and Maas-line) of the country, hence the 'border' prefix to their name.
Royal Navy	*Koninklijke Marine* – the (Netherlands) Royal Navy operated a significant fleet, a quite strong fleet-air-arm and a marine corps (*Korps Mariniers*). The *Koninklijke Marine* was the eighth navy in the world. It was composed of two major commands (and a couple of smaller local commands) of which the biggest was situated in the Dutch East-Indies (Surabaya) where the heaviest units (3 cruisers and 8 destroyers, numerous smaller units) and the majority of the sub-marine fleet (14 sub-marines) of the navy were stationed along with most of the fleet-air-arm (*Marine Luchtvaart Dienst*, MLD in short) comprising more than 80 flying-boats. The second largest component was the homeland command which consisted of the home fleet that had a couple of larger units but mostly coastal gun-boats and smaller units, and a couple of older sub-marines as well as s number of ships under construction. For patrol duties there was

	also a MLD component stationed in the homeland but largely equipped with older type of flying-boats. The Marines Corps – which was an all-professional maritime fighting force of high standard – had about 1,000 men stationed in the homeland, most of which were in Amsterdam, Rotterdam and Flushing. The about a battalion strong Marines complement stationed in Rotterdam and the Hook of Holland would play a major role in the battle of Rotterdam. The OLZ was Supreme Commander of the Dutch navy forces in the homeland and home waters.
Strategic Security	*Strategische Beveiliging* (SB) – the complex of measures, fortifications and mobilisation directives developed in 1935/1936 to protect the Netherlands against a strategic surprise attack by the German army 'out from its barracks'; in other words, without a prior mobilisation and concentration of troops. The SB included construction of heavy concrete bunkers on the west-side of the Meuse- and IJssel-rivers near all the bridges, the permanent stationing of Police Troops (*Politietroepen* – a professional corps of security troops wearing the green of the army) elements at these strategic positions and a pre-mobilisation scheme for a quick mobilisation of around 30,000 - 50,000 men to secure the border-regions and Meuse- en IJssel-lines, facilitating a more or less protected general mobilisation in the hinterland.

French armed forces

Entente	The Anglo-French alliance is referred to as Entente. With the German invasion of the Low Countries and France on 10 May 1940 the in-

vaded countries Luxembourg, Belgium and the Netherlands would become allies of the Entente as had Poland since March 1939, Denmark and Norway since April 1940.

GQG — *Grand Quartier Général* – the French General Head Quarters in 1939/1940. The French high command was divided into three bodies. The French Supreme Commander was General Maurice Gustave Gamelin, who remained in office until his resignation on May 19th, 1940 after which he was succeeded by Weygand. Gamelin and his staff resided in the Vincennes castle on the eastern flank of the city Paris. General Georges commanded the entire north-eastern theatre of operations and had his large HQ a little more to the east, at La Ferte-sous-Jouarre, east of Paris. The actual commander of the GQG was General Doumenc who served both Gamelin and Georges. His HQ was situated exactly in between that of Gamelin and Georges, in Montry a suburb on the eastern side of Paris.

French 7th Army — This Army under General Giraud had initially been formed as a strategic reserve, in May 1940 pre-positioned in the Pas-de-Calais in France, able to interdict in the lower half of the north-eastern front that stretched from the Dyle-river in the north-western region of Belgium to Metz in the north-eastern border area in France where the Maginotline – the famous French fortification line – commenced. Shortly before the German invasion, 7th Army became part of a dominance game between Gamelin and his direct subordinate, General Alphonse Georges, who commanded the armed forces in the north-eastern theatre of operations. Gamelin wanted the 7th Army to become the most northern asset in a bold strategic move to extend the

French disposition to the Dutch Meuse region near Breda, whereas Georges was much opposed to that plan, assessed it too risky and insisted on maintaining a ready and adequate fast reserve to the rear of the front in Belgium and the north of France. Gamelin won and thus 7th Army became the pivotal force behind the 'Hypothese Breda' – the GQG's strategy for a deployment of allied forces from Breda to Metz. The 7th Army did get a substantial reinforcement of which the strong mechanized division 1.DLM was the most prominent. On May 10th 1940 the Army consisted of two motorised infantry divisions (9.DIM and 25.DIM), two regular infantry divisions (4.DI and 21.DI), the mechanized division 1.DLM, two additional battalions with 90 *Renault* R-35 infantry tanks and a regular division of the reserves for the coastal defence between the Dutch sector of Walcheren and the north-western coast-line of Belgian (60.DI). Most of these units were organised in the 1st and 16th Army Corps.

DLM *Division Légère Méchanique* – Light Mechanized Division. These very capable units were entirely motorised or mechanized, hence referred to as a 'light' division. In fact they were the most capable fighting units of the entire French armed forces and on paper more capable than the average German *Panzer Division*. These divisions were composed of an armoured recce-regiment (45 off armoured cars and motorized hussars), a heavy armoured brigade (90 off *Hotchkiss* H-35 light tanks and 90 off *Somua* S-35 medium tanks) and a light armoured brigade (70 off *Renault* AMR-35 light tanks). Motorised infantry and artillery complemented both brigades. The French had three of these DLM's active in May

	1940 and a fourth under construction. These divisions represented tremendous fire power and considerably more operational value than French tank divisions. The 2nd and 3rd DLM were combined in the French *Corps-de-Cavalry* under General Prioux and designated to (forward) defend the plains around Gembloux in the heart of Belgium. The 1st was attached to the 7th Army, the 4th was in France in the process of build-up when war broke out.
GRDI/GRCA	*Groupe de Reconnaissance de Division d'Infanterie / de Corps d'Armee* – Reconnaissance Group of an Infantry Division / Army Corps. Mobile unit of about a battalion strength, usually composed of a couple of squadrons mobile infantry and motorised or armoured recce vehicles. Of these, two were designated as independent tactical reconnaissance formations in the Netherlands, 2.GRDI (of 9.DIM) under Colonel De Beauchesne and 2.GRCA (of 1st Army Corps) under Lieutenant-Colonel Lestoquoi.

Photo 1: Bofors 10-veld gun (10,5 cm)

Photo 2: Krupp 7-veld gun (7,5 cm)

Photo 3: Typical blockhouse as a strategic bridge defence used along the Meuse and IJssel rivers.

Photo 4: Maas-Waal-canal defences – a Dutch MG-casemate

Photo 5: German 9.Pz.Div crossing the Willemsbrug in Rotterdam

*Photo 6: Immobilized French Panhard P-178 (M17587)
of 6.RC in Etten, west of Breda*

Photo 7: The crucial bridges in Rotterdam

Photo 8: the traffic bridge at Moerdijk

PRELUDE TO A STRATEGY

In this chapter, the cold and hot strategy[1] of the Dutch Supreme Commander, General Henri Gerard Winkelman – who took up his post in January 1940 and who led the Dutch armed forces in May of that year – will be examined. Very tantalisingly put, the question to be answered is 'how, against a German *Blitzkrieg*, during the preceding *Sitzkrieg* the Dutch strategic choices degenerated into a *Witzkrieg*[2]'. In answering the question, extensive use is made of source references[3].

The relatively short length of this treatise on Winkelman's strategy does not allow for a broad and deep discussion of all the introductory aspects and therefore a considerable amount of prior knowledge is assumed by the reader. Nevertheless, it is important to consider the circumstances and events that tempted General Winkelman to choose a strategy that would have resulted in defeat in all realistically conceivable scenarios. Winkelman had explicitly failed to take into account the limitations that followed from the *Grand Strategy*[4] behind his strategic choices. This is a weighty conclusion and it requires a good foundation. It is important to outline the international position of the Netherlands and to consider the state and status of the Dutch armed forces. From this background it follows what '*Grand Strategy*' could best serve the Netherlands. An additional factor was the change of army command during the *Sitzkrieg*. This was a symptom of ambivalent administrative thinking and acting, but in reality did not improve the development of strategy and resulted in an uncompensated loss of expertise and time as a new leadership took charge. It did, however, provide political peace of mind. A vain Minister of Defence and an administrator in uniform found each other and patched things up resulting in an unrealistic cold strategy followed during the May Days of 1940 by hot strategic policy that, under the most favourable assessment, should be labelled as 'weak'[5]. Against the German *Blitzkrieg* that poured out over continental Europe, stood Winkelman's '*Witzkrieg*'.

The Netherlands and its neighbours

The Netherlands, as a nation within Europe during the course of the 19th and the first decades of the 20th century, had positioned itself in an introverted manner[6]. Economically, the Netherlands was a self-centred country, although its exports increased after the First World War. The powerful colony of the Dutch East Indies now brought in money again. The wealth of raw materials in the colony gave the Netherlands the opportunity to lock itself up within its own empire and to be rather cautious in many international processes. Moreover, the events leading up to the Belgian independence in 1830-1839 created a poor relationship with its southern neighbours. The country's defence suffered greatly from the enormous costs incurred since 1830 and the long mobilisation because of the Belgian revolt. During this period the Netherlands lagged far behind industrially and was poorly developed in terms of infrastructure. Although considerable investments were later made to modernise industry, infrastructure and society, the Netherlands was not at the forefront of Europe. The armed forces were and remained small, and in the second half of the 19th century they were confronted with one weapon revolution after another as a result of rapid technological changes, so that the small armed forces had to reinvest quickly in order not to fall behind again[7]. The artillery saw rapid technological changes, changing the entire arsenal. Muzzle-loaders became breech-loaders, iron to bronze artillery, smoothbore to rifled tubes, the revolution of breech-blocks and finally, around the turn of the century and for some time afterwards, the transition to better steel alloys. Fortifications then had to be modernised, because the new artillery not only increased its range, but also gained penetrating power and force. From earthen walls to concrete, then reinforced concrete and armoured steel. The massive investments required by the new fortifications of the coast, the Dutch Waterline and the Fortifications of Amsterdam were budget-consuming. All this without any enemy ever showing up, which dampened the enthusiasm for defence investments. After all, the Netherlands managed to remain neutral during the European crises between 1839 and 1939. Even when major wars such as the Franco-Prussian War (1870-1871) and especially the Great War (1914-1918) arose. On the eve of both those wars, the armed forces and the national defence had been weak[8]. Despite this, the Netherlands did not become directly involved in these conflicts[9]. This gave hope for the future. Apparently we did not need such an extensive investment in defence in order to remain neutral after all[10], an opinion that was widely shared in a nation that traditionally did not like to invest in its defence, although this met with resistance from many experts[11]. It is a dynamic that is still relevant today. The British intervention in South Africa (the Boer War) and the understandable Dutch moral commitment to the British's opponents (the Boers who were of Dutch ancestry) further aggravated the already frail Dutch-British relationship. Relations with our western and southern neighbours had thus become poor. However, Germany, which since 1871 had become a united eastern neighbour in the form of the German empire[12], pulled the Netherlands into a period of economic growth that was very much needed. The Netherlands even came out of its isolation to the extent that it actively participated in processes to promote international law and peace. In connection with the intended neutrality, this led to a number of conventions in the Hague and to the establishment of the Peace Palace in the 'City of Residence' for neutral administration of international law. Meanwhile, the orientation towards Germany became stronger and stronger. This was not only due to the general negative feelings towards the Belgians and the British, but the economic interaction between the Netherlands and Germany became intensive, mainly due to the expansion of the port of Rotterdam as the entrepot of German trade and cultural conditions that the two countries shared. However, the Netherlands had a large trade deficit[13]. At the beginning of the 20th century, Germany accounted for approximately half of our country's exports and almost a third of our imports. In those days, by the way, there were still large imports of wood and grain from Scandinavia; the Netherlands could hardly provide for its own food supply. These were issues that, naturally, also featured prominently in political discourse. In this period, the Netherlands also necessarily invested in its defence. At the end of the 19th century the small arms had already been replaced, and at the beginning of the 20th century new artillery was acquired on a large scale and machine guns were purchased. The fleet required reinvestment and so did the fortifications. The enlistments were increased and a cadre militia army was chosen. Shortly before the impending World War, the periods of basic military training were considerably extended, the need for an army air force recognised. The aircraft gradually made its appearance and thus increased the need for investment in the armed forces[14]. In 1914, before the outbreak of the war, the Netherlands was on good terms with Germany, but was at a cool distance from Belgium and the United Kingdom, likewise with France.

Following the re-ordering of Europe after the World War, the Netherlands was surprised by claims to territory from Belgium. These concerned the territory of Dutch Flanders (Zeeuws-Vlaanderen, on the south-western borders with Belgium) and the south of the province Limburg (Zuid-Limburg, the appendix on the south-eastern border with Belgium). During the preparations for the Treaty of Versailles, Belgium had submitted this claim to the Entente and - bizarrely enough - the Netherlands as a neutral nation was summoned to put up a defence against the Entente. Although Belgium would not get its way, the Netherlands was forced to improve access to and from the sea to Belgian waterways. The Netherlands reluctantly gave in, but seriously delayed the measures. Relations with Belgium became very cool as a result. The Netherlands felt betrayed, all the more so because during the war it had offered safe accommodation to approximately one million Belgian refugees[15]. The Belgian action - which was understandable from the point of view of the national strategic interest of the southern neighbour[16] - led to conservative upheavals in the Netherlands, from which many a national-socialistic party emerged[17]. Not least was the NSB (*Nationaal-Socialistische Beweging* – National-Socialist Movement), whose founder, as chief engineer of the water works at the time, was fiercely opposed to the opening up of Belgian waterways. The affair made relations with Belgium very cool, while the Belgians in turn still held a grudge against the Dutch. It will be shown that both parties showed little understanding for each other in

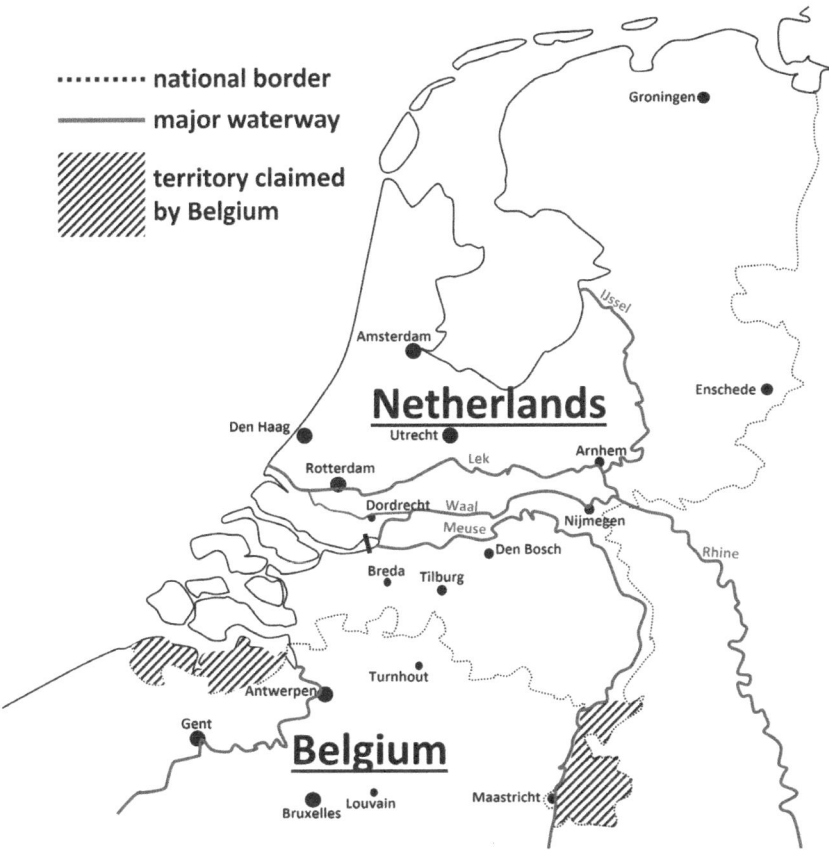

Map 1: General map of the Netherlands 1914-1920

the second phase of the interbellum, during which the Belgians kept a closer eye on the question of security against a German threat than the Dutch[18]. The relationship with the French was not cordial either, but from a military point of view, the French - partly thanks to their own good marketing - were seen as victors of the First World War. The Dutch General Staff showed itself on the former battlefields and adopted much French doctrine. Talented officers with an HKS education[19], both from the army and - remarkably - the navy[20], were sent to French staff schools. The Netherlands kept many army traditions from the French era[21], but by the second half of the 19th century had shifted more towards German doctrine and weapon systems. After the First World War, the revised field regulations and customs were to be based on French principles again[22]. Of course a Dutch sauce was poured over everything so that coherence and quality were largely lost. It was important that the armed forces of the Low Countries, based on the French model, used the 'command principle' ("*Befehlstaktik*"); the principle of centralized directives from above. A hierarchical method of command in which lower ranks were drilled and deployed. This was an archaic method of command, which in fact had lost all its authority and value by the 19th century. However, it was maintained in order to command large but poorly trained mobilizable militias with small professional cores. These militias, it was thought, could only be trained in execution, not in independent tactical manoeuvre. The Germans proved as early as 1914-1918 that this could be done more effectively, but in the period 1939-1945 they would systematically get more performance out of their units by applying the principle, that would become known as 'mission command' (or in German, "*Auftragstaktik*") under which low-ranking leaders did have freedom of action. In this way, the momentum was maintained on the battlefield and opportunities were seized.

From the outbreak of hostilities between Germany and the Allies in September 1939 the Netherlands maintained contacts with other neutral countries, but not intensively and rarely on its own initiative. Except for some economic agreements - such as securing bank gold and the Dutch merchant fleet in foreign ports - the Netherlands kept to its neutrality requirements. By doing so, it further jeopardised the already lukewarm relations with the surrounding countries. Moreover, the Netherlands did not appear to be anti-German in its stance, although one could not objectively call the Dutch army, which in September 1939 had concentrated heavily in the East facing Germany, strictly neutral. The Entente, however, was not convinced of the Dutch loyalty to the 'good' cause and took all scenarios into account, including a possible unsolicited German occupation of parts of the country[23]. The fact that the Netherlands, even after the Polish capitulation, continued to refuse all coordination with the Entente and Belgium, reinforced the Entente's uncertainty as to whether the Netherlands would join the right camp. Winkelman's policy would certainly not have a positive influence on the images held in London and Paris. The Netherlands was not prepared to lift a finger.

The Germans, in turn, did not trust the Dutch either. The German intelligence service had observed Dutch officers abroad and foreign officers in the Netherlands. Moreover, they were convinced that the Netherlands would join the Entente side, or would not (or could not) resist an aggressive occupation of its territory by troops from those countries. The German army staff was also convinced that at least the south of the Netherlands was necessary for an attack on the West, so that the only question before the German command was whether or not to conquer the entire country or only the part below the river Meuse. The Netherlands, for its part, was extremely prudent in its dealings with the Germans and, by the standards of what a neutral power should resist, endured many provocations. The Netherlands witnessed many infringements by German military airplanes of restricted Dutch air space, and quite a considerable number of German spies were caught as well as a couple of intelligence-games acknowledged. The Dutch reacted composed or with silent diplomacy. As a result, the other countries suspected the Netherlands of secret German sympathy. However, the Germans felt that the Netherlands did not take sufficient action against RAF penetrations of airspace[24]. Administratively, the Netherlands was lenient towards the Germans and considered that no reason should be given to provoke an invasion. But in the end things went wrong and the British and Dutch intelligence services blatantly fell into the trap of a German spy game. The Germans needed a *casus belli* to justify an attack on the Netherlands in terms of international law. The SS (*Schutz Staffel*) was prepared to supply this case and, via the SD (*Sicherheitsdienst*), set up a game in which the Dutch and British secret services were jointly lured into a trap[25]. A contact was made in which the British service was told that a high-ranking German officer was prepared to participate in a conspiracy against Hitler. After some probing, an appointment was made. At the cafeteria Backus next to the border post near Venlo, on Dutch territory, a meeting between both sides would take place[26]. During the discussion - that took place on the night of 9 November 1939 - the British Major Stevens and Captain Best and the Dutch Lieutenant Klop were surprised by an SD-commando and GS-III Lieutenant

Klop was killed in the ensuing firefight. Both British officers were taken prisoner. Klop's remains were taken onto German territory and would later be buried in an unmarked grave, never to be re-found after the war. This rather clumsy action from the British side led to the fact that the Netherlands, after the case had been made public by the Germans, was hard-pressed to explain its actions[27]. Meanwhile, the Germans had set a date of 12 November 1939 for their attack. This was eventually postponed, later cancelled. It would not be until six months later that they would cross the border. If the invasion had taken place on 12 November, as was intended at the time, the Venlo incident, like the Gleiwitz incident, would have served as the *casus belli*[28]. After the shocking incident, the Netherlands replaced the head of GS-III, Major-General J.W. van Oorschot[29] and re-activated Lieutenant-General H.A.C. Fabius to become the new head of the service[30].

The fact that the Netherlands did not have a good image among the allies, that it was not trusted in principle and that there were doubts whether the Netherlands would resist a German attack, became clear in January 1940. On 10 January, a German Bf-108 liaison aircraft made an emergency landing near Mechelen on the Meuse in Belgium. It had two *Luftwaffe* Majors on board of which one was the liaison officer of the staff of *Generalleutnant* Kurt Student[31]. He had been on his way to a staff meeting in Köln to discuss the then current scenario of a German airborne landing. Because of the bad weather, a friend from the *Luftwaffe* offered to fly him there. This was done, but the two got lost in the white landscape, which had lost many landmarks due to snow and frost, and force-landed on the Belgian side of the border. By the time they realised that, it was too late. Only part of the plans could be burned. The plans were mainly for *Luftflotte* 2 but contained all kinds of instructions and directions[32]. They included aspects of then planned operations in Belgium and the south of the Netherlands, especially instructions concerning the then planned airborne operation behind the Meuse in Belgium[33]. The Belgians captured the papers and quickly established that they were - in all likelihood - genuine. On 11 January the French GQG was informed and so was the British General Gort.

They then received the complete contents of the documents[34]. The Netherlands did not receive any direct information, but received an impression containing few details that was transmitted via the military attaché to the Hague[35]. Belgium was not prepared to share the documents with the Netherlands, because they did not trust the Dutch sufficiently[36]. Moreover, the Netherlands reacted with remarkable optimism to the scale of the issue[37]. The Entente was not unanimous about the authenticity of the German papers, but they welcomed the opportunity to bring onboard the Low Countries once more. Without success. The Low Countries held on to the neutral status. Troop movements and communications were eagerly observed and deciphered by the Germans. This yielded a wealth of information and the Belgian Chief-of-Staff Van den Bergen would lose his job[38]. Hitler turned the same issue into an opportunity by ordering his OKH to design an entirely new plan. This was to make the German approach to the invasion a surprising one. That thoroughly revised plan would eventually come to fruition in May 1940. Thus, the "Mechelen-on-the-Meuse issue" had become a remarkable pivotal point.

In its relations with its neighbours, the Netherlands adopted an uncompromising and often unrealistic attitude. The only country with which relations were felt to be strong, certainly economically speaking, was in reality planning to invade the Netherlands. The Dutch General Staff was divided about Germany's intentions, although the majority of senior members did believe that Germany was ultimately the only aggressor to be taken into account. Moreover, an important part of the General Staff was concerned that the government was so rabidly opposed to any form of consultation with other countries. On the other hand, the leading class of officers did not like the 'propositions' of the French and Belgians concerning the common defence. Thus, the Netherlands manoeuvred itself into a position where it was not only in check, but also allowed itself very few options to get out of it.

The Grand Strategy

Grand Strategy defines the set of conditions and means that determines for a state what is strategically possible. This goes well beyond what an armed force can offer in material terms, although this obviously determines much of its value. It also includes geographical conditions, economic, logistic and social elements, political and international relations, legal frameworks and all these in conjunction. These elements also have the extra dimension of the (potential) opponent and his probable *Grand Strategy*. It is about opportunities, but especially about limitations and restrictions. The defensive or offensive strategy of a country is derived from its *Grand Strategy*. The Netherlands did not do this enough under General Winkelman. It is remarkable that no credible analysis of this can be found in historical reviews, while it seems to indicate a fundamental failure of the military leadership in those days. The insufficient testing of the defence plans against the possibilities and limitations of the *Grand Strategy* had to do with the lack of modern insights or the lack of operational and tactical skills that the army obviously had after one hundred years of peace. Here the issue of lack of fundamental qualities in the army leadership - but also the government and Monarch - seems to have played an emphatic role. These are fundamental qualities, because one may expect from a Commander-in-Chief and his operational right-hand man that the *Grand Strategy* determines the palette with which to paint.

In the early 1930s, the Dutch armed forces were in poor condition. They had been neglected, but above all they had been eroded from within by a General Staff that was far removed from reality and more concerned with its own dynamics than with the heart of the matter in a militia army: the proper training of the militia and its leaders. Materially, the armed forces were also in poor condition, but while this is important, material elements rarely prevail unless the imbalance becomes great or grotesque. The Finns would resist the Russians very convincingly in the Winter War (1939/1940) and make the attackers pay a huge price for the defeat of Finland. Even today, the effective defence by Ukraine against invading Russia speaks volumes. These Finnish and Ukrainian achievements would have been unlikely on the basis of a quantitative assessment of the mutual material balance. What matters most, however, is what an army does with its resources. From a material point of view, it is of course essential for the military to have ammunition. At the time of the general mobilisation in August 1939, the Dutch armed forces had very little ammunition[39]. For many weapon systems, there was only a fraction of what was considered necessary for warfare. Although this had been determined earlier, by 10 May 1940 the need was far from being met. On the contrary, the production had fallen seriously short of expectations, and practice and training of the mobilised armed forces and the large armies of 1939 and 1940 had cost ammunition[40]. No less than 150 Dutch companies were involved - under the auspices of the *Artillerie Inrichtingen* (AI) - in the rearmament and re-equipment of the armed forces and the production of ammunition[41]. However, much of the ammunition was still produced by the AI itself. Raw materials were scarce, especially copper, bronze and nickel[42]. The stock of raw materials was reasonable, but despite the fact that the finished ammunition stock was not overflowing, the AI did not work extra shifts. As far as can be ascertained, there was no indication or instruction from the Hague to speed up ammunition production. It was not possible to work shifts during the dark hours of May 1940, because on 10 May 1940, the AI complexes had not even been blacked-out. The policy pursued did not in any way reflect the realisation that an army without ammunition was no army at all. There was no sense of urgency or preparedness to produce additional ammunition quickly.

There was enough rifle ammunition (6.5 mm) for three to four weeks of intensive warfare[43]. For the heavy machine guns (7.9 mm) a similar stock was available[44]. This stock was relatively favourable because the premise was that ammunition for approximately 400,000 men should be available, while in reality only about 240,000 men in the army had to be supplied[45]. There were few hand grenades available: exactly one of each type per mobilised soldier[46]. For the artillery, the standard 7-veld (7,5 cm gun), 10-veld (10,5 cm gun) and 12 cm howitzer-types had a supply of ammunition that could last them one to two weeks of intensive action[47]. For the mortars, a supply of ammunition was available that was only good for several days of battle.

The *Böhler* 4,7 cm anti-tank guns (PAG) had a good supply of ammunition, especially when one considers that almost all of its stock was armour-piercing[48]. On the other hand, the PAG almost completely lacked HE shells. For the older guns, only small stocks of ammunition were available and the quality was sometimes poor[49]. The new anti-aircraft guns had a very low stock of ammunition; for the 7.5 cm *Vickers* guns there was a reasonable stock, but some of it was of poor quality[50]. The modern 2 cm rapid-fire guns were purchased with ammunition, but only part of it was delivered. Nevertheless, some 4,000 rounds per *Oerlikon* were still available for this purpose[51], which was quickly used up against numerous low-flying aircraft that would appear. The rate at which the artillery works of the AI could produce ammunition was a maximum of 5% of the daily war consumption[52]. Since stocks of most types of ammunition were available for less than three weeks' fighting, the rate of manufacture after the start of the battle would make little difference.

The small army air force had a modest supply of bombs, most of them of the lighter types, but it also had few means of dropping them. Spare machine guns to replace worn or unserviceable weapons were not available. Spare engines and many necessary spare parts were barely available. In the short term, cannibalism could work by stripping inactive aircraft, but on 14 May 1940 it appeared that what was left of flying material could in fact already be technically written off[53]. The air fleet was in part modern[54], but in quantitative terms far too limited, and even a doubling of the fleet would probably have had little effect. In this respect, the relationship with the opponent was extremely lopsided and the Netherlands, especially with the strategy of 'everything on Fortress Holland', had no room to accommodate a large air force. It would all be exposed to destruction on the ground. It is probably safe to say that an army air force of about 150 to 200 reasonably modern aircraft would have been the practical maximum.

Geographically, the Netherlands had an impossible task if it wanted to defend its entire border. After all, that alone meant over five hundred km of land border and another four hundred km of sea border[55]. Strategically it was impossible to defend the entire coun-

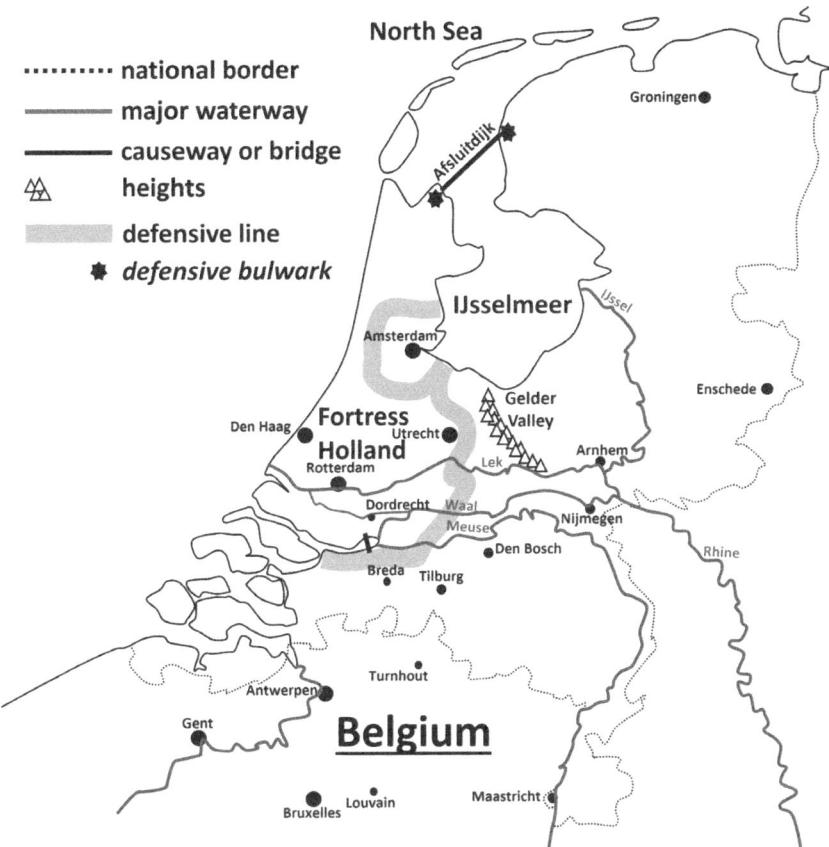

Map 2: The existing Dutch fortifications and defence-lines

try, partly because large concentrations in the east could easily be cut off. Because of its large inland sea (from 1933 an inland lake, the IJsselmeer), the Netherlands had a narrow waist where there was an excellent opportunity to defend the country effectively, the more so because the Gelderse Vallei (Gelder Valley) - formed during the last ice age - lay here. It offered opportunities for camouflaged concentration of resources and the development of a line of defence. The greatest natural strength lay in the rivers that cut through the landscape. As a low-lying river-delta country, the Netherlands was a water country, which certainly gave the defence a lot of strength. For an aggressor to reach the west of the country, assuming the defences there and their outposts were in order, would be a great challenge[56]. For the Netherlands, therefore, the main line of defence would be behind the Grebbeline and above the Meuse and Waal rivers. This had traditionally been the case for so long that it could be seen as the fundamental and historical position of national defence. An inner citadel had been created, an even smaller fortification, the *Stelling van Amsterdam*. That citadel was abandoned after the First World War. Fortress Holland was generally accepted as the castle fortress. It covered the provinces of Holland and Utrecht, the beating heart of the country. On that doctrine of the foundations of national defence, there were differing opinions as to the degree of defence and the locations where it would be carried out. Finding the balance between military utility and necessity in combination with the government's professed 'neutrality' determined part of the boundaries of the *Grand Strategy*. Naturally, this doctrine was strongly influenced by the people and resources of the armed forces. In principle, there was no lack of resources, but there was a lack of people. During the interbellum period, the Netherlands had a very low mobilisation rate, so that in 1939, with 280,000 men in the fully mobilised armed forces, only a small army was available[57]. The approximately 240,000 men available for army functions in fortresses and fields were insufficient to fight a prolonged battle, let alone an isolated one. This low number of available troops was a strong drawback of the *Grand Strategy*[58].

Despite actual shortcomings and imperfections, the armed forces of May 1940 are often overly caricatured in many historical reviews. This is largely unjustified. It was mainly caused by two elements. The first is the armed forces themselves - or rather their senior ranks - which refused to blame themselves for the debacle of the May Days of 1940. They blamed politics and the militia. However, it were the armed forces themselves that wrote their history with many publications during the war and in the first decades thereafter. This cast a false light on the matter, because of the armed forces' refusal to accept blame for the quick defeat. The second cause was that the Dutch people looked back on their own armed forces negatively. This was not in the least caused by the very cleverly orchestrated and highly publicised victory parade of the German 9th *Panzer-Division* and the motorised *Leibstandarte SS Adolf Hitler* on 16 and 17 May 1940 after the defeat of the Netherlands. As they moved towards the eastern border on their way to France, these units were ordered to parade through the centres of the Hague, Amsterdam, Utrecht and also passed Arnhem and Nijmegen. These modern formations made a deep impression and left the impression that the German army, with all its motorisation and mechanisation, was far ahead of our military. The reality was much more nuanced. The differences in quality in the field had relatively little to do with sophisticated equipment, but much more with training and mentality. It was not what one had, but what one did with it. The General Staff had failed hopelessly in training professional and reserve officers. The field regulations were in some respects archaic, training and practice focused mainly on hierarchy, reporting and administration but hardly on manoeuvre in the field and exercises with larger units and tactics. The field commanders were therefore often tactically incompetent and, moreover, were trained in the doctrine of obedience to orders and certainly not to develop their own initiative. There was one holy grail: to realize and maintain a fire plan commanded from above[59]. Fire and movement - what would emerge as the most important development from the Second World War - was non-existent in the practiced doctrine. The Netherlands had drawn its own plan and - literally and figuratively - had completely buried itself in its limitations, thereby limiting itself even further. This was a classic self-fulfilling prophecy. The wailing of General Staff officers about funds and resources, before and after the war days, was unimaginable. The average Dutch soldier had been pre-trained for six to eleven months and had often been on reserve recall to duty twice afterwards[60]. Except for the professional core of the German land forces, most of the German reservists who came in between 1936 and 1939 had only had three months of initial training[61]. In addition, divisions in the *Dritte Welle* (the third wave of mobilisation) were supplied with a large contingent of *Landwehr* (Territorial Reserve), a small proportion of whom had even fought in the previous war[62]. In this way, the German army could grow from 100,000 men in 1935 to 3,500,000 in May 1940[63]. When both countries mobilised in August 1939, the Dutch army was better prepared on paper in terms of initial training than the massive German reserve army. Another persistent myth is that the soldiers of the Dutch army had a high average age. One often reads or hears in jest that the Netherlands had 'house fathers' in the trenches[64]. The reality is surprising. The Netherlands had on average the youngest army of all belligerents involved in May 1940[65]! Nor were the divisions of the *Dritte Welle* and above any better equipped than the Dutch divisions, with the sole exception of the contingent of anti-tank guns[66]. Relatively speaking, the German army was as dependent on horses and ordinary foot soldiers just as were the Dutch, Belgian or French army. The great difference in the field between the two sides therefore lay in the concentration of resources in the vanguards, the concentrated attack on the centres of gravity with fast units and the operational tactics. Moreover, it was often not even the resources that determined the differences, but the way they were used. The greatest difference lay in the people, who were not only more efficiently trained, but, thanks to the joys of the *Auftragstaktik* and the excellent German cadre training, were led by (junior) officers who were instructed and motivated to achieve the tactical goal anyway and, if possible, more. Key words were "*Ausnutzen!*" ("Exploit!") and "*Immer weiter!*" ("Push forward!")[67]. Those German forces opposed allied formations that were not unified under a single command, that lacked determination and unity, and that were not prepared for a ground-breaking, aggressive war.

The contemporaneous fact remains that the effectiveness of the German army and air force[68], despite the Polish campaign, remained largely unknown to the Dutch. We had no foreign intelligence service of any significance and cooperation with services of allied powers was mediocre. The Netherlands had the main outlines, but partly due to a lack of insight they saw little of the finer points[69]. Although the strength of the German army was recognized, the French army was seen as the most powerful in Europe by most of the General Staff[70]. Therefore, the *Grand Strategy* was based on the assumption of a confrontation between Germany and France in which the French would be able to resist and perhaps defeat the Germans. Moreover, the French could spare some troops for our country[71]. This idea would develop from hope into concrete planning, at least with Winkelman and his Chief-of-Staff. Winkelman would not show any interest in the German concentrations south of the rivers. He considered them of little relevance to his cause which may have had something to do with his strategic choices but also with the fact that his general military knowledge and interest seem to have been modest[72]. Winkelman seems to have had the attitude that *'what will be, will be'*, so that he concentrated on using the means he had as efficiently as possible. This approach at the very least raises a number of questions.

Grand Strategy determined the serious limitations that applied to the Netherlands. Every supreme commander had to deal with it, regardless of his own desires and choices. Given the above, the following picture emerges. There was a modest armed force, of which the majority of the General Staff realised that the manoeuvring power of the Field Army was limited[73]. The size of the Field Army meant that it had too few reserves to sufficiently support troops at the front. It had to be supplemented by troops from the fortified positions. There was no capacity for strategic reserves, so that these would have to be formed from operational reserves, placing a serious burden on the frontline units[74]. There was a very limited ammunition supply, which could hardly be replenished by new production during the battle. After one week of war, it was necessary to reckon with sharp reductions in ammunition for various weapon systems; after two weeks, important weapon systems would run out of ammunition completely. The country lent itself well to a defence only at its narrowest width - between the IJsselmeer and the Belgian border and - secondarily - above the rivers Meuse and Waal. The relationship with the (presumed) allies was weak, while the 'neutralism' of the government did not allow for any form of formal exploration of a combined strategy. The chance that the Netherlands would not be attacked by Germany if it attacked France seemed virtually nil, but the chance remained that the Germans would operate exclusively below the Meuse. The likelihood that a strong contingent of troops would be placed at the disposal of the Dutch defence of the Fortress Holland by the French was extremely small, certainly in the short term. This was a fact that weighed heavily because this allied replacement was a requirement due to the minimal ammunition supply and the lack of reserves[75]. One had to take into account that the enemy would soon gain supremacy in the air, especially after a few days of battle when not much would remain of the small army air force[76]. The expectation of

German air supremacy over the western Netherlands was partly due to the fact that this theatre was far away for RAF and French aircraft and the availability of the French air force for the Belgian theatre was already limited in principle[77].

Based on these *Grand Strategy* limitations, one would expect the Netherlands to consider three options. One option was immediate capitulation if Germany actually attacked. Although unheroic, this option could save many Dutch lives. It had become the chosen scenario for Denmark - which, unlike the Netherlands, did not have a serious armed force at its disposal[78] - when it was invaded on 9 April 1940[79]. Direct capitulation, which would also be a government capitulation[80], had two major disadvantages. The Netherlands had its colony, the Dutch East-Indies, where it had realised from the start that only allied defence would lead to any chance of success if Japan would attack[81]. Immediate capitulation in the homeland would have a clear negative impact on the allies. The second major disadvantage was that it offered the Germans an immediate occupation of the Netherlands, which would not only come across as a veiled genuflection towards Germany but would also confront the allies with an immediately threatened left flank. The Netherlands did not want to allow this to happen[82]. The capitulation option was discarded. The two defensive options were those of alliance or isolated combat. Commander-in-Chief Reijnders had been aiming for the former[83]. He did not see any point in an isolated defence and considered it *a priori* in conflict with the allied obligation he saw of defending the Belgian left flank (the north flank)[84]. The third option, to withdraw to Fortress Holland as soon as possible and to offer resistance from there in isolation, was the one Winkelman would choose. Of the three options, the first - direct governmental capitulation - was the mildest in terms of human lives and war damage. It had major drawbacks politically and internationally and was therefore not a realistic option. The second option was probably the most expensive, but offered a chance of success. Standing shoulder to shoulder with the Entente and Belgium, meant that it was at least reasonable to demand that the allies also contribute to the survival of the left wing and thus send troops and resources to the Netherlands. The third scenario was actually hopeless. It might not be as costly in advance as prolonged combat with the allies[85], because the isolated battle could not last very long, but it would in fact always lead to a defeat in the relatively short term unless a miracle of quick and decisive support from the newly acquired allies was obtained. Nevertheless, Winkelman and Minister of Defence Dijxhoorn would choose the latter option. They did so, however, by ignoring the negative aspect. They trusted that unrealistically large and fast allied support would be forthcoming to continue the fight in the Fortress Holland. Moreover, those allies would virtually take over the defence of the Netherlands after a few weeks, because the Dutch army had very little ammunition and reserves in any case. The choice of the latter scenario pointedly ignored the key questions of whether (*i*) the allies would send such substantial troops and resources and especially whether (*ii*) they would do so within one, at most two weeks. The point was the watershed that divided between realism from wishful thinking[86].

General Reijnders

It makes sense to give some background on the policy of the first Commander-in-Chief, General I.H. Reijnders[87]. In May 1934, Reijnders had succeeded Lieutenant-General Seyffardt[88] as Chief of the General Staff, which was the highest military-administrative position in peacetime[89]. Not long after Reijnders took over in May 1934, a governmental change took place with regard to defence policy and rearmament. Adolf Hitler's seizure of power, after the death of President Hindenburg, was perfected in August 1934 when he became Chancellor and President, which, together with the Enabling Act of March 1933, gave Hitler all power in Germany. His subsequent appointment as *Führer* and the announcement of rearmament even awakened many pacifists. This demanded analyses by Reijnders for the improvement of the armed forces and the Dutch defence. It is not useful in the context of the subject to elaborate on this, but a brief consideration is necessary.

In February 1935, Reijnders wrote a formal recommendation[90] to Minister of Defence Deckers[91], in which he warned about Hitler's rearmament quest and the limited power that a Belgian-French alliance could oppose if the German army ambitions were realised[92]. He anticipated a German offensive in which he indicated that, without a doubt, this would at least partly take place over Dutch territory. Reijnders pointed out the necessity of an adequate Dutch defence and the large effort that would be needed for this. At the same time he pointed out the doctrine, which played a prominent role within the General Staff; that of the Strategic Surprise Attack[93]. With its militia army, the Netherlands would not be able to resist such a raid[94]. In 1936 and 1937, the General Staff and the staff of the Field Army were busy making an inventory of wishes and necessities. In 1937, this led to a written request to the government for an emergency programme to expand and modernise the army[95]. By May 1940, this would only be partially realised, partly due to policy choices[96]. As early as 1934, Reijnders showed that he was steering on a good compass and moreover that he understood that the motto for the Netherlands would be joint defence with allies. During this period Reijnders came into intensive contact with the then Major of the General Staff A.G.H. Dijxhoorn[97]. He had first met him as a regular staff officer at the Ministry of Defence, later as the head of Section IIB and chief of cabinet of the Minister of Defence. A few years later Dijxhoorn himself became Minister of Defence and thus formally the administrative superior of the Chief of the General Staff. In the first phase of their collaboration, Dijxhoorn would particularly attract Reijnders' attention because he had very outspoken, authoritarian opinions of his own and, substantively, advised the (then) Minister of Defence Van Dijk not to purchase any tanks, which advise was followed. Dijxhoorn thought that the defences against tanks at the time already dominated these weapon systems, thus, in his opinion, they were no longer relevant, or at least other priorities should prevail[98]. Although he nuanced this view and his scepticism about light tanks in particular was largely correct[99], he should have had every reason to look for room in the budget for medium tanks and to actively propagate them. He failed to do so. It is culpable that he obstructed this, although in 1938 it would almost certainly have been too late to have sufficient tanks available in time to make a significant difference in May 1940[100]. The suggestions that one sometimes reads - that in this phase before August 1939 the relationship between Reijnders and Dijxhoorn had already been thoroughly ruined[101], or at least was under serious pressure - finds little support in contemporary sources[102]. Rather, besides the issue about the necessity of procuring tanks, there seems to have been a fairly large degree of agreement between them during this phase[103].

When the general mobilisation was announced in August 1939, a Supreme Commander of the army and navy (OLZ) also had to be appointed. This would finally put an end to the paralysing *ex aequo* principle and all commanders would come under one head. It was logical - although not a necessity or a rule - to appoint the serving Chief of Staff to the supreme command. All this happened against a political-administrative background of division and chaos[104], so that partly for this reason it was decided to take the short route and appoint General Reijnders. However, the new cabinet had one surprising minister and that was the one in the department of defence: A.Q.H. Dijxhoorn. Previously the adviser of the previous minister and frequent interlocutor of Reijnders, he was suddenly his administrative superior[105]. The first item on the agenda was the instruction that the OLZ received from the government. Much has already been said and written about this[106]. It serves no purpose to repeat this because after his successor Winkelman took office, Reijnders' strategy was not implemented. For the perspective, however, the main points should be discussed.

The starting point for the strategy seems to have been a written consideration by the then Prime Minister H. Colijn from May 1936. It was addressed to Chief of Staff Reijnders and contained a consideration of what, according to Colijn, should be the starting points of a Dutch strategy. It is striking that this memo in fact reflects the choices of both Reijnders and Winkelman. Colijn indicated that in his opinion the only realistic threat would come from the east. He considered it impossible that in case of a war, in which the Netherlands would be involved, this could be fought by the Netherlands alone[107]. However, he indicated that if the Dutch Field Army were to offer itself for direct action and thus fight the German attacker with force immediately behind the border, that would lead to a serious deterioration of the fighting power or even the destruction of the units concerned. Therefore, the army had to focus on a strong, but above all deeper front. The existing Concentration Blue[108] did not position the Field Army behind the Maas- and IJssel-lines, but in concentrations in the Gelder Valley position or Grebbe-line (*Grebbelinie*), as it would later be called, and the Peel region below the Meuse river. Between 1936 and 1939, not much changed in this line-up, except that the Peel concentration developed into the Peel-Raam-line (*Peel-Raamstelling*)[109] and thus this concentration, like the other Field Army positions, became also a fixed defence-line[110]. For lack of funds, however, too little work was done on permanent reinforcements or finalizing even the basic construction of these positions. Apart from the measures at the Afsluitdijk and the Strategic Security (SB - *Strategische Beveiliging*) sectors[111], no final choice had been made until August 1939, nor had any spades been put in the ground[112]. Neither the government, nor military leadership had yet finalized its choices – a risky situation[113]. Without prepared positions, the Field Army would actually have to defend itself in the field and not in prepared positions, which was considered an extraordinary risk by the General Staff, considering the limited qualities that were ascribed to the Field Army. On the other hand, there was a lack of resources and a desire not to abandon strategic choices prematurely[114]. There was also something to be said for the latter. So this seemed - certainly until August 1939 - to be a classic dilemma.

The appointment of Reijnders as Supreme Commander led to a governmental instruction conceived by Minister Dijxhoorn on the basis of prior consultations between the monarch, the Prime Minister (De Geer) and the Ministers of Defence and Foreign Affairs (Van Kleffens) as well as Reijnders himself[115]. Meanwhile, the general mobilisation in the period 25-28 August 1939 had gone extremely well[116]. However, the planned proclamation of the State of Siege after a mobilisation of the armed forces was not initiated by De Geer. The much more limited State of War, which the Prime Minister did allow, was moreover limited in a number of respects[117]. This immediately led to great tension between the government and the armed forc-

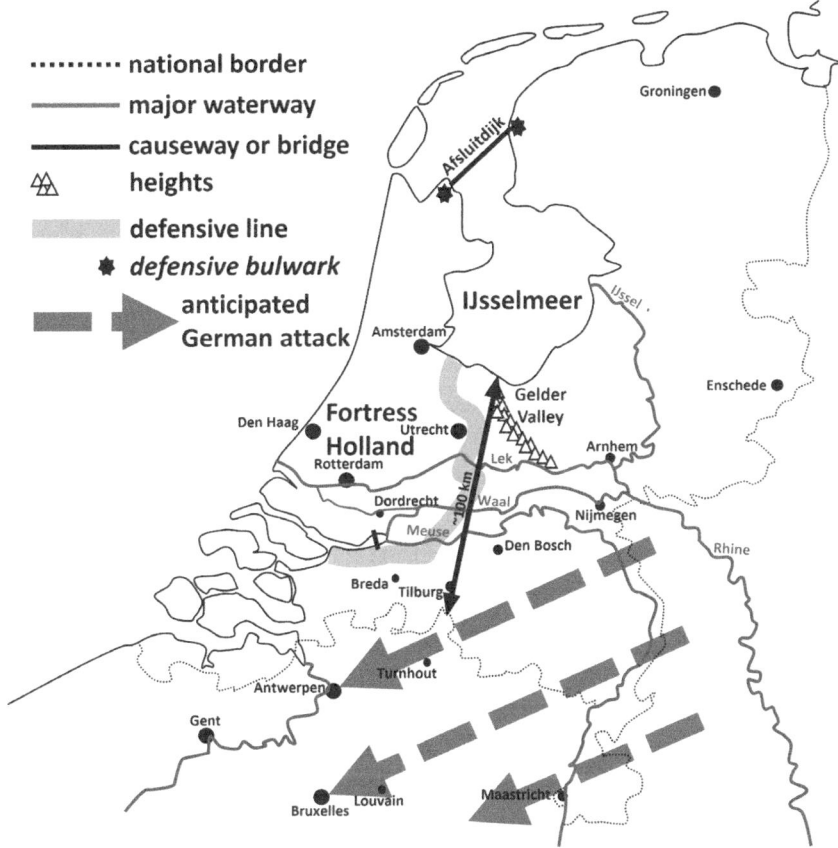

Map 3: The anticipated Meuse variant of the German invasion

es, moreover, it kept the crippling budget and licensing laws of the peacetime government[118]. The concentration of the mobilised army also led to the need to make strategic choices, a process in which the Minister of Defence exceeded his authority by constantly intervening in both the strategy and its tactical elaboration.

Reijnders insisted on a concentration of the Field Army in the Peel-Raam-line. North of the rivers, his preference was for a preliminary defence in the Grebbe-line with the eventual main defence in the east front of the Fortress Holland[119]. Especially in the central part he did not want to bind the troops to one of the two positions (Grebbe-line or east front of Fortress Holland). The concentration of an army corps and the Light Division in Brabant, as well as the disposition of two army corps in the centre, would become the friction point par excellence between the Minister of Defence and OLZ. Other matters that one often reads as prominent points of contention were merely side issues[120]. Moreover, the Minister changed his mind along the way and started to intervene more and more strongly on the content and the execution by the OLZ, pushing through his basic wish - for a direct concentration of resources in Fortress Holland and only a weak preliminary defence further forward. The Minister considered concentration of troops in Brabant irresponsible[121]. This was in fact an extreme interpretation of Colijn's memorandum, of years earlier. It had stated that the Field Army - while awaiting allied assistance - should not let itself be tied down too soon. The OLZ attached great importance to the defensive component in Brabant, and in so doing he honoured not only the obligations of neutrality[122], but especially the other component of Colijn's memorandum: the necessity for the Netherlands to conduct its defence in active alliance with other countries. In pushing through his own views, Minister Dijxhoorn came to the wrenching situation that as a Lieutenant-Colonel, who until recently had been an active General Staff officer, he allowed his strategic views to dominate those of the OLZ, who outranked him by four ranks. Dijxhoorn aggravated this dispute by undermining, wilful actions. He and his adjutant, Captain of the General Staff Kruls, used to carry out unannounced inspections without consulting or coordinating with the OLZ to test troop readiness. Even more objectionable was a visit initiated by Dijxhoorn to the Commander of the Field Army and the commanders of the 2nd and 4th Army Corps, without informing them that his visit was not informative but dealt with matters of strategy and, moreover, had not been coordinated with the OLZ[123]. The information that Dijxhoorn received during that Field Army session, he used in a confrontation with the OLZ during a meeting with attendance of the Queen and Prime Minister. The minister thereby put the OLZ in a corner in a completely unacceptable way[124]. This confrontation was of great importance in the demolition of the OLZ's reputation by the Minister of Defence[125]. The Queen did not remain silent either and asked her adjutant in special service, Lieutenant-General J.J.G. van Voorst tot Voorst (who was Commander Field Army), to advise her bilaterally without the OLZ's knowledge[126]. This strained Reijnders' working relationship with the CV. The latter was strongly opposed to the Peel-Raam-line and very much in favour of the Grebbe-line[127]. Van Voorst tot Voorst opted for the Orange-position (*Oranjestelling*) on the diagonal between 's Hertogenbosch and Tilburg, as an alternative for the Peel-Raam-line. This Orange-position which, in his opinion, met the possibilities and the known wishes of the informal French-Belgian axis much better. As an advocate of this solution, he opposed the Peel-Raam-line, which he considered indefensible because of its vulnerable right flank. Dijxhoorn also became increasingly demanding in pushing his strategic view, while Reijnders did not want to adjust his strategy under the circumstance in which an invasion could begin at any moment[128]. Reijnders had not been provided with funds for a new position and thought that giving up the Peel-Raam-line as main position would be a blow to the allies[129]. He was convinced that the only meaningful battle was that alongside and with the allies. Reijnders refused to budge. Reijnders also refused to choose between the Grebbe-line and the eastern front of Fortress Holland and wanted to defend both in sequence, but found no support for this in the consultations with the government. Minister Dijxhoorn caused the net around Reijnders to close more and more. Although De Geer managed for some time to prevent Reijnders' dismissal, which Dijxhoorn had wanted in December, he ensured that the case blew up in January. Reijnders was forced to resign[131]. Carstens offered his functional as Chief of Staff out of loyalty with his OLZ and returned to the Field Army. In the middle of a major crisis, the Dutch army top leadership was replaced.

THE COLD STRATEGY

General H.G. Winkelman[132] - the Supreme Commander of the Dutch armed forces during the war days of May 1940 - has been characterised in books and in the only published biography to date as a diplomat, an organisational talent, an energetic man and an amiable commander[133]. One could call this a typical Dutch quality character. The question is whether these are the qualities a war-time commander should have. Apart from organisational talent and an energetic spirit, probably not. The shared qualities of great war generals seem to fit the profile of his predecessor Reijnders more than that of Winkelman. It will be seen that his claimed organisational talent is open to question and that his profile of an amiable, liberal commander in many ways led to unconvincing policies, certainly at the General Headquarters (AHK) itself[134]. Winkelman was a remarkably liberal commander in a world where authority - certainly at that time - was expected and necessary. He delegated a lot of responsibility and seemed to pay little attention to the competence of his subordinate commanders or to how they used the delegated authority. His approach to delegating authority was not in step with the centralising character of the armed forces. People were trained and formed to follow, not to create and decide independently. In addition, the leading decision-makers were elderly senior officers with little understanding of modern conflict and modern armed forces. This situation would lead, when the cold strategy suddenly became hot, to some remarkable effects[136].

The change of supreme command - a huge risk in itself[137] - required a transition process that was unavoidable[138]. The change of both the Commander-in-Chief and the Chief-of-Staff was in fact unacceptable. That it happened anyway was the government's fault and would have had a devastating effect if the German invasion had occurred shortly afterwards. The replacement of one of the two officers would have been unwise, but not result in a complete break in continuity. Replacing both made the armed forces temporarily ungovernable. Such a replacement is only justifiable in such international circumstances if there is real incompetence or such diplomatic circumstances that replacement is imperative. In all other cases, this double replacement is irresponsible. The replacement of Reijnders and Carstens definitely falls into this category. There was absolutely no question of incompetence. It was a conflict over control and direction between the Minister of Defence and the Supreme Commander, which the Minister settled in his personal favour.

Winkelman and his Chief of Staff (Major-General H.F.M. van Voorst tot Voorst), after their formal appointment on 6 February 1940, spent weeks being informed by the staff sections at the GHQ and by the staff of the Field Army. Numerous inspections were organized during which the state of the positions and the readiness of the troops was examined. The incoming and outgoing commanders-in-chief had only a very brief meeting at the handover. Very little love was lost between them[139]. The chiefs-of-staff had a more extensive handover. The Minister of Defence was responsible for this imperfect transition-process[140]. The heads of the sections at the AHK also had to inform the new leadership. There are strong indications that this was done imperfectly[141]. Winkelman and his Chief-of-Staff agreed on one fundamental principle beforehand. They wanted to concentrate the troops in the heart of the country[142] in and behind the positions they would tenaciously defend and thus not - as Reijnders had done with the central front - leave the choice open and distribute troops[143]. This was therefore the only distinctive strategic change made at this stage[144]. Operationally, however, Winkelman's choice was almost identical to Reijnders' idea. The latter had rightly argued that if the Grebbe-line was chosen, the eastern front of Fortress Holland should also be strengthened because this would always serve as a fallback option after a defeat on the Grebbe-line. Dijxhoorn refused to go along with this, but in doing so he denied the obvious. Reijnders stated that if the eastern front was the only one that could be strengthened and the main defence would be formed there, the extensive inundations of the Waterline (in combination with the large evacuations of civilians in the inundated areas) would have to be initiated immediately. In addition, Reijnders had stated that he would have to leave a security occupation in the eastern front if the preliminary defence was in the Grebbe-line. This was all correct. Dijxhoorn had dismissed this reasoning but Winkelman's choices operationally amounted to the same thing. Curiously enough, Dijxhoorn would not only support Winkelman's choice but praise it and present it to the Dutch Cabinet with the words "you see - this is also a way to do it". Winkelman, by the way, was forced by Dijxhoorn to choose between the two defence-lines for budgetary reasons - that had not changed[145]. However, after Winkelman's progressive study of the strategic situation, a dramatic shift would soon follow, which was received with remarkable mildness by post-war historiography, but which would in fact make the Dutch national defence a lost cause from the outset.

The government instructed Winkelman when he took office that the defence of the heart of the country was essential and that persistent resistance had to be mounted there so that the Fortress would be defended to the hilt[146]. This included the province of Zeeland[147]. An alliance with the allies was to be sought but this was emphatically not to be done in advance of the opening of hostilities. This directive instruction was equivalent to the one given to Reijnders, but more pointed. Since six months had passed - a period in which shortly after a Russian-German alliance had been formed, Poland had been invaded[148] - the directive to Winkelman was even less helpful than that given to Reijnders. The Polish campaign made it clear that the Germans were capable of bringing a sizeable army to its knees within a few weeks by means of overwhelming and rapid concentrated attacks, accompanied by prominent air support. The Hague should have realised - the case of Poland made this very plausible[149] - that without an alliance, the Netherlands would be completely hopeless and would probably only be able to resist for a few days. However, an alliance and any exploration thereof remained out of the question and the resistance of Dijxhoorn (and the rest of the government) against a prolonged defence in Brabant - which would be essential for a joint allied defence - also remained intact. Only the defence of

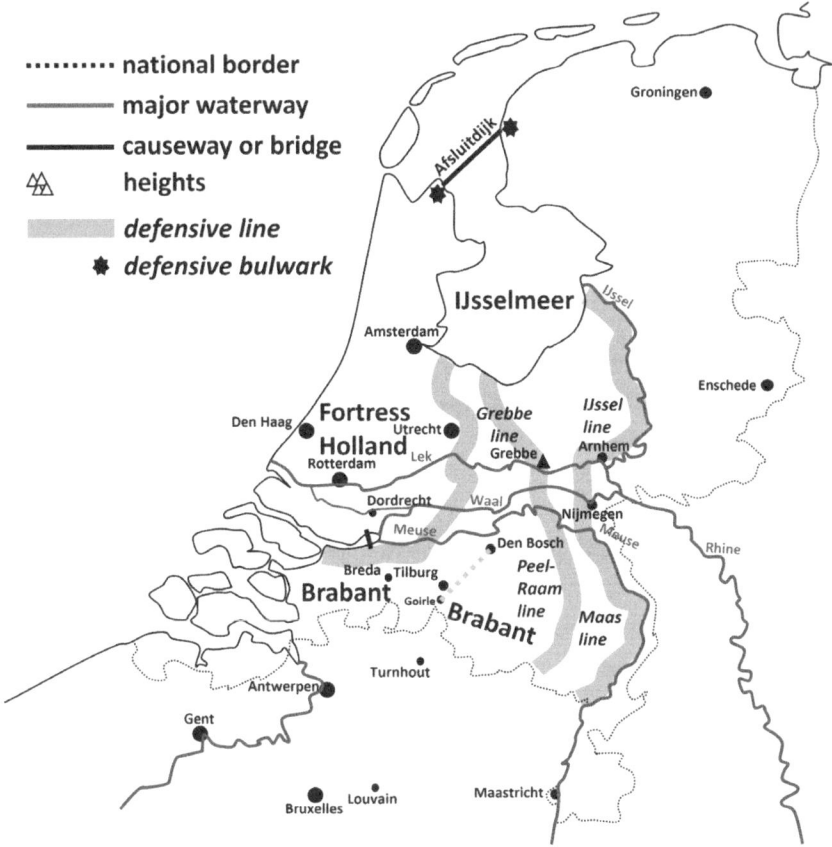

Map 4: Projections of Dutch defence-plans 1939-1940

Zeeland remained, because it was realised that giving this up would mean that the Netherlands would expose access to Antwerp, which the British and Belgians could interpret as covert support for the German cause[150].

It was a governmental instruction that thus set up the isolationist policy of the Netherlands, but Winkelman himself poured it into concrete! Winkelman did not oppose his instruction and would even pick up the bridge to allied defence of the south. Remarkably enough Winkelman was given much more room for manoeuvre than his predecessor when it came to the implementation of his strategy. His final strategy would only come to full maturity during the first two weeks of April 1940, and was fully supported by Dijxhoorn. Winkelman would soon, partly at the insistence of the CV, speak out for a firm defence of the Grebbe-line. He gave instructions to continue the previously suspended trench works there with great urgency[151]. He also reduced the concentrations of troops on the border and in the northeast of the country that his predecessor had kept remarkably large. Although the question is legitimate as to why Reijnders left so many troops on the border after the concentration of the Field Army, the reduction of these formations under Winkelman was in any case a wise action. In his conviction that concentration of resources was essential Winkelman, however, kept a relatively large number of troops in frontier positions even though their usefulness was questionable. The OLZ and many field-commanders would complain about the shortage of professional officers for Field Army battalions, but then leave all border troops - which after the concentration of the Field Army only served as sacrificial units - under the command of professional Majors[152]. This situation was maintained even when Winkelman tied all troops above the great rivers to fixed positions. The issue of the border battalions can safely be called a policy blunder of the army leadership[153]. However, this would not be the only blunder with the border troops, whose tasks were insufficiently adapted to the changing circumstances[154]. Winkelman himself struggled with the issue of defence in Brabant. He and his Chief-of-Staff - to the dismay of the Head of the Operations section of the GHQ Wilson[155], promoted to Lieutenant-Colonel on 1 May 1940 - did not believe in the Peel-Raam-line. Winkelman thought it was not deep enough, too weak in certain sectors and in his opinion lacked sufficient troops to occupy the position adequately[156]. The OLZ found the lack of link-up with a Belgian defence-line unacceptable[157]. There was a risk that German formations would pour through the gap between the Dutch and Belgian forces, hence the risk of being outflanked. These arguments were all valid, although they applied in most cases equally well to the Grebbe-line and its connecting positions. In fact, the Peel-Raam-line was in a better position than the barely constructed Grebbe-line at the time of Winkelman's findings, where even parts of the tank ditch in front of the defence line were still missing and where near Rhenen (at the Grebbeberg) no inundation could be established due to an unfinished pump-house[158]. In principle, the quality of the Dutch defence line construction was inadequate. It was a stripped-down derivative of the French trench construction from the First World War. The Dutch version lacked depth, sufficient space between the successive lines and connecting trenches between the lines[159]. In general, Dutch defensive positions lacked the capacity to absorb sufficient troops in the front-line trenches, adequate and strong fortifications and prepared capacity to concentrate reserves and staff & support facilities[160]. In that respect, the Peel-Raam-line was stronger in March 1940 than most parts of the Grebbe-line. What stood out as an argument was that there was a major weakness on the right flank of the Peel-Raam-line. The Light Division was available as a mobile force to counter outflanking manoeuvres by the aggressor. It could be supported by two available border infantry battalions. This was an adequate remedy against enemy reconnaissance movements on the right flank but far too weak a safeguard against an enemy encirclement *'in force'*. The Division had to cover a 45-km wide gap between the cities of Weert and Tilburg. In addition, the position lacked - as argued earlier - an alternate position behind it. The fact that there were too few men in the defence line also applied, albeit to a lesser extent, to the Grebbe-line and intermediate defence lines. This was due to the low absorption capacity of the trench systems[161]. However, under Winkelman there were still no less than 34 battalions (around 22,500 men) of infantry in border positions or in the outer defences. If those border troops had been greatly reduced[162] and the thin Maas- and IJssel-line positions had been occupied only at the bridges and road-junctions behind them, and the freed up troops had been placed behind the Peel-Raam-line, then the latter and the border with Belgium would have been well occupied at all important locations by the standards of the time[163]. It would have remedied most challenges except for the open flank. Another relevant factor was that the French and Belgians wanted a defence of Brabant near Tilburg. Reijnders had actually investigated that possibility, but ultimately rejected it as the first option[164]. Winkelman rejected the allied demands immediately. He apparently did not want to choose the construction of such a line because he stood in a quandry in the matter of whether or not there would be a firm defence in Brabant. In this respect, Winkelman seemed hardly to have believed in the allied defence from the outset. To make sure that he did not miss out on a small chance for significant French assistance, he had the attaché in Paris verify (again) what the French were prepared to do while the Belgians were approached to see if they could be persuaded to link up with the Peel-Raam-line[165]. On behalf of Winkelman the proposal was made to the French GQG to advance as far as the Zuid-Willemsvaart, which was a compromise between the French support in the Peel-region and the French wish to join-up only at Tilburg. Initially, these contacts took place without the government being informed[166]. The Belgians, after a covert inspection of the Peel-Raam-line, again declined support, but did indicate that they wanted to link up with a Dutch position at Turnhout from Goirle-Tilburg. The OLZ then asked the attaché in Paris to approach the GQG with a final request, this time after having obtained political support in advance for such an action[167]. The attaché Lieutenant-Colonel Van Voorst Evekink contacted General Gamelin at the French headquarters once more[168]. Meanwhile, Winkelman was pessimistic about a French reversal. Together with his Chief-of-Staff, he developed the idea to strip the province of Noord-Brabant of all important army units during the first war night and to evacuate those units to Fortress Holland, in order to have more troops available there. This provisional strategy was, for security reasons, kept a closely confined secret, but would soon be firmly established in Winkelman's mind. A strategic plan was born.

It is important here and now to say a few words about the strategy of the French and British, the old *Entente Cordiale*. They had endeavoured - especially by the end of 1939 - to devise joint strategic plans to counter the hypotheses of the German direction and nature of attack. The preservation of Antwerp and its Scheldt access was one of these objectives. Therefore, most French strategic scenarios included elements that involved at least the southwest of the Netherlands. In concrete terms, this concerned only the Zeeland and West-Brabant territories. In 1939, the French – eventually supported by the British – had opted for a basic strategy known as *Hypothèse*[169] Dyle[170]. This was a plan that called for the alignment of the French, British and Belgian field armies on the line from Sedan in north central France to the Fortress of Antwerp, thus including the Belgian "*Réduit National*" (National Redoubt – a Belgian version of the Fortress Holland). The name for this strategy came from the fact that the northern part rested on the natural barrier formed by the small river Dijle (hereafter 'Dyle'). An important natural ally was the river Meuse, because behind it, between Sedan and Namur in Belgium, a strong position was to be held. The intermediate section between the Dyle and the Meuse, the 30 km wide segment from Wavre to Namur, partly formed an elevated open ridge of terrain devoid of meaningful natural defenses[171]. This became an area where the main defence relied on improvised elements such as railway embankments and streams and whose raised plateau was called the "Gembloux gap" after the gap the elevated terrain posed in between the river-lines. It was equipped by the Belgians with a few permanent fortifications and a large linked iron fence consisting of so-called Cointet-elements, intended as a kind of anti-tank barrier[172]. The northern part of the position was occupied by the *British Expeditionary Force* (BEF)[173]. The central part was to be occupied by the French First Army of General Blanchard, who had as front defence on the plateau of Gembloux the strong French *Corps de Cavalerie* of General Prioux. This corps consisted mainly of two very strong mechanized divisions (2.DLM and 3.DLM) and was supported by some additional artillery units. It had to buy time for the advancing French and British armies to reach their intended main positions. The Belgian field army was to carry out the remaining preliminary defence and slow down the retreat to the main line, which could properly be called the Belgian equivalent of Fortress Holland[174]. The French, in addition to the room behind Gembloux, also occupied the front south of Namur down to Sedan, and further east to Metz where they linked up with the Maginot Line. The French strategy was not new, but it had been elaborated in 1939 and 1940. It was not until 12 March 1940 that Gamelin added a daring variant, the *Hypothèse* Breda[175]. The Dutch GHQ was aware of the main points[176]. Reijnders and Winkelman knew the framework of the strategy that would apply to the future allies. The component that was less known, but elements of which were known, was the expansion of the *Hypothèse* Dyle into the *Hypothèse* Breda[177]. The latter did not change the main strategy, but moved the French 7th Army, until then the strategic reserve of the French North-East Theatre of Operations, from Pas-de-Calais on the Franco-Belgian border to the sector Antwerp-Breda. The 7th Army was now to advance there as far as the Dutch river Dintel/Mark and behind that form a front. A forward defence was to be formed from Tilburg and Turnhout, linking up with the Belgian line of defence along the canal of Turnhout, occupied by the Belgian 18th Division. The essence of this French plan was to support the Belgian army on the Albert Canal defence on its north and south flanks. In this way, Gamelin thought the Belgian army command, which had no arrangement in advance for its subordination to allied command, would be operationally bound. Moreover, this would entice the Dutch army to actively defend its southern territory and thus contribute to the French cause[178]. However, because the *Hypothèse* Breda was uncertain until mid-March, a repeated coordination of the attaché Van Voorst Evekink with the GQG was necessary and meaningful[179]. The French regularly shared the outline of this plan with the Netherlands, so the Dutch GHQ was informed of any significant adjustments to the plans[180]. They also knew about the Belgian considerations. Winkelman's requests to the Belgians were aimed at convincing the Belgian high command to extend its front along the Albert Canal to (the Belgian) Zuid-Willemsvaart so that the Peel-Raam-line would be in contact with the Belgian front. In spite of the Dutch popular belief that the Belgians would reject this out of hand, General Van Overstraeten, the military advisor to the Belgian King Leopold III, did consider complying with Winkelman's requests[181]. In March, a Dutch officer took the Belgian attaché in civilian clothes for a few days on an inspection through the Peel-Raam-line. When the Belgian attaché Colonel Diepenrijckx delivered his final report in Belgium, the conclusion was that it made no sense to assume that the Dutch army would be able to hold out for a long time in the Peel-Raam-line, which was assessed as a weak position[182]. This assessment was followed by a Belgian refusal and a counter-request, which was in line with the French strategy, to take up a unified position on the line Leuven - Turnhout - Tilburg. Winkelman rejected the counter-request and did nothing about building positions in this area, although he knew the French strategy[183]. The rejection of the Belgian and French wishes was not only to the Netherlands' own disadvantage, but also prominently to the disadvantage of the Belgians and French. This rarely seems to be the subject of discussion in Dutch historical reviews[184]. The case is always presented in a one-sided way, namely from a Dutch perspective. This seriously hinders objectivity. During the May Days it would appear that despite the knowledge of the French strategy, its essence and the vulnerability of the northern front in connection with the developments in the field, at no time the general command in the Hague managed to asses the situation right and objectively. On the contrary, they made a huge mistake and systematically derived false expectations from the cooperation with the French. They expected fundamental support from the French and did not expect to have to give it themselves. The Dutch Supreme Command in fact relied on French support. This would have a disastrous effect on the quality and effectiveness of the operational directives from the Dutch GHQ and the Commander of Fortress Holland (C-VH) just before and during the May Days[185]. More about this will follow when the 'hot' strategy is discussed.

The period of March and the first week of April 1940 constituted the crucial period for Winkelman's strategy. Winkelman had set his sights on concentration of resources from the outset. He wanted to make the defence as compressed as possible. In March, his final plan took shape. He wanted to conduct firm resistance at the Afsluitdijk[186], the Grebbe-line, the intermediate defences on the islands between the rivers[187], including the Waal-Linge-position, and the south-front of Fortress Holland, representing mainly the defences behind the Meuse estuary up to the coast of the North Sea. The unstated assumption here was that the Field Army would have to retreat from the Grebbe-line and intermediate defences onto the east-front of Fortress Holland if the central front in the Gelder Valley was about to fall[188]. However, the proverbial 'Alamo' would then have been reached. There they would wait for relief by the allies[189]. Opinions differed as to how long this would take, but none of the senior command had a realistic idea of the limitations imposed by the ammunition supply. Some spoke in terms of a few weeks or even three months![190]

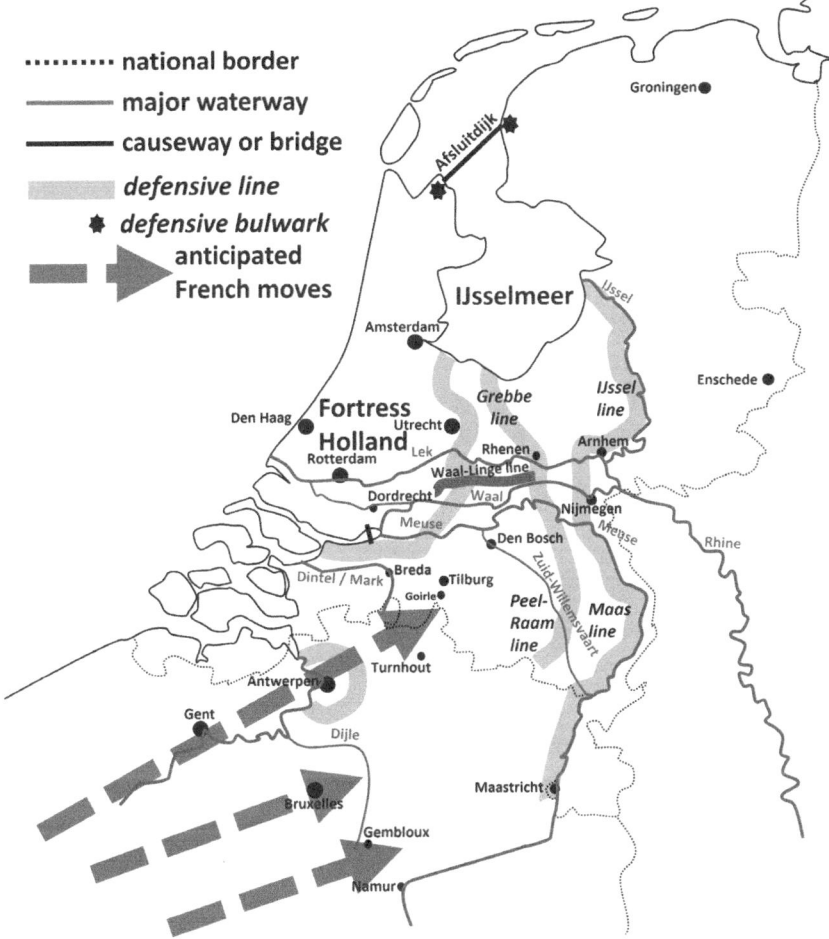

Map 5: The Winkelman and allied plans combined

Superficially, the 'Winkelman Plan' may seem plausible, especially given the government's directive and the small size of the armed forces. That is probably also the reason why the critique of this strategy is not very pronounced regarding the surrealistic content of the 'Winkelman Plan'. However, when comparing the elements of the *Grand Strategy* with the defence theory of the OLZ, the key question soon arises "*and where is the Dutch army, withdrawn to the Fortress Holland, without an ally, going to get the necessary ammunition and reserves?*" The General who was praised by so many historians and some contemporaries for his methodical working method, who supposedly had his qualities in logistics in the armed forces and who was supposedly so thorough, could not have arrived at this strategy if the aforementioned qualities had actually been present in him. The only remedy Winkelman had for (in principle) realising his Alamo strategy was a request to send many units and extensive ammunition transports to Fortress Holland, the request actually being processed by the leading elements of the allies in the midst of their own chaos and challenges and – last but not least – the request getting the envisaged positive result. However, such a scenario was, mildly speaking, unrealistic[191]. France was asked for many troops, the United Kingdom for ammunition and aircraft. It was extremely inappropriate for a commander-in-chief, who first raised the bridge to the allies in front of their noses, to then beg for extensive help. Moreover, it was logistically impossible to transport the four requested divisions by sea, quite apart from the question of whether the French could spare such an amount of troops in the first place[192]. The second request discriminated against the logistical reality that the Netherlands mainly used its own weapon systems and calibres. No foreign party could actually supply arms and ammunition there except for some obsolete foreign weapon systems that the Netherlands happened to have kept as standard[193]. Winkelman apparently did not test his ideas against reality[194], and shifted gradually over a mere three months to the strategy of total isolation[195]. Moreover, he was inconsistent in his concentration of resources and his arguments in defence of his choices only hit home in isolated or local contexts at best, but rarely against the background of the *Grand Strategy*. The key question - what was the point for the country of defending itself in isolation for (at most) one or two weeks and in so doing causing a great deal of needless destruction and sacrifice, while the end result would certainly be defeat - was apparently not posed by Winkelman[196]. Or perhaps only implicitly. He thought that Dutch resistance according to this plan was a sacrifice that could be justified, although it would always lead to defeat. After all, there was no possibility of a victory in isolation over Germany and the chance that the French would completely take over the defence of the Netherlands was nil, especially after the Netherlands had turned its back on the French army in Brabant. Therefore, the question arises why a joint allied defence was so firmly rejected by the same Winkelman. Had he opted for joint action with the allies in Brabant, the concentration of troops in Brabant would indeed have increased the risk of the Netherlands running out of reserves in the north, the ammunition supply would not have improved and many troops in the south would have died[197]. However, the big difference with the final Winkelman paradigm was that in the joint allied scenario there would be a more realistic chance of a successful defence against the German invasion. Moreover, and at least as important, in that scenario one would have had every right to appeal for and probably would have received some allied help, because the continued Dutch defence would have been of use to the *Entente*. If this scenario turned out to be a failure, which of course was a real prospect given the relationships and the uncertain allied commitments[198], then on balance no more would have been lost than in the scenario where the Netherlands pulled up the bridges and withdrew into a siege for which it did not have the means of survival and was doomed. The only potential way out of the dilemma for Winkelman was that the Germans would only pass through the south of the country, but he himself had considered that unlikely[199]. The strategy eventually envisaged by Winkelman had no realistic chance of success. Nevertheless, the Winkelman strategy took shape and remarkably did not meet with any noticeable resistance. Winkelman's strategic plan seemed to be 'supported' on 29 March - when attaché Van Voorst Evekink confirmed that the French would 'only' advance towards Tilburg and not further east - by the repeated French refusal to commit to reinforcement of the Dutch Peel position of which Gamelin had no high expectations[200]. Winkelman asked Van Voorst Evekink again to ask explicitly if there would be no French support in the direction of Eindhoven - Den Bosch, or at least up to the Zuid-Willemsvaart. Only a clear French 'yes' to this question would stop Winkelman from his strategic choice to evacuate Brabant at the end of the first day of war[201]. This typified the remarkable Dutch position in a period so close to the German invasion. The Netherlands demanded from others, but was not open to the wishes of the Belgians, French and British[202]. It was a one-way street. This was a tendency that would continue in what the Belgian General Van Overstraeten already referred to in February 1940 as 'the Dutch isolation policy'. When on 5 April

1940, Van Voorst Evekink called from Paris to tell Winkelman that the French would indeed not march as far to the east as desired, but would act in the surroundings of Breda with a preliminary defence up to Tilburg, the attaché was summoned to drive to Eindhoven that very day for a meeting with the army command.

On Friday 5 April 1940, Winkelman sat with his Chief-of-Staff[203] in the Hotel *Royal* in Eindhoven[204]. They held several meetings here[205]. Van Voorst Evekink arrived in the late evening. At the end of March Winkelman and his Chief-of-Staff had already had a number of meetings with Colonel L.J. Schmidt[206], the commander of the Peel-Division[207], as well as with the commanders of the Light Division and the 3rd Army Corps[208]. Only the commanders of these units were allowed – and their seconds-in-command – to learn about the Winkelman strategy for Brabant. The rest of the staffs were not allowed to know anything, which made operational planning extremely difficult. The new instruction started with the order to direct the 3rd Army Corps and the Light Division[209] to a more rearward position, under the guise of an exercise[210]. Each of the six infantry regiments of the divisions of the 3rd Army Corps was to leave a battalion to occupy the Peel-Raam-line. After the opening of hostilities on the first day of the war, after darkness had fallen, the Army Corps would move from Brabant to the area above the rivers. The Army Corps – north of the rivers supplemented by six reserve battalions to fill the gap of the battalions left in the Peel-position[211] – would then be positioned on the Waal-Linge-front, facing to the south and supported on its left flank by the independent Brigade B. The Light Division would become available as a strategic reserve after it had been taken back into the Fortress. In northern Limburg and the eastern part of Brabant a rear-guard would remain, which would be formed by the battalions of the Peel-Division, supplemented by the already mentioned six battalions of the 3rd Army Corps and one battalion of Brigade B. Every regiment of the 3rd Army Corps was instructed to leave behind a battalion in the regimental sector, so that the entire frontline of the northern two sectors of the Peel-Raam-line would remain occupied by these six battalions. The lower three sectors of the Peel-Raam-line – which were less likely to be attacked in force

– were occupied by battalions of the reserve[212] which fell under the Peel-Division. The whole came under the authority of the commander of the Peel-Division – Colonel Schmidt. He would get the overall command over all troops in Brabant and the north of Limburg. He would be directly subordinate to the OLZ and its GHQ-staff and not under the command of the Field Army[213]. This meant that the Maas-line from Mook to Roermond and the entire Peel-Raam-line, including the border with Belgium behind it, had to be defended by 23 infantry battalions supported by two battalions of engineers with just one battalion of vintage artillery and completely without anti-aircraft defence[214]. This force would have a strength of infantry battalions that normally exceeded that of an entire army corps, but led by a Colonel[215], who did not even have a full divisional staff, not even an adequate operational staff to coordinate an army corps' worth of combat troops. Moreover, the total frontal width of both defence-lines to be occupied was 150 km. With hardly any means of communication available beyond existing telephone lines, there could be no question of *'command and control'*. The whole force had to hold its own during the first day and the following night, so that when darkness fell on the first night of war – with the supposed calm that would then develop in the air – the 3rd Army Corps and the Light Division could evacuate northwards across the major rivers. As soon as this manoeuvre would be completed, the resistance of the Peel-Division could be carried on as it wished and its continuation could be coordinated at will with the Belgian or French troops. Further instructions about that phase did not follow, and that situation remained so during the May Days. The Commander of the Peel-Division was told to act as he saw fit from the point where the Field Army formations would have left the territory. In the eyes of the army command, this division had become irrelevant to the war effort from that point onwards.

Colonel Schmidt was perplexed when he received his new instruction and, moreover, was firmly instructed to share this instruction only with his chief of staff[216]. No one else was to know. The side effect of this was that the Peel-Division could not work out and test any alternative scenarios. Thus, no plans and instructions could be worked out for a regular retreat to the projected re-assembly and secondary defence position behind the Peel-Raam-line, on the western bank of the Zuid-Willemsvaart (a narrow canal)[217]. Furthermore, Schmidt asked the logical question of whose orders he would be under after the 3rd Army Corps had withdrawn and – in all likelihood – French troops would be at his back. As for defensive instructions, all that he was told was to retreat in a controlled manner after a breakthrough of the Peel-Raam-line[218]. Schmidt received no reinforcement of his staff and no instruction on how to deal with French or Belgian allies, let alone a liaison staff with French-speaking officers[219]. The promotion of Schmidt to the rank of Major-General (even if only titular), which would have been more than reasonable in view of his duties and the relationship with the expected French, was apparently not considered, or at least not carried out[220]. As a result, a Dutch Colonel would be representing the Dutch armed forces vis-a-vis French forces[221]. Another clear sign on the wall that the allies were not taken very seriously by Winkelman. The whole plan and execution bore the signature of haste and remarkable disinterest in the continuation of the battle after the retreat of the 3rd Army Corps. This anomalous situation would conspicuously continue during the May Days whereas one would have expected a complete change in the approach of the Dutch high command as the invasion developed[222]. This makes it even more tempting to conclude that Winkelman's strategy was not a responsible military strategy – that would be adapted to actual developments – but a fixed concept, from which the general could not be dissuaded. To the contrary – on 10 May 1940, he doubled down on his instruction by ordering the evacuation from Brabant half a day earlier than his original instruction had specified.

The Winkelman plan demanded absolutely that the defence of Fortress Holland be in good order, especially on the southern front of Fortress Holland, which due to the evacuation of the Field Army from Brabant, had the worst preliminary defence of the entire system. This south-front was not in order[223]. By its very nature, the fronts of the Fortress were occupied only by troops of the Fortress Army[224]. These were the older regiments of infantry and artillery; units where the average age was higher, where almost all officers were reservists and where the organisation and armament was more modest than in the Field Army[225]. This was especially true for artillery. The Fortress Army artillery regiments usually had older artillery, sometimes pieces that had been taken out of mothballs and were two generations old. Although in 1940 more than half of the Dutch artillery was modern or at least of acceptable quality, somehow these oldest pieces in particular received all the attention, as if they symbolised the entire arsenal[226]. This created a myth of antiquated armed forces. Moreover, all belligerents (except the Germans[227]) had a relatively large number of artillery pieces of older design. These were bulky and slow-moving, but for that very reason still useful as quasi-static fortification artillery. Many such artillery pieces found their way to the south-front of Fortress Holland as well as the connecting Merwede-front between Sliedrecht and Gorcum. Following the events in Scandinavia in April 1940, the security force that occupied the east-front of the Fortress – which consisted of Brigades C and D – was redistributed, with a significant part of it being placed on the south-front, while a few other elements were placed on the Waal-Linge-front as a security force and, together with a few other battalions, formed Brigade G[228]. This saw the south-front of the Fortress being occupied by about a brigade strength of infantry, supported by quite a strong artillery component. Curiously, the southern front was not given its own sector command, but was led – all the way from the Hague – by the Commander Fortress Holland (C-VH) and his small staff. The other active fronts of Fortress Holland had their own sector command. Until April the southern front had had one integral staff quarter that had operated as a sector command. However, in April it was stated that no suitable officer and staff were available to set up an integral sector command. Remarkably, the deserted eastern front of the Fortress held its sector command, the reason for this being that if the Field Army would eventually reach that position there needed to be a controlling staff. The southern front, which according to the Winkelman Plan would be by far the most vulnerable because the defence in Brabant would become symbolic, was not given a local integral command. This decision was fundamentally wrong, as would become convincingly clear during the May Days. In principle, however, this was the domain of the Commander of Fortress Holland, the reactivated Lieutenant-General Jan van Andel[229]. However, he played no visible role in most strategic decisions before the May Days, nor to have sought information on peripheral matters that would eventually end up on his plate. His decision not to establish an integral command on the southern front of the Fortress resulted in the creation of three significant autonomous concentrations there. These were from the coast to the Nieuwe Merwede (river) near Gorcum respectively the Group Spui, the Group Kil and the cantonment (regional command) Dordrecht, where 1,500 troops were cantoned. All these entities were directly subordinate to the C-VH and had no formal connections to units on their flanks. In addition, initially Winkelman had determined that the redeployment of troops from the east-front of the Fortress would only take place after the beginning of hostilities. That changed when the Germans invaded Denmark and Norway on 9 April 1940. This accelerated the decisions of the OLZ, so that many instructions of 30 March were put into effect immediately. Thus, in the month before the German invasion, a considerable movement of troops took place. That kept many commanders and units busy. Thus less time could be spent on exercises and positioning. Troops that did arrive in the new position were employed right away. Work was being done with great haste to improve positions or even, in some locations, to start construction[230]. The major vulnerability was the pair of bridges across the Muese estuary[231] near Moerdijk, although bridges across the river at Keizersveer, Ravenstein and Grave were also of some importance[232]. The Moerdijk bridges were provided with a security detachment, but this was only meant to secure the bridge on the north side. On the south side they had a forward guard post and a number of barricades could be placed on the (railway) roads a few kilometre from the bridges. A proper bridgehead defence on the south side was constructed in April 1940[233]. This was no more than an outward looking perimeter defence of semi-permanent quality. Shortly before the May Days it was decided to concretise it. Outside of earthen emplacements, only a few concrete casemates were ready and available in May, but due to the German airborne landing in the heart of the bridgehead, it would ultimately serve only the German occupiers. The bridges had been prepared for destruction, but Reijnders and his successor Winkelman both refused to permit detonators to be connected until the last moment. The Generals were afraid of premature destruction by nervous soldiers. That would prove to be a fatal decision on 10 May 1940[234]. An occupation of the northern banks of the Hollandsch Diep (Isle of Dordrecht) and Haringvliet (Hoekse Waard) – the actual south-front of the Fortress – was to be carried out by the infantry of the 28th and 34th Regiment Infantry. The seawalls and dikes were not to be affected by position construction, so the position work there had to remain limited. The artillery placed to the rear was largely placed in poorly prepared open positions. Winkelman's 'Alamo' was a thin perimeter defence. This was to be reinforced with Field Army units as these would have withdrawn to the Fortress, but no positions had been constructed for this purpose, not even shelters or staging posts. There were no immediate reserves on the southern front so they would have to be brought in from far away. Ammunition distribution points were completely absent[235]. During the May Days of 1940, it would become clear how disastrous all these imperfections in military planning were. The first of the security forces from the east-front arrived on the south-front on 12 April 1940. A defence-plan had to be set up, trenches had to be expanded, firing-plans drawn-up, artillery fire-missions prepared and communications established. The Group quarters in Puttershoek, that had been chosen as an HQ for Group Kil, suffered from vermin and had to be treated first, hampering the effectiveness of the coordinating Group-staff and support units. Telex lines had to be set up and in order to secure at least outgoing messages, a pigeon loft was brought along for a section of homing pigeons[236]. The south-front, which was so prominently in the danger zone because of the Winkelman Plan, was on the eve of the German invasion still under construction. Moreover, standing orders for the troops were that ammunition was to be stored by company and not distributed to combatants, unless the highest degree of combat readiness had been ordered. Only the part of the detachment at Willemsdorp (located at the northern abutment of the Moerdijk bridges) that had active duty as well as the guard pickets had ammunition on them[237]. The regular infantry did not. Moreover, in Willemsdorp ammunition was stored centrally in a shed near the barracks camp. In the bridgehead Moerdijk (located south of the Meuse and south-east of the village Moerdijk) ammunition had been stored in a decentralized way so that all platoons could be supplied quickly. Group Kil had failed to make suitable arrangements for all positions and, despite warnings from subaltern officers of the infantry units, had not taken any proper measures by 10 May 1940. All this fitted in with the way in which, due to a lack of proper direction from above, there was too little improvisation and awareness within the Dutch armed forces at that time[238].

The German invasion of the Scandinavian countries on 9 April 1940 – which had been predicted in the Hague by the Dutch military attaché in Berlin, Major Sas, who was not appreciated by the intelligence service GS-III[239] – did not miss its effect. After this event, the government stopped daydreaming and finally, after a further ten days of meetings, dared to proclaim the State of Siege (from Dutch '*Staat van Beleg*': Martial Law). By then it was only three weeks before the German invasion of the Low Countries. The *Staat van Beleg* was of little use then. Winkelman accelerated measures that he had planned to take after the opening of hostilities and so troop movements were already being carried out, as we saw. Meanwhile, the KLM pilot Van Dijk[240] witnessed the German airborne landing on the airfield near Oslo in Norway on 9 April and returned to the Netherlands on 16 April. After being debriefed by KLM, he gave Minister of Defence Dijxhoorn a detailed account of his experiences. The GHQ initially showed remarkably little interest in civilian observations and accepted the report of the eyewitness lukewarmly[241]. Dijxhoorn's intervention in military affairs turned out to be positive this time as he wished to have through roads blocked within Fortress Holland. After all, German planes could land there. Unused airfields were ploughed up. Pickets were stationed on highways, airfields were reinforced[242]. Winkelman, except for the reinforcement of airfields, in spite of the similar wishes of the Commander Air-Defences, Lieutenant-General Best, felt little urgency in the blockade measures[243]. Dijxhoorn asked him to be allowed to initiate it himself and got Winkelman's approval. The road blocks turned out to be efficient measures that contributed to the failure of the German air-landings around the Hague, especially the large landing at Ypenburg[244].

By now, the OLZ and his Chief-of-Staff were taking an imminent German invasion seriously. However bizarre it may seem, there were still General Staff officers who did not take it seriously. Winkelman was not the man to impose strict discipline. Neither was his Chief-of-Staff. This meant that at the GHQ there was no clear expectation concerning the impending invasion. Staff officers were given quite a lot of leeway and used it. A year of frequent alerts had made many cynical. There were also other sentiments at play. Generals Carstens and Reijnders had been popular with many officers. Chief-of-Staff Carstens in particular was well liked and appreciated for his skills. The new leadership had less support and seemed to have sought less interaction with the staff. The head of the operations section, Lieutenant-Colonel Wilson, was dedicated but pecked in the ribs that the Peel-position would be sacrificed. Van de Plassche, head of the foreign intelligence section, one of the most important officers of the army command, had hardly any contact with the new OLZ. Both these staff officers influenced many other officers on the GHQ with their attitude. There was animosity among them. Then Captain Somer[245], also of GS-III, wrote an exposé about it in London[246]. It would be disputed, but many sources indicated that the situation at the GHQ was disputatious and that there were tensions. Although in the Reijnders period too there was sometimes talk about certain choices of the OLZ, Reijnders and Carstens were both thoroughbred army commanders that were respected. This was much less true of their successors. However, it is difficult to judge this matter *ex post facto*. What is certain is that this impression is strongly supported by the events on the eve of the German invasion, which will be discussed below.

In the second half of April and early May, there were all kinds of incidents. They were not critical in and of themselves, but they formed an exciting prelude to the 6th of May. Tension was very high. Major Sas and other sources[247] warned of an imminent German attack. This led to an increase in readiness and the cancellation of all leaves. General Best ordered that the air defence be ready daily from one hour before sunrise until one hour after sunset. For the armed forces, all leaves were cancelled on 7 May, which was the first time that measure was taken[248]. Winkelman ordered remarkable measures. He found it so obvious that the threat came from the east that when the alarm sounded the troops within the Fortress – with the exception of the coastal and air defences, and along the southern border – were excluded from the highest degree of readiness. This would also be the case on the evening of 9 May 1940, when the border troops reported much activity on the German side; also then the troops on the southern border with the exception of the Peel-Division were not alerted[249]. The incomplete alerting had a whole range of undesirable side effects[250], some of which Winkelman had considered but some of which he simply did not see. Certain measures had also been delegated to lower commanders - such as certain arrangements for ammunition stocks and distribution and the granting of particular leaves and the setting up of readiness grades at higher echelons. Here again the arrangements that Winkelman ordered were at fault. He did not adequately oversee the effects of his decisions. In this he deviated from the policy of his predecessor, who proclaimed the preparedness measures centrally – and was right in doing so because in the constellation of those days only one authority had the overview of the whole situation, the GHQ[251]. The exclusion of Fortress Holland and the southern border, however, showed how little the OLZ understood about modern warfare and how little he had learned from the invasions of Poland and Scandinavia[252]. The same could be said of the Chief-of-Staff and Commander Fortress Holland.

It is interesting to compare the Dutch procedure with the alerting of the Belgian and French units. They had an even greater challenge than the Dutch. Their large armies had so many men on leave that on 10 May 1940 there were units missing 15% of their strength, and in some units even higher[253]. A salient detail: the Germans also had to deal with furloughs and other absences. The stealth of the German invasion – which permitted increased readiness only 24 hours in advance – also surprised the German units. The Netherlands permitted only sick leave, so all units (except for vacancies) were at full strength. Thus, the preparedness at the borders was very good by international standards. But this was not the case in Fortress Holland. When on 9 May it seemed for a moment that the tension was easing a little, in the evening came the report from Sas that the invasion would really begin that night. Sas, after he noticed the disbelief at the Hague, did not mince his words when the head of GS-IIIA, Van de Plassche, called him again to ask if it was really that bad. Nevertheless, Van de Plassche still did not believe a word of it[254] and head of operations Wilson did not believe him either[255]. Winkelman and his Chief-of-Staff did[256]. They gave all necessary orders to the subordinate commanders and were convinced of the German invasion during the night[257]. So convinced that a great deal of demolition in the border region with Germany could already be carried out. Afterwards, they left the GHQ around midnight, convinced that things were in order[258]. They had decided not to spend the night at the headquarters and to let the Deputy Chief-of-Staff Colonel Van Alphen run the headquarters with a small security staff at the most important sections[259]. Even the head of operations was not on standby[260].

No convincing authority emanated from the way in which Winkelman and his Chief-of-Staff managed the GHQ and the immediately subordinate commands during these last 24 hours, although both radiated calm and deliberation[261]. After the war, they would reaffirm everything they had done (and left undone) in those days and firmly claim that their presence or absence at the GHQ had made no difference[262]. That was an untenable claim considering that the OLZ had linked a number of strategic instructions only to his personal actions or those of the Chief-of-Staff[263]. The fact that both Generals spent the night at home and one (Chief-of-Staff) chose to travel from Wassenaar to the GHQ on his bicycle the next morning and the other, because he did not have a driver at home, had to travel with his civilian neighbour, can hardly be explained in any other way than as naive and irresponsible[264]. Both eventually arrived at the GHQ well after the beginning of the German invasion[265]. The first hours of such an operation are golden hours. As a responsible army command in such a centralised organisation, one could not run the risk of being absent in that crucial phase[266]. The fact that Winkelman denied this even after the war shows his stubbornness, and if he really held this opinion, it is also a confirmation of unsuitability for the job. After all, without too many twists of fate, things could have turned out quite differently for the two officials, given what was going on in the air above and on the ground around them. The massive German air-landing operation around the Hague was in full swing when both Generals were – exposed and unprotected – on their way to the GHQ. Under no circumstances should they both have been absent, even though they were convinced of the German invasion at the crack of dawn. The effect signalled to other staff officers was that many saw the alert ending in a fizzle, as had happened so often before, although the remarkable orders to carry out much demolition along the eastern border convinced some. The question may therefore arise as to what would have been necessary to alarm some cynics[267].

Save all the criticism that can be levelled at the army command, it must be said at the same time that none of the other invaded countries were as prepared as the Netherlands at H-hour. The challenge of large leave-quotas has already been noted and also the alerting of the southern neighbours had not gone well. In Belgium, the warnings from Sas were not taken very seriously any more and although the belief in an impending German invasion grew stronger during the night, action was so slow that most of the border troops were not yet in full readiness when the German assault took place[268]. In addition, at the fortress of Eben-Emael, the German attack had started a little earlier to achieve total surprise. The Germans actually attacked directly from the air at the bridges and the fort thus surpassing the buffer of first having to cross Dutch territory. In his quarters in Vincennes the French Supreme Commander Gamelin was sleeping. He had brushed aside every warning in the evening of 9 May, even ignoring his own French intelligence about movements of German concentrations at the Luxembourg border[269]. He felt there was still time enough to act. The BEF entrusted to him was not even informed that things had become tense again, so that it was in a low state of readiness when suddenly, in the morning of 10 May, it received the alert. Precious hours were lost. When in fact the German border-crossing had long been underway, Gamelin finally decided to respond to the messages from his staff and get out of bed. After some thought, he decided on the execution of the *Hypothèse* Breda. It was then about 06:00 hrs, two hours after the German assault had started. By his slow action the French plans to come to the aid of Luxemburg in time had failed[270]. German '*Vorausabteilungen*' – including covert commandos who had crossed the border well before the hour of attack[271] – were quicker than the belated French cavalry, so that Luxembourg was immediately occupied and important roads for the German advance had fallen into German hands. The start of the mass movement of the BEF and most of the north-eastern French field army formations was also delayed by hours. The speed which the French would nonetheless achieve towards the north would prove to be the only favourable surprise of the first days of the campaign.

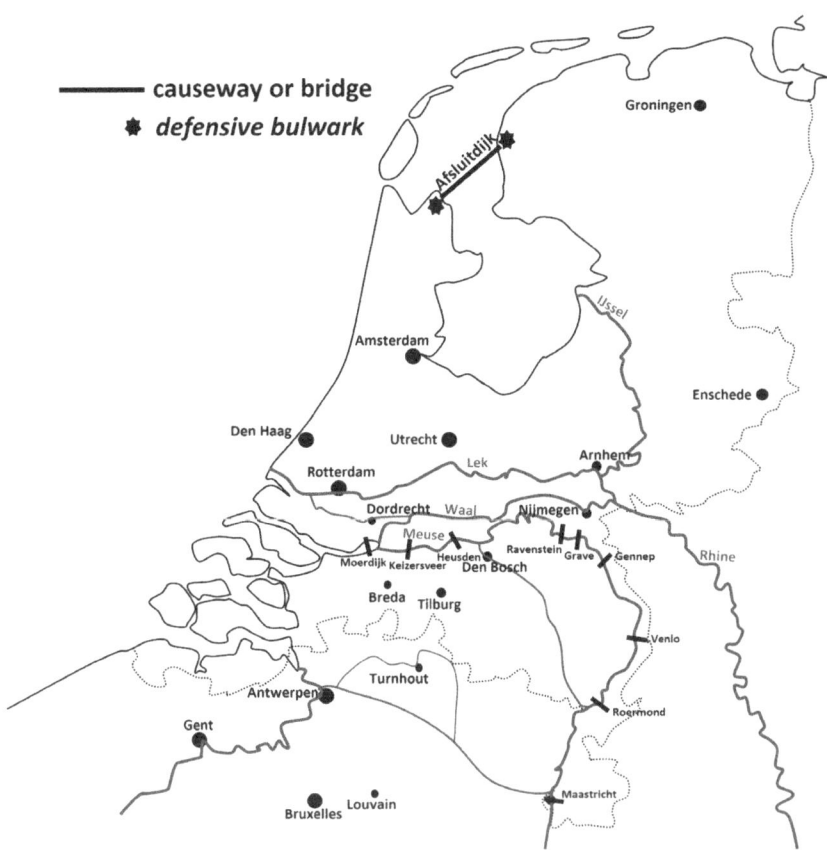

Map 6: The bridges across the Meuse (Gennep and Mook combined)

THE HOT STRATEGY

The essence of the discussion is the crucial strategic decision-making during the five-day war in the Netherlands in May 1940 and how the hot strategy related to the cold strategy, the *Grand Strategy* and especially to actual developments in the field.

On 10 May 1940 at 3:55 a.m. Dutch time[272] the war became a fact for the Netherlands. The German invasion of the Low Countries had begun. The Dutch defence along the eastern border reacted adequately. The last acts of demolition were carried out and even the bridges over the Meuse near Venlo and Roermond, both very close to the German border and targets of German raids, were destroyed just in time – although the order to destroy from the OLZ was not sent to his subordinate commanders until 04:40[273]. The IJssel defences further from the border did not yield any intact bridge.

On the Maas-Waal canal, one bridge (at Hatert) was destroyed imperfectly – a malfunctioning explosive charge was the cause – while the bridge near Heumen was treacherously captured by German *Brandenburg commandos* in flagrant violation of the law of war[274]. However, the lost bridge was defended tenaciously until late in the afternoon. The German objective had been to capture the bridge at Grave behind it and thereby gain an extra route to the west for motorised units. This effort failed, partly because the bridges further west over the Meuse at Grave and Ravenstein were destroyed in time. Across the Meuse, all bridges were destroyed except the one railway bridge between Gennep and Oeffelt on the single track line Boxtel - Wesel (the so-called 'German line'). There, around the exact invasion time of 03:55 hours, a raiding party of *Brandenburger commandos* succeeded in ambushing the bridge guards after having misled them on the spot, disguised as German POW's and four Dutch MP

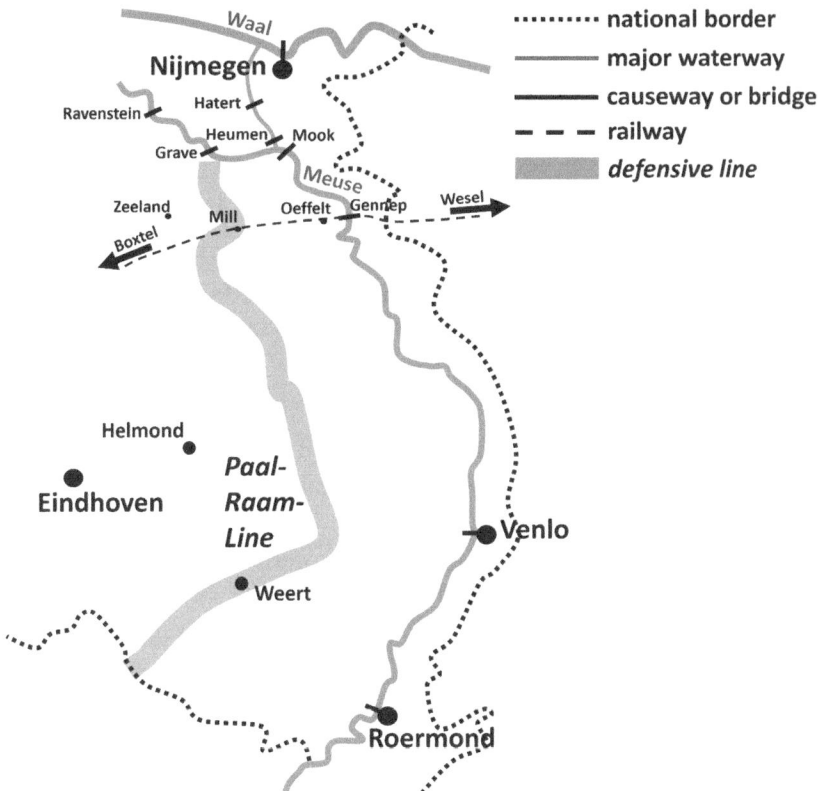

Map 7: The Meuse theatre between Nijmegen and Venlo

guarding them. The failure to destroy the bridge was not due to late instructions from the GHQ, but was related to decentralized local command-structures and a weak bridge-commander[275]. Some other strategic bridges had been targeted by *Brandenburger commandos* or similar covert operations, however, apart from the above-mentioned bridge, the Germans were unable to capture another intact bridge over an important waterway, as things also went against them around Maastricht[276]. This was a serious setback for the Germans and a compliment to the defence[277].

The capture by the Germans of the bridge at Gennep did not provide the Germans with any real operational success or benefit[278]. It did lead to a panic reaction in the Hague though. The news of the capture arrived simultaneously with the news that two German military trains had driven through the Maas-line and even through the Peel-Raam-line near Mill, to unload troops at the train-station of the village Zeeland (slightly west of Mill), although this event did not become known until later. This endangered Winkelman's strategic plan. He now feared that the Peel-Raam-line would not be able to cover the retreat of the main force of the 3rd Army Corps and the Light Division. The decision was taken to deploy the 2nd Regiment of Hussar-Motorcyclists from the Light Division to counter the breach. Meanwhile, the large-scale aerial assault on the western part of the country was already underway. The Netherlands was the first and at that time the only country to be on the receiving end of such a large scale strategic air-landing raid[279]. This presented the GHQ an operational reality for which theory books had not yet been written[280]. A classic operation with an enemy that moved from the border to the Fortress – which had been the premise of Winkelman's cold strategy and policy – was no longer. The enemy had boots on the ground in the heart of the Fortress Holland before Winkelman had finished his first briefing on his GHQ. From 04:30 hours onwards, real and false reports of parachute landings on the south-front and around the Hague swarmed the operational staffs. After 05:00 hours it was reported that Rotterdam had been attacked in its heart by infantry that had landed using seaplanes and that the Moerdijk bridges were being attacked by paratroopers. Airborne troops were reported landing south of Rotterdam. Winkelman put the 1st Army Corps (1.AC), which was located inside the Fortress as a strategic reserve, at the disposal of the C-VH to fight new expected airborne landings and – in the first instance – to fight the already landed Germans[281]. The situation in Rotterdam became clear the quickest. To remedy the situation the C-VH asked for a battalion of 1.AC as early as 05:15[282]. At 05:30 the CV asked the OLZ to allow the 3rd Army Corps and the Light Division to withdraw directly to Fortress Holland, which request was denied. At 07:00 hours this order was given by the OLZ[283] after all. At 07:45 hours the Commander Air-Defence (C-Lvd) Lieutenant-General P.W. Best received a partly burnt briefcase that had been found in the Tweede Adelheidsstraat in the Hague in a crashed Ju-52 with a part of the plan for the attack on the Hague[284]. These papers revealed that the Germans focussed on encircling the residential city and capturing members of the Government, the Army Command and even the Monarch. This information was shared with the OLZ and C-VH after which orders were given to seal off the Hague. At 08:00 hours the 10-veld artillery battalion (modern 10,5 cm *Bofors* howitzers) of 1.CA was made available for the bombardment of the seized airfield Waalhaven south of Rotterdam[285]. Meanwhile – probably between 06:00 and 07:00 - the military attachés of the UK, Belgium and France arrived at the GHQ. Both the British and French attachés reported that liaison missions would be sent[286]. The French attaché reported about the main lines of the Dyle-Breda plan and the projected French troops in transit to Brabant. This information was shared with the CV and C-VH. Around 09:30 it became clear that the Moerdijk bridges across the Meuse estuary had probably fallen into German hands, upon which the OLZ sent a telex to the CV that the Light Division, that was planned to retreat via those bridges to the Fortress, would instead move via Heusden and Keizersveer. Probably shortly afterwards Winkelman had a telephone conversation with Gamelin in the presence of the French attaché in which he asked the French General to have his troops retake Moerdijk so that the Netherlands could focus on other matters. Gamelin supposedly agreed to this, although he probably spoke in general terms[287]. At 10:20 hours the entire army air force was placed under C-VH with the intention for it to be used exclusively for the battle within the Fortress[288]. Attaché Van Voorst Evekink reported by telephone from Paris that the French GQG had firmly rejected the Dutch requests of sending troops to the Fortress[289]. The British attaché made it clear that requests to station RAF aircraft on Dutch bases were out of the question[290]. With that, the principles of Winkelman's cold strategy were in fact completely swept away[291]. What his strategy became afterwards has remained unclear and was not part of the questioning by the PEC. It is clear from the events and decisions, however, that Winkelman continued to follow his cold strategy as if nothing had changed. He did not adjust his overall plan, but continued to steer strongly towards an isolated defence within Fortress Holland. In the afternoon orders followed that underlined this. Not long after noon, the OLZ promised the C-VH that the CV would hand over infantry in the strength of a regiment for the defence of the Nieuwe Maas river near Rotterdam. This commitment would soon be doubled. The seized AFB Waalhaven was to be retaken. The C-VH requested the C-Lvd to make contact with the RAF and ask for air raids on the AFB's Ypenburg and Waalhaven[292]. These attacks and the shelling by 10-veld howitzers[293] from Hillegersberg ensured that from the evening of 10 May[294] until the end of 11 May only some fragments of the planned airborne troops and part of a reserve battalion of air-landed infantry (I./IR.72 of the 46th Infantry Division) could land on Waalhaven with a very modest supply of ammunition and equipment[295]. Waalhaven could be kept out of action by the Dutch by indirect means, which is why recapture should not have been a priority at all. From the 12th onwards the Germans themselves considered it no longer responsible to land there, although the need for it had also largely disappeared. On that day troop landings ceased and only occasional aircraft landed[296].

Let us take a closer look at the frenzy of often conflicting reports which reached the Dutch GHQ. The mosaic of messages at the GHQ created a picture that in no way resembled the intended disciplined retreat of a Dutch army to its Alamo. On the contrary. This

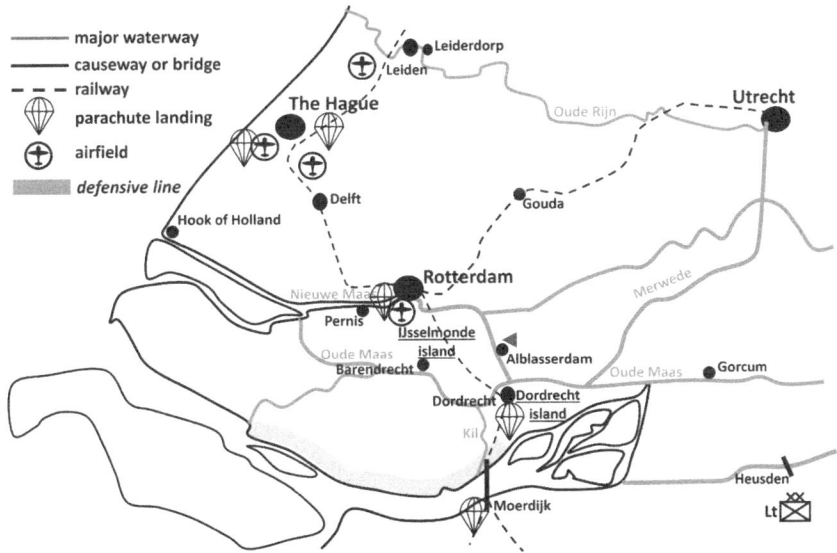

Map 8: The airborne theatre of operations within Fortress Holland

was something nothing like what they had been trained for. The total lack of adequate training and war experience, as well as the confrontation with underestimated or unknown new means and tactics, took the GHQ by the throat. It was the realisation of Clausewitz's theory in optima forma[297]. There was a picture that showed that from the crest of Groningen to the junction of the Netherlands, Belgium and German near Aachen, the German war machine came massing across the Dutch border[298]. The aggressor had become active from Luxembourg to the Wadden Sea and had therefore launched a major offensive. As an unexpected extra dimension, an ambitious airlanding had taken place right within the supposedly secure Fortress – and seemingly all over it. The German airborne troops were reported from every corner of Fortress Holland. The war literally coming over Holland had not been foreseen, let alone on this scale[299]. This demanded immediately all focus on the moderately staffed GHQ and the totally understaffed HQ of the C-VH. From underestimating the scale of the possible airborne landings beforehand, they then turned to overestimating it. Winkelman and his Chief-of-Staff intervened. Winkelman tied 1.CA to the interior of the Fortress, would later that day do the same with the Light Division. Moreover, as mentioned above, he had asked the CV – who protested vehemently – for troops to reinforce the Nieuwe Maas front in Rotterdam. The request grew from one regiment to a total of seven battalions and some smaller units[300]. Another three battalions were designated for the protection of the capital on 11 May[301]. This meant that behind the main defence in the Grebbe-line and on the east front of the Fortress, the already weak tactical reserves were weakened even further. These reinforcements were mostly for the benefit of the Nieuwe Maas defence in Rotterdam and beyond, where in reality only a few hundred airborne troops were opposing the Dutch. The additional troops were also intended to counter expected further landings elsewhere[302]. Because of this overreaction on the Dutch side, the German airborne operation was a strategic success. The landing on the first day of the war of at most 8,000 to 9,000 paratroopers and airborne troops[303] generated a countermeasure worth 25,000 men of 1.CA and another 9,000 men in called-up reserves of the Field Army at the expense of the concentrations behind the Grebbe-line and on the outer-fronts of the

Fortress. This was in addition to the depot troops already involved and the Fortress Army on the western and southern fronts of the Fortress. Despite this large force of troops and firepower, little initiative was developed. There was mostly occupation of positions in anticipation of new landings, hardly any fighting[304]. Here *'the fog of war'* really was the devil for the GHQ and particularly the C-VH, because they not only grossly overestimated the *'boots on the ground'* of the German airborne formations, but especially their intentions[305]. There was so much disinformation, so many additional airborne landings were reported[306], that decision-makers in the Hague got the picture of an overwhelming German airborne operation. The logical result was the overreaction, only the overreaction arose in such a form and lasted so long that the logic gradually disappeared from the course of action. The overreaction, however, was reinforced by the earlier mentioned discovery of German papers in the wreckage of a downed Ju-52 – namely that the Hague with its staffs and authorities was the target. The airborne operation thus became central to the Dutch hot strategy and its clear and present threat to the GHQ itself and other officials in the Hague was experienced as much more invasive than the operation itself really was, while the most strategically dangerous component (the intended link-up with ground troops near Moerdijk) was insufficiently recognised. The operational and strategic policy pursued here had profound implications beyond the operational response within the theatre attacked with airborne troops[307]. The war over Holland dominated the decision making at the GHQ.

The fact that every strategy requires immediate adjustment after the first bullet has been fired left, with regard to Fortress Holland, a very deep footprint on the operational plot-table of Winkelman and his Chief-of-staff[308]. Winkelman immediately had to improvise and his strategic talent was immediately put to the test[309]. The capture of the Moerdijk bridges and the falling into German hands of four airfields were five dangerous wounds from which blood ran[310]. A sixth wound was the rapid encroachment on the Peel-Raam-line, which Winkelman saw as only a preliminary defence, but which had the weighty task of covering the retreat of the 3rd Army Corps and the Light Division during the first night of war. The latter touched on the basis of Winkelman's plan to retain the Field Army as much as possible for his Alamo strategy. As both the Maas- and Peel defence-lines seemed to have been breached in the crucial north at 04:30 hours, the durability of this cluster of defences was suddenly of great concern. The evacuation from Brabant could be foiled by a quick and deep German penetration along the northern Meuse or it could be hit halfway in the flank. This led to a series of decisions that in many respects seemed logical from Winkelman's strategic plan, but curious from the desirable strategic reaction. There was, after all, now every reason for the OLZ to revise his strategy. There was talk of a broad German attack and the GQG had announced they were sending forces to the south. The French would come to the area of Breda, the Germans had not just invaded the south-eastern territory but invaded the entire country. The French would not send reinforcements to Fortress Holland, which meant that the basis for the Alamo strategy from the *cold strategic plan* had in fact been completely swept away[311]. Moreover, the south-front of the Fortress had been forced open by the seizure of the Moerdijk and Dordrecht bridges. That back-door stood wide open. There was therefore every reason to change strategy and to conduct the defence in Brabant with the Field Army and offer the French every chance to operate in the sector Breda and Moerdijk. Without this preliminary defence in Brabant the German wedge on the door at Moerdijk was even more dangerous. Winkelman, however, stuck to his plan and even accelerated it. He decided to start the retreat of 3.AC and the Light Division onto Fortress Holland not only after dark but immediately[312]. In order to ensure that the ongoing defence sealing-off the German breach at Mill would not prematurely collapse, the small but able 2nd Regiment of Motorized Hussars was temporarily separated from the Light Division and sent to Mill as to intervene[313]. It would later move towards Fortress Holland after the front line at Mill had restored. When it became clear that the Moerdijk bridges had fallen Winkelman did not react by an order for the Light Division to move with one of its battle groups[314] through Brabant towards Moerdijk. Instead he chose to give the 6th Border Infantry Battalion, that had guarded the Belgian border south of Breda, the task of retaking the bridges. Because the OLZ realized that the chances of success for that artillery-less border battalion were minimal he trusted – after having spoken to General Gamelin – that Moerdijk would eventually be retaken by the French[315].

Here one touches the pivotal point of Winkelman's hot strategy, in which he stuck to his Alamo strategy at all costs. Of course, one must look at events in a nuanced way. The diffuse nature of the German airborne operation made everything confusing. The raid on the government centre distorted the operational strategy to the point where presumably only a better strategist with war experience would have made the right decisions. The determining fact was presumably – the exact contemporary considerations cannot be verified because of the burning of the GHQ-records at the time of the capitulation[316] – that with the loss of the Hague (with government and staffs) the defence of the country would also break down. From this point of view, the primary reaction of concentrating everything on the Fortress as quickly as possible seems explainable. However, the crucial southern front and the operational area in Brabant fell victim to this. That theatre degenerated – especially after Gamelin's promise – for the GHQ to a side issue, partly because the battle within the Fortress had been delegated by the OLZ to the C-VH, General Van Andel. Brabant had already been written off as a manoeuvring area, had been taken away from the CV before the war, and received no further attention from the head of operations or the Chief-of-Staff[317]. The strategic cornerstones, however, were determined by the OLZ. He saw to it that the airborne landings around the Hague and Rotterdam would be fought, with the occupied and used AFB Waalhaven as the centre of attention for counter offensive action. It was realised that the Germans had encroached on the southern front and thus threatened Fortress Holland. It was already thought that the idea behind this was to lead German troops into the Fortress via the chain of captured bridges. However, the GHQ left the restoration of the initiative and the repair of the breach entirely to the C-VH and the French. As was assessed before, additional troops were allotted to General Van Andel to enable him to achieve the operational goals set for him. 1.AC first, then some regiments of the Field Army reserve and finally Van Andel got the Light Division as a genuine manoeuvre formation. The C-VH was instructed to retake Waalhaven above all else. That was the umbilical cord through which the German operation was fed and it had to be cut.

The operational pivot point in the operation of the Germans, Dutch and French in the Netherlands was the Moerdijk bridgehead. This was the only location where a tactical change could significantly alter the operation for all sides both operationally and strategically. The interests of controlling this location remained partly as before for the Dutch and entirely the same for the Germans. For both, possession of the intact bridges was essential in principle. For the Germans this remained essential, for the Dutch it became a threat after 12 May around 15:00 hours (arrival of German ground troops near Moerdijk) and the destruction of the bridges became suddenly crucial. To the French, the Dutch possession of these Moerdijk bridges on 10 and 11 May seemed an ambition to be supported secondarily, but on 12 May, German possession was more to the advantage of the French cause. After all, it could then divert the force of the oncoming German formations towards Fortress Holland instead of the whole of the French 7th Army and subsequently the allied northern front of Antwerp and the Westerscheld bank. Curiously, for the Dutch, the retaking of the bridges until the evening of 12 May would not have led to their destruction. Winkelman ordered a ban on firing on the bridges and wished to keep them intact to allow the French to gain and maintain contact with the Fortress. It is hard to know why, because the French had systematically indicated that they would not make any troops available above the Meuse estuary at Moerdijk. Recapture by the French would not have led directly to destruction, which would have allowed the Germans to regain control of the bridges with ground troops. The question is, especially with Winkelman's proviso not to destroy the bridges, whether the Dutch could have prepared them for destruction in the meantime[318]. Possibly the bridges would have fallen back into German hands. The French, on the other hand, suspected in all likelihood that the Dutch would have blown up the bridges the moment they were recaptured. The Germans would have faced a considerable deterioration of the operational situation if the bridges had been destroyed. Not only would their strong 26th Army Corps – that was issued orders to enter the Fortress as well as push the

French away back into Belgium – have been side-lined for the battle in the Fortress, but the fragile airborne corridor would have been seriously jeopardised. With all the other bridges across the Meuse destroyed, an amphibious crossing of the more than 1,000 m wide Meuse estuary (Hollandsch Diep) with its strong current would not have been a plausible option, or at least one can assume that the Germans would have handed the battle for Fortress Holland over to their 10th Army Corps that was fighting on the east-front of the Fortress. It is obvious that a reinforcement of the latter army corps would have followed, presumably with SS formations and one of the infantry divisions[319]. Such an event would probably have stretched the battle in the Netherlands by at least a couple of days, although even in this scenario a strategic air bombardment could have speeded things up. The element that was uncertain for the GHQ was the possible French consideration that the German possession of the bridges at Moerdijk would at some point be beneficial to the French operation. It is almost certain that the AHK did not – or did not seriously – consider this. This is clear from the complex of Dutch instructions before and after 13 May 1940 around 01:00 hours. In that light, it is interesting to look again at the Franco-Dutch military relations and the developments as a result of it.

Essential was the (first) telephone conversation of Winkelman with Gamelin, that Winkelman says to have had on 10 May. The exact content of this conversation has not been documented and has never been clarified either, although other Dutch staff officers confirm it took place in the presence of the French attaché. Gamelin says nothing about it in his memoirs and only recalls to have spoken with Winkelman on 11 and 12 May. The lack of reliable information on particularly this first conversation is a major gap in the source material. The nuances of the discussions are historically essential, because the essence of the first conversation touched a foundation in Winkelman's strategy, namely the abandonment of Moerdijk from a Dutch operational perspective. The first conversation between the two CIC's presumably took place somewhere between 09.30 and 11.30 hours. At that time it was already clear that the Moerdijk bridges were almost certainly lost and occupied by the Germans[320]. Both parties had previously exchanged their strategies through their attachés and probably repeated them that very morning. According to Winkelman Gamelin reacted to the Dutch strategy without dismay[321]. It was announced that liaison missions were being sent back and forth, although Gamelin (also) stated in his memoirs to have requested a Dutch mission to be sent to the 7th Army HQ but this request is untraceable in Dutch archives and never materialized either[322]. Winkelman requested Gamelin to retake Moerdijk, which he apparently promised[323]. This solved the problem of the open backdoor for the OLZ. Winkelman would also hardly consider it further, by which he made a capital mistake[324]. He would direct the attention of the C-VH on Waalhaven and leave Moerdijk to the French. It is very curious that the open door at Moerdijk was like a castle with the bridge over the moat left unguarded. After all, the Germans were lords and masters of the gates as far as the courtyard at the bridges of Rotterdam. They could reinforce their positions with subsequent airborne landings. The entire 1.AC was concentrated almost exclusively in the sector around the Hague. Further south, the Light Division was the only unit available for further action. The GHQ therefore saw more risk in the Hague sector than in the Moerdijk-Rotterdam sector, which it apparently considered secured by assigning the Light Division and by the French promise to intervene at Moerdijk. The result of the assessment at the GHQ was that the solution chosen was not to send a combat group of the Light Division from Brabant to Moerdijk to clear the German bridgehead but that intervention against the German operation was organized from the inner lines of Fortress Holland. Winkelman defended that decision before the PEC with the answer that after all the French would restore the situation at Moerdijk[325] and that Waalhaven "... *where enemy airborne infantry was constantly being landed was an extremely important point. If that continued and the Germans got sufficient troops, even for the Germans the immediate possession of the Moerdijk bridge would not be so urgent anymore*"[326] . Whether Winkelman was trying to mislead the laymen of the PEC with this reasoning is unclear, but his argument was paper-thin and it did not answer the question posed[327]. After insistence by the PEC chairman, Winkelman blamed the French. They had promised to retake Moerdijk but had not kept word[328].

Winkelman's reasoning was flawed and he also ignored the extremely weak leadership of his subordinate, the C-VH, which failure came for Winkelman's account and not for that of the French. The German use of Waalhaven could have been largely suppressed with artillery[329] and troops could have been moved via Vlaardingen across the Waterway to Pernis to defend on the island of IJsselmonde – the island on which the south of Rotterdam and Waalhaven are situated – against the Germans operating from the corridor[330].

The Light Division was ideally suited to the type of action required here on the south-front of the Fortress against the light German troops. It was a unit which had all the resources to develop one or more fast attack(s) with sufficient firepower against the German airborne troops. As said before it should have been sent with a combat group to Moerdijk in the morning of the 10th[331]. If they had retaken the Moerdijk bridges – which, considering the recorded qualities of the Division during the May Days, is doubtful[332] – it could have pushed on to Dordrecht where another German airborne battalion had taken two crucial bridges. It could have taken the other battle group of the Division, that was concentrated near Papendrecht and Alblasserdam on the north side of the river Merwede, and jointly execute a classic encirclement of the German bridgehead near Dordrecht. The great advantage of this would have been that the initiative would have been regained and on the south-front decisively severed. After all, waiting for the French not only meant the question of whether that door would be closed, it also allowed German troops to dig in for at least two days at Moerdijk and elsewhere in their small bridgeheads. In reality Winkelman asked something different of 3.AC and the Light Division. The latter had to evacuate over the Meuse and Merwede rivers and regroup at Gorcum. The 3rd Army Corps was to make the same move via other routes and then occupy the south-eastern sector of Fortress front[333]. The Light Division was initially to move west to act as a mobile reserve for the GHQ, but when its most forward elements reached Gorcum it received the order around 16:00 to go to Alblasserdam and place itself under the direct orders of C-VH. Until that moment it was completely uninformed of the strategic situation[334]. At Alblasserdam – where a brand new traffic bridge across the Noord river connected to the island IJsselmonde – the Division would have to give up a battalion to the defence of Dordrecht – that was under siege of German airbornes – and push with the main force across the Noord river and subsequently retake AFB Waalhaven during the night after that airfield had first been raided by RAF bombers[335]. Hesitant action by the Commander of the Light Division (Colonel Van der Bijl) led to missed opportunities when he postponed the operation to the early morning of 11 May. This was a crucial tactical blunder. The Germans had not known of the Alblasserdam bridge which had not been indicated on their maps. General Kurt Student – who commanded the airborne operation between Moerdijk and Rotterdam – had been furious when he found out that this bridge appeared to be right in his bridgehead. He lacked sufficient troops to safeguard this side of his corridor and only had one platoon of infantry and two light guns at the bridge in the evening of 10 May. There were no German reinforcements nearby and *Luftwaffe* intervention could be expected only by daylight[336]. When the airbornes noticed the arrival of Dutch formations in the evening they called for additional troops, which strengthened their defences at night. This event caused the Dutch action in the morning of 11 May to falter, although even with that stronger German garrison, hesitant action and lack of courage on the part of Colonel Van der Bijl was to blame for the failure. Two Dutch shore parties had reached the other side of the river but a handful of casualties had made the Colonel call of the action. He called General Van Andel and stated that the crossing of the Noord river was a mission impossible. The General yielded but insisted on the Division still reaching the island of IJsselmonde. A truly bizarre alternative plan was developed between the C-VH and the Colonel. The Division was to leave two battalions and an artillery battalion along the Noord and to cross over the Merwede river to the Island of Dordrecht with the remainder of its formations. There they first had to roll up the German occupation around the city of Dordrecht. After that was done, the river Kil had to be crossed at Wieldrecht. Subsequently the combat group would have to try to get across the Oude Maas near Barendrecht. This location was defended by the Germans, who also held the only fixed bridge across the Oude Maas there. Yet the Division would have to deal with them.

When that step would have been taken, the Division would have to attack the Germans at Waalhaven. It was an absurd plan. There is no rational explanation for so much wishful thinking, particularly not since the Light Division had, just before this new plan was designed, not even been able to cross the barely defended Noord river[337]. The C-VH should not have given any other instruction to the Division Commander than to cross the Noord again and succeed, regardless of losses[338]. No document or interrogation reveal how they thought they could successfully execute the extremely complex new operation. It is not surprising that nothing came of it. The Light Division would disperse more and more in the following days and bog down in an almost continuous city battle in and around Dordrecht and eventually a weakly developed offensive over the Island of Dordrecht on the 13th. The poor performance of the Division stunned many after the war. It was the best equipped unit of the Field Army, modern for its day and age. It had the best officers and NCO's, most of its senior ranks were professional soldiers. Nonetheless, in reality, the unit was poorly led tactically at almost all levels, fell victim to panicked senior officers who suspected treachery everywhere and then, through inertia, would suffer an unnecessary encounter with German tanks and *Stuka's* on 13 May, which cost it almost half of its strength on the island[339]. The only real operational case of *Blitzkrieg tactics* in Holland during the May Days hit the battle group of the Light Division on 13 May in the morning when it ran into German armour and tactical air force south of Dordrecht. It was completely overrun without a chance. The reason for this was the fact that the Moerdijk bridges had not been retaken and the Division had exhausted itself for four days in difficult manoeuvres with hardly any initiative. The deployment of this Division – which was supposed to be the elite of the Field Army – was a complete failure. The whole operation demonstrated the tactical and operational weakness of the Dutch General Staff and the C-VH. However, it was also a failure on the part of the OLZ and his Chief-of-Staff who tolerated the total failure of the C-VH within the Fortress. The term 'total failure' seems to be very strong here. However, when one considers the balance of forces within the Fortress with a large Dutch supremacy in all but the third dimension, one cannot help but conclude that in the three days of fighting preceding the German link-up at Moerdijk, nothing had been achieved in restoring the situation. After the mostly locally initiated recaptures of the airfields in the morning and early afternoon of 10 May 1940, nothing had been achieved and there was no sign of the development of initiatives[340]. Nothing!

The misjudgement at the GHQ of the importance of the bridges near Moerdijk in the various battle plans of the belligerents is the pivot point of the story. However, the fundamental intention of the Belgian defence and the French Breda strategy – and the strategically correct assessment of the connection these had with the Dutch theatre – seems to be the point where things went completely wrong at the GHQ. There is no trace of any integral consideration of the allied operational plan. The Dutch leadership seems to have reasoned purely from the Dutch point of view. Although no French liaison-party had arrived at the GHQ yet – they would not reach the Hague until 14 May and had to flee immediately to Scheveningen to escape the Germans – there were the French and Belgian military attachés. Their role is unclear, but it is certain that they passed on at least basic information to the GHQ. The Netherlands did not participate in the decision-making process of the allied countries and was always informed late about (relevant) decisions[341]. Apart from three missions to the Belgian, French and British general headquarters, the Netherlands had no liaison teams ready to link up with lower allied staffs – such as the 7th Army staff – so that no coordination at field army level was possible. Not even a French-speaking staff-team had been added to the already undersized Peel-Division staff, which may be considered a fundamental mistake of magnitude. What effects developments in Belgium had on the French plans in the Netherlands the GHQ was thus always informed late. This made it difficult to obtain an up-to-date situational picture. However, by barely showing any interest in the events below the south-front of the Fortress, the army command did not actively gather any information either. The information mosaic concerning matters outside the Fortress was never a priority. It was therefore impossible to make a meaningful estimate of what considerations on the part of the allies might change. Moreover, Winkelman thought that Gamelin could steer the war operationally, which was not the case. Gamelin was also at a great distance and in principle not meant to command the north-eastern theatre. General Georges was supposed to fill that role. He was the commander of the French field army forces and – by delegation – of the BEF in Northern France, Belgium and the Netherlands. Gamelin was not supposed to intervene in this, except for the main lines of strategy and weighty decisions[342]. Thus, a promise by Gamelin about an operational matter such as the retaking of Moerdijk was of limited value because Giraud, as the commander of the 7th Army, had to make his own operational considerations. By the way, until the afternoon of 11 May he himself was still convinced of the possibilities in the sector Antwerp - Breda[343]. Gamelin's supposed promise to Winkelman is only echoed in one instruction. That instruction was carefully worded and left Giraud the opportunity to measure the instruction against the circumstances in-situ, just as it should have been[344]. If Gamelin did make a firm promise to Winkelman, this was done out of underestimation of the speed that things would take or perhaps only to secure Dutch support for the allied – read 'French' – cause. Winkelman apparently attached much more importance to this promise than Gamelin did. It was wishful thinking on Winkelman's part. This was logical, but at the same time logic dictates that the Dutch Supreme Commander should also have realised that the issue was for him a central issue and for his French counterpart at most a side issue. The fact that this open door through the Dutch southern front was so important for the preservation of the Dutch defence made it unreasonable that Winkelman left the whole initiative to close it to a third party whom he could only suspect of having a limited interest in its success. Winkelman should also have kept this in his own hands due to the nature and development of the Belgian defence plans. The defence plan with the southern neighbour was, as far as the first phases were concerned, as it were an inflated balloon. If penetrated anywhere, it would collapse. The Belgian defence plan called for the main resistance to hold on the line Antwerp - Namur - which meshed with the allied Dyle-Plan[345]. The preliminary defence system had a semi-spherical shape which ran from the north-east of the Antwerp region along the Antwerp canals, the Albert Canal and then along the Meuse to the south. The latter actually ran in a south-westerly

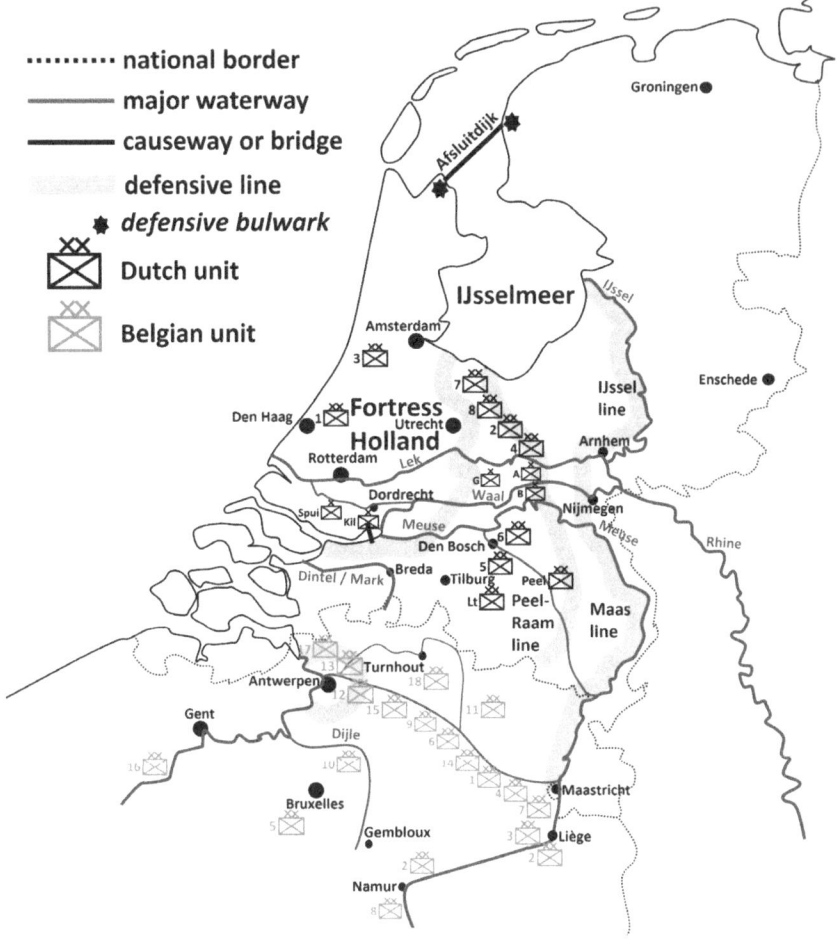

Map 9: Disposition of the field army units of the Low Countries

direction from Venlo, then bent sharply to the west near Liège and only then turned south again near Namur. The Dyle-base had Namur as its pivot point. Below Namur, the Meuse was still followed, but from Namur onwards, the river was abandoned for the main defence and became the forward defence largely (to be) occupied by French light formations. The Belgian forward defence-line thus ran in a balloon-shape from Namur over Liège, Visé and then behind the Albert Canal to Antwerp. In front of that line were some security units that had to report breaches of the border by enemy forces and execute demolitions. The crucial point was that once the Belgian

Meuse-Front had been breached[346] the balloon would immediately deflate for lack of intermediate defence-lines. When it deflated, the entire defence system in the north of Belgium up to the Dyle front – which was situated to the east of Antwerp – would immediately have failed. When one looks at the position that would be created for the French 7th Army one immediately recognises that in the event of a breakthrough on the Meuse and a Belgian retreat onto the Dyle-defences it would be in danger of being cut off in Holland[347]. The scenario that Winkelman so feared for his own 3rd Army Corps and Light Division in Brabant – that it would be cut off from the main defences by a German penetration – he did not recognize, or not sufficiently, regarding the French troops in the Netherlands. It was a fact that the Netherlands had not prepared itself for an allied defence, had not sent a liaison mission to the 7th Army, and therefore had not been able to participate in the conference on 12 May near Bergen, Belgium, where the other allies did meet[348]. This created a huge information gap. Winkelman could have been all the wiser would he have delegated a mission to the 7th Army.

The turning point for the Breda-variant was in fact the capitulation of the Eben-Emael fortress, which took place around noon on 11 May. The Belgian retreat order onto the main defence followed shortly afterwards and caught the French by surprise[349]. Although German troops had been advancing through the region just south of the Dutch border (the Kempen) before, the strong German 6th Army broke out into the Meuse valley on 11 May and in one day advanced with an advance unit of a tank division to the area of Tongeren and even west of it[350]. In terms of timing, this was simultaneous with the arrival of the French vanguards in Brabant that made contact with German reconnaissance units below Den Bosch. The 7th Army was still in the process of deploying to the north[351]. In the evening of 11 May and the morning of 12 May, the gravity of the situation became clearer, but it did not yet lead to a retreat order for the 7th Army. In the course of 12 May this did happen. In the afternoon, after the major allied meeting near Bergen the threatening integral picture was clear to everyone present[352]. For the 7th Army it meant that the position behind the Breda-Mark-front in the Netherlands would be untenable. This position would have to be abandoned to withdraw onto the Scheldt front, north of Antwerp. The Netherlands was not informed about this, which was another sign that there was no real alliance between the Dutch and the allies[353]. The allied countries did not expect much more from the Dutch armed forces and it was estimated that an isolated Netherlands would hardly be able to hold out for more than a few days.

The role of the French forces northeast of Antwerp thus changed on 12 May. The 7th Army was to go back. The French reserve troops along the coast, in Zeeuws-Vlaanderen (Dutch Flanders) and on Walcheren, had to stay to prevent a possible quick German conquest of the access to Antwerp[354]. With the imminent German threat in the north, it was clear that a rapid advance of German mechanised and motorised formations was imminent in both the Netherlands and Belgium[355]. The Netherlands had disappointed the French by abandoning the defence of the Peel-Raam-line and filling it only with light troops, so that it did not hold even twenty-four hours[356]. Subsequently, the French observed that the Dutch resistance in Brabant totally crumbled in the afternoon of 11 May after the Germans managed to penetrate the improvised Dutch fall-back defence behind the Zuid-Willemsvaart[357]. From that moment on, coordination between the Dutch and the French largely disappeared. Many Dutch units in Brabant experienced this, which particularly was felt after Colonel Schmidt and his entire staff were captured by the German vanguard in the morning of the 12th. Moerdijk played for the French from the point on that the Breda-strategy was abandoned, only the role of a relief valve. If the French were to retake the Moerdijk bridges, the Dutch could (from the French point of view) follow this up immediately by destroying those crucial bridges. This would mean that the German formations storming to the west would likely fall entirely on the 7th Army. To entice a considerable part of them to cross the Moerdijk into Fortress Holland was in the French and Belgian interest. Nowhere do French sources reveal these considerations, so the above is a conclusion which is plausible but unproven. On 12 May, however, the French would implicitly choose this course of action by their dispositions. The screen of troops of 1.DLM, built up on 11

May between the Turnhout Canal, Goirle and the Wilhelmina Canal up to the Mark Canal (a 6 km long connecting channel between the Wilhelmina Canal and the Mark river north of Breda), was dismantled and withdrawn southwards. In the morning of 12 May, except for destroyed bridges and a single stray Frenchman at two bridges on the south side of the Wilhelmina Canal, the Germans found no French defence of Tilburg. The previously taken position in front of Tilburg was cleared and the reconnaissance group which had held the positions between Tilburg and Oosterhout (*Groupe Lestoquoi*) was withdrawn and placed south of Breda. Before that, the French had not cared for the part of Brabant north of the Wilhelmina Canal, not even on 10 and 11 May. When the Commander of the Peel-Division, Colonel Schmidt, in the early morning of 11 May at the HQ of the French commander of 1.DLM in Oostmalle (Belgium) discussed cooperation, French General Picard was not keen to listen to Schmidt after he heard that the Peel-Raam-line was already abandoned. He asked the Dutch to hold on to the north of the Wilhelmina Canal in their retreat and to keep the south side free for French troops. The only interest there for the French side was the front defence behind the canal at Turnhout extended to the Wilhelmina Canal and south of the Mark Canal on Dutch territory. Where this canal joined the river Mark at Terheijden the French main defence (25.DIM and its reconnaissance unit) took over the position. The French however never took any position above the Wilhelmina Canal, Mark Canal or Mark/Dintel river. The route north of the Wilhelmina Canal to Oosterhout and Geertruidenberg was thus wide open. The French kept exactly to the boundary of the Breda Strategy and thus the lower and rear side of the Mark and the waterways connected to it. Moerdijk was left open all that time and nothing changed after Gamelin's supposed commitment. On 10 May not a single French order came which would go beyond instructions to reconnoitre the German bridgehead at Moerdijk[358]. On 11 May, the most far-reaching instruction came to assist the Dutch in retaking the Moerdijk bridge, if the operational circumstances justified it and if it was in the interest of the 7th Army, but it was made very clear that in principle no action should be taken beyond the front near Breda[359]. However, by 12 May, the French already assessed the Dutch situation as hopeless.

Nothing more was done and French forces already began taking the first steps back. The last order issued concerning Moerdijk was an instruction in the afternoon of 12 May to 2.GRDI to reconnoitre the German bridgehead from the area of Zevenbergen. However, they had sight and fire contact with armoured reconnaissance troops of the 9th *Panzer Division*[360]. These scouts, who were reinforced with a company of motorized infantry, a battery of artillery, a platoon of mechanized *Flak* and a platoon of pioneers, linked-up with the commander of the German paratroopers who occupied the Moerdijk bridgehead on 12 May at 15:30. As mentioned earlier, in the evening and night the first tanks and artillery of the main force arrived. During the late night of 12 to 13 May and the next morning, the Moerdijk bridge was crossed by half of the 33rd Tank Regiment of 9.PzDiv. The French were spared a confrontation with these forces. Fortress Holland was then decisively penetrated by strong German ground forces. At that moment – the morning of 13 May 1940 – the fate of the Netherlands in this campaign was sealed. That this moment came so soon was due to a failed hot strategy. The GHQ had bet on the wrong horse and had done nothing to retake the Moerdijk bridges or to exploit its troops in Brabant after 10 May. Moreover, there was hardly any attention paid to the deteriorating field intelligence concerning the situation in Brabant. The French, already withdrawing from Breda had their retreat hampered by German armour on 13 May when the second half of the 33rd Tank Regiment drove them out of Breda and the surrounding area. Those tanks were then sent into Fortress Holland to join the rest of the Tank Division that was about to move into Rotterdam. The motorised regiment *Leibstandarte-SS "Adolf Hitler"*, recruited from the German 10th Corps, also joined the troops crossing the Moerdijk bridges into Rotterdam on 14 May. The *SS-V Division* attached to the 26th Corps was given the task to expel the French from West-Brabant[361]. They would have remarkably little trouble doing so. The first serious battle they would have to fight was around the Belgian settlement Essen and the Dutch Zanddijk-line in Zeeland on their way to Walcheren.

There is another element that deserves to be discussed because it touches on the extremely weak strategy of the Dutch army command in those days. Therefore, we will go back to the 12th of May. After the aborted attempt to cross the Noord on the 11th, the Light Division had its hands full crossing the Merwede and getting out of the fought-over town of Dordrecht to execute the first phase of the complex new operation plan. It did not succeed and found itself tied up in street fighting in Dordrecht on 12 May. Meanwhile, in the morning of 12 May General Student had sent a battalion of air-assault infantry (I./IR.72), that had landed at Waalhaven shortly before, to seal off the east side of the inner city of Dordrecht and then to roll up the Dutch defences there[362]. Student had not expected the Light Division in Dordrecht[363], but his plan parried the Dutch ambition to prepare a battle group southeast of Dordrecht to advance across the full width of the Island and sweep up German resistance. As mentioned above, the Dutch plan lacked any up-to-date field intelligence and thus ran aground in unexpected severe encounter battles. The battle in Dordrecht was fierce. Two battalions of the Light Division were caught in the middle of it, the rest did not intervene but lay ineffectually to the south-east of the city awaiting the other two battalions to free themselves. Meanwhile the German battalion (I./IR.72) moved in between the two battling battalions and the pair laying to the southeast of Dordrecht. The latter two could have easily denied access to the German battalion by simply closing the gap. However, the Dutch divisional command was so preoccupied with alleged betrayal and Fifth Column panic amongst its own troops as well as, by its own doing, fragmentation of its tactical command, that it had no overview of the battlefield. Three battalions stood idle all day between Dubbeldam (east of Dordrecht) and the Zuidendijk (south of Dordrecht), while their intervention might have hurt the Germans badly. That did not happen. In the evening of 12 May, the Division-battlegroup decided to attack the next day with the rest of the units. Meanwhile, as seen, the 9th *Panzer-Division* had arrived at Moerdijk and would be met in the morning of 13 May.

Group Spui was the neighbour of Group Kil. It was the command responsible for the south-front sector between the Spui waterway and the west coast (Voorne-Putten) north of the Haringvliet (Meuse estuary). It also occupied a forward position at Willemstad across the

Haringvliet, on the Brabant shore. At some point contact was made with Captain Isaacs of the Position Willemstad. He was commander of a heavy machine-gun company and coordinated his actions on his own initiative with the French. During a field meeting with a French senior officer at a bridge in Steenbergen he witnessed how motorized and mechanized units of the French 25.DIM drove past[364]. He reported this by telephone to Group Spui, but the forwarded message quickly transformed into 'a French armoured train is in arrival', causing undesired effects[365]. Because the GHQ had been feeding the morale for days with exaggerated messages that mechanized French assistance within the Fortress was imminent[366], this message was immediately passed on to GHQ and C-VH. There it was modulated in such a way that soon the message from the C-VH was passed on to the subordinate commands of Group Kil, the Commander of Dordrecht and the Light Division that at any moment a French armoured column could come over the Moerdijk. At the same time reports that were received – among others from the Light Division – that in fact German armoured cars had been sighted were dismissed as false. Also reports from Brabant that a 'German armoured column' was moving through the province towards the west were not believed and – if true – the French would deal with it[367]. But Winkelman had no idea of the actual French position in Brabant, so he counted on a '*dark horse*' that was supposed to win the race for him but in fact never appeared. There was little effort in the Hague to verify the state of affairs in Brabant, but they were eager to believe anything that spoke in favour of the 'French scenario'. Thus a single field report, which in essence was not exaggerated, accumulated mythical proportions on the way to the top of the chain-of-command, gave rise to an instruction to lower commanders which was totally disconnected to that originally observed and reported by Captain Isaäcs[368]. This led not only to the field commanders becoming confused[369], but also to the failure to realize that Moerdijk still lay open and could at any moment decisively fall to the German ground troops. Blinded by hope, the Hague actively turned a deaf ear and a blind eye to what they did not want to hear and accept. So it was that only when after midnight (12 to 13 May) that the intelligence radio-monitoring service in the Hague reported to the GHQ that the Radio Bremen confirmed the arrival of the 9th *Panzer Division* at Moerdijk, that the army command started to give credence to the facts[370]. By then it was too late. They had literally bet on the wrong horse: the French '*cheval noir*'. However, it was the German cavalry horse that had won.

Winkelman tried to intervene at Moerdijk after all. Shortly after midnight on 13 May, when the message from Radio Bremen had been processed, the GHQ gave a direct order to Group Kil to lay heavy artillery fire on the traffic bridge at Moerdijk. The hope was to hit the demo-charges. The air force was ordered to carry out a bombardment. The British were asked to attack the bridge from the air too[371]. It led to little. The last operational *Fokker* T-V[372] bomber would be sacrificed when it unsuccessfully attacked the bridge at 05:35 in the morning with two 300 kg HE bombs[373]. One bomb just missed the target, the second seemed to have grazed a pillar but did not detonate. On its way back the bomber was intercepted and crashed along with one of its escorting fighters. The bomber's volunteer crew perished. The artillery was useless. The shells themselves were at best only good for damage and the German airborne engineers had already thrown

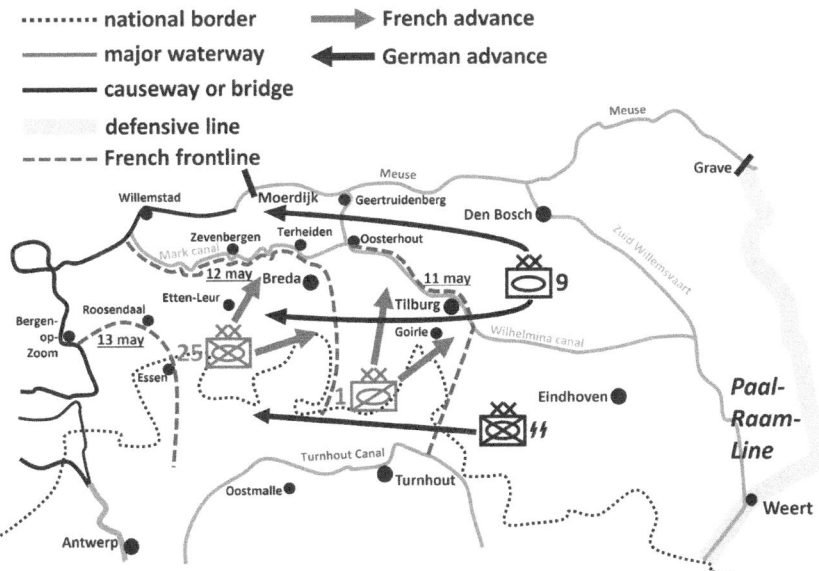

Map 10: French and German positions and manoeuvres in the Brabant region

all the explosive material found in the designated explosives-compartments into the Hollandsch Diep on the first day of the war[374]. The bombardment of the approaches to both bridges was all that remained but was to little avail. The RAF did not appear[375]. Sources on British considerations are lacking but it would make sense to believe that the RAF and the French army made equivalent analyses and on strategic points knew each other's considerations[376]. An intact Moerdijk bridge and a diversion of the German attack formation towards Fortress Holland were more important to the allies than the German force acting on the north wing of the front in Belgium, which would eventually threaten not only the French 7th Army, but also the BEF[377]. Since the rest of the corridor captured by the Germans had remained untouched during the first days of fighting, by the morning of 13 May Fortress Holland had been decisively penetrated on its southern front. That situational picture also landed on the table at the GHQ and led to the urgent advice from the OLZ to the Queen and the Cabinet to leave the country. Minister Dijxhoorn said that he had already had the impression on 12 May that the French would not recapture Moerdijk and that the situation at Rotterdam would not be restored either[378]. Winkelman was said to have sighed to him in the evening of 12 May "*it can't go on like this*"[379]. The next morning the government was informed that the situation was very precarious. On the south front, the Germans had already entered the Fortress, on the Grebbe-line's southern segment at the Grebbeberg position the situation was dire too. The allied countries could not help and in Brabant and the north of Belgium the French were already in retreat. What remained of Winkelman's plan after the morning of 10 May 1940 and the refusal of support from allies within the Fortress had been reduced to nothing. After all, there was no further hope of a relief by allies and meanwhile the army air force had practically ceased to exist, while the ground-to-air defences hardly had any ammunition left. On the Grebbeberg in the early morning of 13 May, only the rear-side of the defences (stop-line) was still more or less intact, but it was hanging by a string, so that it was foreseen that the Field Army would have to take a huge step back to the eastern front of the Fortress. And this front, due to the policy of Dijxhoorn, had been unable to make any preparations for further reinforcement after Winkelman had opted for the Grebbe-line. What goal did the government and the army command still have at this point? Was it not obvious that what remained was to negotiate with the Germans for a capitulation?

Remarkably enough, it was Winkelman who wanted to fight on. The General who had chosen to fight the war in isolation in case Germany attacked, suddenly became the General who started thinking in terms of allies. And that while, from his perspective, the allies had 'let him down'. After all – the British had offered almost no support and the French had promised something in Brabant, but had not delivered (what Winkelman believed to have been promised) with all the consequences this entailed. Support for the defence of Fortress Holland had not been forthcoming, as had been made clear on 10 May. When, from a strategic point of view, the Dutch had committed themselves to resistance to the German invasion, the allies took no further interest in the country.

Were the allies, particularly the French, to be blamed for this? Of course not. The Netherlands had played the isolation card, both in terms of government and military leadership, and had selfishly believed that it would be able to escape, only to jump aboard the allied sloop at the eleventh hour (or even later). Logically, the allies felt no need – had they had the capacity to do so – to help the Netherlands prolong her defence for a few days. Gamelin himself would be forced to resign a few days after the Dutch capitulation. His very risky strategy had proved fatal to France. Removing the 7th Army from the Reims sector without replacing it with an adequate mobile reserve played right into the hands of the Germans. The speed and availability of those units was exactly what was lacking when things went wrong around the Meuse river at Sedan on 13 and 14 May 1940. Despite promises to his Generals to the contrary, Gamelin had not arranged a new ready fast reserve for Georges and thus the German breakout from the Meuse valley meant Gamelin came under pressure[380]. On 19 May he had been dismissed from office and was succeeded by his predecessor: Maxime Weygand[381]. However, by then the French forces – and with them the BEF – were in perilous condition. In this way, the French had their own command debacle. Winkelman, however, changed on 13 May from the man who withdrew into isolation and had little interest in the allied cause to a commander who wanted to prolong the hopeless struggle in order to give the allies some respite and to tie up German forces for the sake of the allies. A few days of the reality of war had turned him into a warrior. Whether this worked out well is a question that can be considered in some detail but which essentially falls outside the scope of this analysis of Winkelman's strategy. It is, however, logical to briefly reflect on the sequel.

Winkelman realised during the night of 12 to 13 May that the matter was settled. It was only a matter of days, at most. In the morning, he advised the Queen and the remaining members of the Cabinet to leave the country[382]. Meanwhile, additional anti-aircraft artillery was sent to the Hook of Holland. The Queen with her retinue and the Cabinet would move to Hook of Holland and the *Royal Navy* would take care of their transportation. Queen Wilhelmina was escorted to Hook of Holland around 10:00 by Police Troops and some modern *DAF Pantrado* M.39 armoured cars. The Queen and her delegation left the Hook in the morning[383]. The Cabinet had another meeting at a fort near the Hook and subsequently left Dutch soil. When the government left the country, Winkelman received all authority on his shoulders. Dijxhoorn had urged him not to practise the much used adage 'to the last man and the last bullet', but to be sensible when the futility of continued resistance would become apparent[384]. Winkelman then suddenly opposed him and thought that resistance should be offered to the utmost, but finally he complied with the instruction that continued resistance should not become pointless. The elastic meaning of 'needless' gave room to the OLZ who would make use of it in charting his own course.

The discussion about what to do continued through the morning and into the early afternoon of 13 May. At that moment the heaviest sacrifices had already been made by the Germans, at least as far as the campaign in the Netherlands was concerned. The Germans were at the Nieuwe Maas in Rotterdam, fighting in Dordrecht and – Winkelman did not yet know[385] – had decisively broken through the stop-line of the Grebbe-line near Rhenen. Around 14:00 hours on 13 May the Dutch 4th Division (2.AC) stealthily started to evacuate from the positions in the southern sector of the Grebbe-line and shortly afterwards, around 16:00 hours, the CV had the Grebbe-line in the southern sector officially evacuated. The adjacent 2nd Division (also 2.AC) and the hardly challenged 4th Army Corps had to retreat onto the eastern front of Fortress Holland at nightfall. At the penetrated point of the Grebbe-line, at the highly contested positions on and around the elevated ground of the Grebbeberg, the matter was decided after a poorly planned and executed counterattack had been smothered by German artillery fire and the bombs and sirens of a squadron of *Stuka's*[386] which attacked shortly after noon. However, thanks to the resistance of some brave stragglers and an unexpected infantry charge by a company of the 11th Border Infantry Battalion – that had previously distinguished themselves west of Nijmegen on the first day of the invasion – at Rhenen station, the Germans were still under the impression they had not yet penetrated the Grebbe-line. It was not until dark that a *Waffen*-SS patrol near Achterberg discovered that the bird had flown the coop. The Grebbe had fallen. The Field Army, partly covered from detection by the *Luftwaffe* by thick ground fog, was able to successfully retreat to the east-front of the Fortress. That issue which had caused so much trouble between Reijnders and Dijxhoorn and which the CV had also pointed out, turned out in reality to be no problem at all. For the second time during the May Days a large strategic manoeuvre had been successfully carried out without any noteworthy problems[387]. How wrong Dijxhoorn's policy – also on this matter – had been only then became clear. The Field Army ended up in a position where no occupying troops were to be found, where nothing was ready for battle and where even the inundation had hardly reached an acceptable level. The positions were unfinished, camouflage was lacking, there was no ground-to-air defence in place. New positions had to be constructed above ground due to the high groundwater. This was an enormous disappointment to many. The policy of reinforcing only one position had been irresponsible and lacking foresight, especially with the strategy Winkelman had embraced. A confrontation between German troops and the eastern front, however, was not to come. It took the Germans all of the next day to get there, on the left flank manoeuvring 207th ID into position to do anything, while the 227th ID on the right flank failed to get into position in time like it had done on the days before[388]. The 207th still had the SS-*Standarte 'Der Führer'* in front of them, but it was badly battered by the battle at Westervoort (IJssel-line) and the Grebbe-line[389]. Its combat power was more than halved. 207.ID had to take care of things themselves, had suffered themselves too. On 14 May, late in the afternoon, they were to appear in front of the defenders at Utrecht and demand the surrender of the position on pain of being bombed. Although almost certainly a bluff, this event would initiate the capitulation of the Netherlands.

Twenty-four hours before Winkelman still thought that the battle should be continued. The Grebbe-line still held and the Germans had not yet crossed the Nieuwe Maas at Rotterdam. From a military point of view this is probably a justifiable position. Winkelman had therefore given the order to build up a makeshift 'anti-tank front' through the green heart of the region, from the Hague to the Oude Rijn (Old Rhine) below Leiderdorp, near the city of Leiden. He intended to continue the fight even after a German breakthrough across the Nieuwe Maas. Rotterdam was meanwhile stripped of almost all anti-aircraft batteries which were relocated behind the new anti-tank front. The harbour city remained unprotected against air attacks but in fact had been for several days, partly because there was no anti-aircraft batteries to the south or east, only around the harbour facilities and northwest. From 12 May onwards tactical bombing raids were the order of the day. Head of the operations section at the GHQ, Lieutenant-Colonel Wilson, had been sent to the city to represent the authority of the OLZ. It was two to twelve. The order had been given on 13 May to retake and destroy the bridges over the Nieuwe Maas. Up to that point the two sides had spent four days on the Nieuwe Maas front staring at each other and had done little offensively. This was not the fault of the defenders. It were the C-VH and his Chief-of-Staff themselves who had remained completely clueless and passive. Rotterdam, moreover, like Dordrecht, was a shambles of uncooperative commanding officers. In addition, Rotterdam had a very stubborn Commander Naval Troops, who was also executive commander of the Dutch Marine Corps[390]. A battalion Dutch Marines – professional soldiers – was heavily involved in the defence of their home town. With the regular army troops in the city, nothing was done against the Germans across the river front. That there was still confidence that German tanks could be stopped is understandable since crossing a narrow defended bridge would be no mean feat for the Germans. On the other hand, it could be expected that such an attack would happen with heavy preparation of artillery and/or air support. The city had to be prepared to make that sacrifice. The GHQ in the Hague realised this and so did the mayor of Rotterdam[391]. Winkelman's consideration was that these were sacrifices that had to be made and that would buy time for the allies by tying down German formations and resources. Winkelman's consideration can be followed from a military point of view, but he grossly underestimated the sacrifices required. From his level of knowledge, it seems he could hardly be blamed for this, although a well prepared General should have known better. A basic understanding of modern war was lacking in this General. It is evident from other instructions and decisions, that the military developments in Spain (1936-1937), Poland (1939) and Scandinavia (April 1940) had hardly crossed his mind.

In the evening of 13 May, Hitler had thought in his HQ at the *Felsennest* that the Dutch resistance had to be over. The Netherlands offered more and tougher resistance than expected and a critical battle was underway on the Meuse River in Belgium and France. Although the Germans were in a favourable position, the German headquarters OKH and OKW did not fully realise this. There too, '*the fog of war*' was the order of the day. In his personal instruction of the morning of 14 May, Hitler instructed *Heeresgruppe* B – responsible for the operations of the 6th and 18th Army – to use all necessary means to finish the battle in the Netherlands quickly. Although Holland was on the verge of being 'nazified' and therefore no excessive incidents were desirable, the 18th Army was given the 100 He-111s bombers of *Kampf Geschwader* 54 to make good on the threat of destruction from the air. Hitler's henchman and supreme commander of the German *Luftwaffe* Hermann Göring's direct role in this is not clear, but his concern for the encircled airborne troops who were in direct radio contact and under a great deal of pressure seems to have contributed to the decision to undertake a carpet bombardment of the north of Rotterdam on 14 May. The intention of this bombardment was clearly strategic, although some historians seem to artificially insist on a tactical element[392]. Moreover, the city was heavily defended and was a crucial position for further German advance. Thus, in principle, a legitimation for the German air attack had been found. The GHQ took this into account to some extent, but a Warsaw scenario seems never to have been seriously expected in the Netherlands. Large-scale bombardments were also a relatively new development, so that the not very modern Dutch army command had underestimated this[393]. It took the German *Luftwaffe* exactly ten minutes to bombard the new reality of war into the minds of Dutch military leadership. The bombardment and the subsequent raging fire-storm would devastate the larger part of the north of Rotterdam, killing around 800 civilians.

After the shocking bombardment of Rotterdam in the early afternoon of the 14th and the capitulation of the city defence and all military formations on the city grounds, resulting in the German crossing of the last major waterway, it seemed logical to capitulate. After all, the Grebbe-line had also been broken through in the meantime. Winkelman thought about this and consulted with his closest subordinate commanders. Remarkably, however, he still saw an opportunity to offer meaningful resistance. This decision of Winkelman seems hard to reconcile with the sober General before the May Days. After the capitulation of Rotterdam and the German crossing of the Nieuwe Maas, there was now an enemy within the Fortress who had no further major natural obstacle before him. No further meaningful resistance was possible. Winkelman seemed to have lost sight of reality here. Shortly after his decision to press on, news reached the GHQ that a German emissary had appeared in front of the position near Utrecht, demanding the capitulation of the city. Leaflets threatening a bombing raid of the city were dropped by an aircraft. There is no evidence of an actual imminent attack on Utrecht. The leaflets may have rolled off the stencil machine of the German 10th Army Corps and been dropped by liaison-aircraft of this unit over the city[394]. But for General Winkelman and his close associates it was clear by then. Sacrificing a second city was going too far. It was time to seek an armistice. The German attaché was summoned to the GHQ.

It was the fifth day of the war. The land forces had expended and also lost a considerable amount of ammunition when the large ammunition storages behind the Grebbe-line were largely abandoned when the line itself was evacuated. The battle had demanded much from the arsenals. What is certain is that the air defence was finished. Aircraft were worn out or destroyed, spare guns and replacement engines were not available. Ammunition for the anti-aircraft defences was virtually exhausted. Many older artillery units were out of stock and the standard guns were given smaller rations. Hand grenades were almost out. Ammunition for mortars, 6-veld and *Böhler* anti-tank guns seems to have been in reasonable order still. It is likely that at least one third of the infantry ammunition was expended or lost. If the Fortress had remained closed, there might have been ammunition for a week or so, but the air defence would have been largely silent.

General H.G. Winkelman – Supreme Commander as of February 1940

General I.H. Reijnders – Supreme Commander until February 1940

Major-General H.F.M. Baron van Voorst tot Voorst – Chief of Staff as of February 1940

Lieutenant-General J. van Andel – Commander Fortress Holland

Lieutenant-General J.J.G. Baron van Voorst tot Voorst – Commander of the Field Army

General Maurice Gamelin – the French Supreme Commander

Lieutenant-General P.W. Best – Commander Air-Defences

Major Gijsbert Sas – the Dutch attaché in Berlin

CONCLUSION

Winkelman's cold strategy compared to his hot strategy like a trial balloon compared to an actual balloon. A virtual balloon stays in the air as long as you believe in it, but a real balloon that does not meet the fundamental requirements for floating will fall to the ground or never ascend in the first place.

Whatever the position of the armed forces, the availability of ammunition determined the end of the resistance. Whether this resistance was done in house (on the fronts of the Fortress) or outside the fences (on the Grebbe-line and in Brabant), the ammunition supply was an absolute limiting factor. The fact that an extremely limited supply was available from the start could therefore not be a reason to start from the premise of defence on the fronts of the Fortress, as Dijxhoorn emphatically pursued. Winkelman was allowed by Dijxhoorn to shift the eastern front of the Fortress to the Grebbe-line, but had to offer the only and final organised resistance there. Only Dijxhoorn found the apparent logic in this that there would therefore not be a second withdrawal and defence on the east-front of the Fortress since he only provided funds for one defence-line. In his own defences after the war, Dijxhoorn constantly attempted to justify his actions, but he had clearly shown at the time of his ministry to have been only a Lieutenant-Colonel and not a General. He had – as a minister – actively interfered in strategy and even operational planning, not only flouting rules of professional etiquette and normality, but also putting his vanity above the national interest. This had led to an irresponsible and unnecessary change of supreme command in the heart of a crisis the likes of which the country had not seen in 100 years. Dijxhoorn has been judged extraordinarily leniently on this by the PEC and the history books and although he was not alone in his actions, he had been the dominant force.

Winkelman's plan may have been born out of necessity, and may have led to wishful thinking that a mighty relief army would soon march towards the Dutch Fortress, but the essence of his plan – the turtle disappearing into his (weak) shell without looking around – was an irreversible '*Vorentscheidung*' (preliminary decision): he could only lose with this strategy. Winkelman's turtle-plan stood in remarkable contrast to Gamelin's Breda-plan, which assumed just the opposite. Gamelin was already considering 'the next step' with the Breda variant, that incorporated the element of holding the low lands in Dutch and Belgian Brabant so that the allies could in time launch a counter-attack from there into the German *Ruhrgebiet* – the industrial heart of Germany. Gamelin was grossly overconfident. As Karl-Heinz Frieser so eloquently put it, Gamelin played '*va banque*'[395], but without his military or the situation necessitating it. The French Supreme Commander was precisely the turtle with the strong shell who stuck out his neck unnecessarily and looked around too long and too far. Both commanders-in-chief planned operations that were almost irreversible and, moreover, they led them in the hot phase so weakly that even the slightest chance of a reversal of course was soon gone. Both commanders-in-chief were far removed from reality, stuck in their own paradigms. But with one, the glass was (half) empty and with the other (half) full. The shards of both glasses lay on the floor before they could take a sip from their glass in the reality of war.

Gamelin, however, was realistic in one respect. He saw that the only remedy against German strength and size lay in waging an allied, integral battle[396]. Belgium, meanwhile, was pursuing a perhaps even more curious course than the Netherlands. The southern neighbours should have been as good as certain of a German attack, for in all war scenarios they would become a battlefield (again). This made it all the more remarkable that Leopold continued to deny this reality and even opted for neutrality in 1936, while the only guarantee for his country was its pre-existing alliance with France. Belgium and the Netherlands were, at that stage, united in their policy that Hitler could be '*appeased*' with neutralism[397]. That a Franco-Belgian alliance was symbiotic in nature and not synergistic, that parties to an alliance have strong egocentric interests and an alliance is not unselfish, is a given. Nevertheless, it is a fact that King Leopold completely misjudged matters, and that, with the wisdom of a country that had suffered so much in the previous war and had to deter the Germans only through alliance. The Netherlands was also isolationist, but in principle still had some reason to be. It had been successfully neutral before and also had a good relationship with its eastern neighbour, while maintaining weaker ties with the other nations. But the Netherlands had another reason to maintain its neutrality longer and more fanatically than the Belgians. It did not have a strong armed force. It kept its armed forces small and lacked the resources to fight a long battle. In that sense, the Netherlands had nothing to gain from risking involvement in an armed conflict. Until the occupation of the entire former Czechoslovakia on 15 March 1939, this argument could probably be justified. When Hitler, by occupying the whole of Czechoslovakia on that day, flouted the Munich Agreement, it became clear that Germany had aggressive intentions. It became equally clear that good relations with the neighbours to the east, German promises and a Netherlands that remained neutral in 1914-1918, offered no guarantees for the future. At that moment, the Netherlands should have considered other scenarios. The fact that the Belgians also continued to focus on neutrality in this phase, albeit informally preparing for allied combat, did not help to make the Netherlands politically enthusiastic for a defensive alliance between them before then. Whether the Dutch would have entered into such a defensive alliance if the Belgians had formalised their alliance with France and the UK is also questionable. The Netherlands seemed to live in a vain corset and to want to shut itself off from the obvious. The attitude that Minister for Foreign Affairs Van Kleffens in particular adopted internationally caused a great deal of irritation and ridicule and left the outside world guessing of whether the Netherlands would defend itself, some even had doubt as to which side the Netherlands would be wearing its coat.

The stubborn attitude of the government centre was an attitude that General Reijnders also came up against when he, like other military chiefs, pointed out that the Netherlands could only conduct a potentially successful defence in alliance with its southern neighbours. On the other hand, Reijnders himself was partly to blame for the fact that the bridge to the Belgians and French was never actually built. Early in 1939 he was asked by the French to take seriously the strengthening of a Mark-defence and the construction of field fortifications in West Brabant. This would make it possible to link up with both a preliminary defence of the French Scheldt Plan and the main defence of the Dyle Plan. Reijnders saw nothing in it – at least in the Hague he did not make a case for it – and stuck to the Peel concentration (later the Peel-Raam-line), whose defects were evident from the start. It became his own paradigm and it made him vulnerable. Departing from his correct principle that an allied defence would be the only right choice for the Dutch armed forces, he should have deepened and improved the defence of Brabant. However, he resisted all other ideas on this and thus lost support. He opted exclusively for the Peel-Raam-line, which was militarily unreal because this line could only be meaningful if it was the front of a whole complex of defence-lines or hedgehog positions and had a defended southern flank connecting to the Belgian positions. Nevertheless, his Peel-Raam-line was a position which would have provided an excellent opportunity for a first line of defence, especially if it had been operated with three divisions and a light division in the open southern area. The Peel-Raam-line was rarely judged fairly because of the military-political charge it was given. The line did not merit an extremely heavy garrison, as its opponents so often claimed. Whole sections – basically the whole lower half of it – were unsuitable for offensive operations. Concentrating men and resources on the parts that were open and putting up light fortifications at nodes behind them in order to slow down local breakthroughs would have been an excellent and credible realisation of Reijnders' rightly envisaged allied defence. As said here before, Reijnders made himself vulnerable by only constructing the Peel-Raam-line and furthermore by not developing anything else in Brabant nor submitting plans for assessment to the minister(s), although the chances of him getting adequate funding would probably have been negligible. There is some proof that in 1939 reconnaissance efforts were made on locations that seem to be connected to the theoretical Orange-line (Den Bosch – Tilburg line), but those efforts stalled quickly and the plan was likely shelfed for lack of funds. In other areas, Reijnders was too often caught between decisions, and that is another point to bring forward against him. His indecisiveness was remarkably at odds with his stubbornness towards the ministers he served. For a General who spent five years in office as Chief-of-Staff and then Commander-in-Chief, his policy towards his political chiefs was undiplomatic and ineffective. His hindsight 'brochures' – elaborate memorandums which he wrote after the Dutch capitulation – were completely devoid of self-reflection and contrasted with a successor who had taken decisions. Moreover, those brochures were not accompanied by a *mea culpa* when it came to the weak occupation of the southern front of the Fortress (in his own disposition of troops), especially in connection with the airborne operation that might also have caught Reijnders unaware. Humanly speaking the brochures were understandable but professionally and morally they were not very uplifting.

Winkelman saw no point in defending the Peel-Raam-line alone, but also refused to look for depth in the defence of Brabant. He too put aside ideas and requests to do so. Winkelman, moreover, was not a great believer in allied defence, although his concept of defence was dependent on timely intervention by a large French army. Winkelman opted for the Fortress strategy and thus lapsed into isolationist medieval practices. His choice to move the troops out of Brabant immediately meant that any alliance was at best a one-sided affair for him. His only explanation for that choice could be that the Netherlands would then wait inside the Fortress for a relief by allied troops. This was an unreal and unreasonable scenario, but curiously enough had the full support of the Minister of Defence. The fact that the Netherlands lacked the means to hold out inside the Fortress for more than a couple of weeks at the most did not seem to prevent Winkelman from opting for this unrealistic scenario, while at the same time daring to demand considerable support from the allies, on whom he had emphatically turned his back in Brabant. The post-war PEC enquiries do not reveal by what right he thought he could count on the desired allied support.

Winkelman's hot strategy also proved weak, but the judgement here is more lenient in the circumstances. All decision-making during those days of war was extremely difficult. It was encumbered by the overload of conflicting information, the lack of overview and the extraordinary weakness of his subordinate C-VH and several other important subordinate commanders. In many ways Winkelman cannot be blamed for this. Winkelman, however, seems to have been an inert figure who did not stand very firmly on the bridge but rather watched from the crow's nest at a distance. He gave much patience and freedom to the C-VH during those crucial first days of the war, while he did nothing at all, besides the fact that the C-VH headquarters lacked adequate staff to conduct a large operation to begin with. That Winkelman decided to stay true to his plan and pulled the troops out of Brabant even quicker than planned, may – from his point of view – have been logical, but it almost certainly hastened the Dutch fate. An important and capable formation as the 3rd Army Corps contributed nothing to the battle and the Light Division achieved practically nothing within the Fortress. The Germans might have taken Dordrecht without the formations of the Light Division present, but that made no difference to this theatre. After all, with or without the city of Dordrecht, the Germans firmly held the corridor to the Noordereiland (the island - surrounded by rivers - that connected the south of Rotterdam with the north) from 10 May. The only influence that Winkelman could have exerted strategically lay in holding on to the Peel-Raam-line. That should certainly have prolonged the battle there by a day, perhaps more. With one-third of the force, without any anti-aircraft guns and despite the absence of powerful artillery, the defence had been sustained for a full day. With triple that and artillery support, double that time should have been possible. Also sending a combat group of the Light Division along the south side of the Meuse to Moerdijk could have made a strategic difference, both in the scenario where the Peel-Raam defence would be evacuated or the scenario where it would remain fully occupied. The scenario where the Peel-Raam defence was abandoned and a battle group of the Light Division directed to Moerdijk underneath the Meuse, was an uncertain one though. After all, given the weak performance of the Division as it turned out, there is little to say about its chances of success. The complete reliance on French intervention to retake Moerdijk might have been justified on 10 May, but on 11 May the GHQ should have taken responsibility for this itself. The integral strategic vision that the collapse of the Belgian defence balloon ended the sustainability of the Breda variant for the French should have been anticipated by the GHQ in the Hague. But Winkelman, knowing the French intentions to enter West Brabant, had no staff officers on standby in Breda to directly represent Dutch interests at various operational levels and Gamelin's personal request to send a mission to the 7th Army was ignored. The total lack of insight, of liaison connection left him strategically and operationally blinded. In this too, he, who had hung the success of his entire strategy on allied help, made major planning errors. This was no coincidence. The disinterest and detachment of the OLZ and his Chief-of-Staff towards the events below the rivers was unforgivable. The paradigm of the defence of the Fortress seemed even to have implied a limitation of the point of view of the GHQ. It typified in particular the person of Winkelman who had constantly shown disinterest in many subjects which was so significantly noticeable even after the war at the PEC hearings. This was apparently his way of dealing with the overload of information, but a generalissimo must deal with the matters that govern the success of his strategy. The quantity and nature of the expected German troops and the strategy of the allied countries were matters that should have been of prime concern to the Dutch Supreme Commander. They were not. That was a limitation which is therefore entirely his.

Winkelman had opted for a defence that in all scenarios – barring a miracle of a liberating army arriving within two weeks – would result in a quick defeat. He merely enticed the allies to turn their backs on the Netherlands by choosing to leave the battle in Brabant to the French. However the battle in Belgium went, the Netherlands turned its back on the allies. It was an arrogant, unreal and above all losing strategy. In all scenarios, the Netherlands should have opted for connected, allied defence. It would have been better to go down fighting south of the rivers, than to go down anyway, but completely alone, above those rivers. If a defence strategy relies for its success entirely on timely intervention by allies, it is unthinkable that those allies should be received by the Dutch with, as it were, their backs turned on the first day while counting on at least serious Dutch preliminary defence, which turns out to be no more than token defence in the end. Winkelman's choice of the battle in isolation was a bitter joke. This leads to the conclusion that his strategy led to a '*a Witzkrieg*' (literaly: a joke war).

Winkelman showed very little self-criticism after the war, not showing any enrichment of his insights. His considerably younger Chief of Staff was, if possible, even less self-critical. We have to consider that they accounted for their policy in an era that men of status were not under great social pressure to confess a *mea culpa*. Besides, most people were no longer concerned with 'May 1940' after the war and in times of a large crisis in the Dutch East-Indies. The PEC did not question any military person keenly and was incompetent in terms of military policy. It was concerned with ascertaining the truth and reconstructing government policy in particular, much less with assessing the content. Winkelman, like all the others, was questioned critically, but apparently – also considering many of his gruff answers – he was disturbed by the lack of respect for his service. He was extremely frustrated that he was not offered any important functions after the war and that he was instead compelled to leave quietly. Self-reflection might have given him answers as to why he had not been received with praise. This self-reflection turned out to be lacking in almost all senior officers who were heard before the PEC. The mistakes had all been made by others. This was a time of vanity and untouchability of authority, unlike our times.

In Winkelman's defence, something also needs to be said. In 1948 all the facts of the German campaign and the defeat of the Netherlands were still far from clear. Moreover, Belgium and France were also looking for an explanation for their swift defeat, which given the scale of their armed forces was certainly shameful for the French. Whereas Winkelman was criticised for his lack of boldness, Gamelin was criticised for the opposite. He was blamed for using the French field army in such an unfavourable and risky way that the battle was decided within a week. The French frustration about May-June 1940 is many times greater than the Dutch and with good reason. After all, France had maintained a large military force and had invested more in its defence than anyone else. However, this also meant that the French opinion after the defeat became verbally aggressive towards Belgium and the Netherlands. This was partly deserved, but also not free from hypocrisy. After all, the French efforts in those countries were almost exclusively motivated by keeping the fighting away from French territory. Cooperation between France and Britain was limited and with Belgium and the Netherlands wholly improvised and lacking any agreed political base. The shaky alliance of May 1940 had little binding force. The whole was little greater that the sum of its parts, so the alliance offered no added value. The French could have remained on their own territory given the neutral position of Belgium and the Netherlands, and perhaps that would have been the wisest thing to do. That the French (and BEF) chose to enter Belgium was in their own interest. The Belgians would not unconditionally submit to the French operational command and the Belgian capitulation infuriated the French, especially because it was felt that it went without proper consultation. That feeling was in fact unjust – the Belgians had prewarned their allies days before – but it did force the Entente to step in where Belgian formations capitulated. The French would, a few weeks later, themselves lay down their arms and bargain a deal with the Germans in fear of total submission. This French ambivalence resulted in the puppet state Vichy France and for the Free French a weak position on the allied table for the duration of the war. The Dutch turning their back caused some commotion, but in the French plan this was eventually of secondary importance. Still, according to their own sources, the French lost some 600 men in May 1940 in the Netherlands and a few thousand prisoners. This certainly gave them some right to speak and Dutch senior officers in German prisoner of war camps experienced this. The animosity that French senior officers showed towards their Dutch peers showed little understanding for the Dutch cold shoulder that was turned toward them. And probably rightly so. The French could not laugh about the Dutch *Witzkrieg*. The Germans, however, could. The swift victory during the *Westfeldzug* (German Campaign in the West) was cause for a German mood of euphoria, which resulted in a scarce photo of a *Führer* stamping with glee and a smile from ear to ear. At least someone was laughing at the *Witz* ...

ENDNOTES

1 'Cold' strategy is the strategy before the act of war occurred, while 'hot' strategy refers to the strategy after the act of war – in short, from the time of the German invasion on 10 May 1940.
2 The terms explained. *'Blitzkrieg'* stands - in principle - for the German application of a surprising, rapid and concentrated manoeuvre or offensive in which firepower, movement, speed, endurance and manoeuvre are the key concepts. *'Sitzkrieg'* is the term given to the period between the Anglo-French declaration of war on Germany in September 1939 and 9 April 1940 (the German invasion of Denmark and Norway). *'Witzkrieg'* is a creation of the author himself. It is meant to point out that (in the author's opinion) Winkelman's strategy was a macabre or cynical joke, because as conceived, this strategy could not bear fruit in any scenario and moreover, completely played into the hands of the Germans. *'Witzkrieg'* as a cynical term is by no means intended to cast aspersions on the soldiers in the field or otherwise from the achievements and sacrifices made. Let that be said!
3 For the sake of simplicity, some frequently used sources are abbreviated in the footnotes. The interrogations of the *'Parlementaire Enquête Commissie voor het regeringsbeleid 1940-1945'* (*Parliamentary Inquiry Committee for Government Policy*) is abbreviated as 'PEC' with the addition of the part used (parts 1 and 2 are relevant); *'De strijd op Nederlands grondgebied tijdens de Tweede Wereldoorlog'* (several volumes, SDU), published by the Ministry of Defence, is abbreviated as 'Stafwerk' (staff work) with the addition of the relevant volume; *'Het falen van de Nederlandse gewapende neutraliteit - september 1939-mei 1940'* (2009, 2nd edition), Tobias van Gent becomes 'Van Gent'; *'De sterke arm, de zachte hand - het Nederlandse leger & de neutraliteitspolitiek'* (2006), Paul Moeyes becomes 'Moeyes'; *'Generaal Reijnders - een miskend bevelhebber 1939-1940'* (2007) by Eppo Brongers, becomes 'Brongers'; *'De wisseling in het opperbevel van land- en zeemacht in februari 1940 - hare oorzaken en hare gevolgen'*, I. H. Reijnders, becomes 'Reijnders'; *"May 1940 - the Battle for the Netherlands"* (Brill ISBN 978-90-04-18438-1, 2010, chief editors H. Amersfoort and P. Kamphuis) hereafter referred to as 'Amersfoort/Kamphuis'; the collection of battle reports of the Dutch army concerning May 1940 in the archive of the Netherlands Institute for Military History (NIMH, MinDef) is referred to as 'NIMH 409-' with the unique archive serial number; *De veldtocht van het Belgische leger in 1940'*, (Dutch edition, De Fabribeckers, 1980) is indicated as 'De Fabribeckers';

'*De Belgisch-Nederlands verhoudingen en het gevaar van een Duitse aanval op de Lage Landen*', Van Waesberghe, 1995 is indicated as 'Van Waesberghe'; "*Blitzkrieg Legende – Der Westfeldzug 1940*" (German edition, K.H. Frieser, 2005) is indicated as 'Frieser'.

4 *Grand Strategy* is a concept that includes the calculation of (all) available resources, people, circumstances, time, space and political possibilities. Of course, the military aspect is dominant, but international law, governance and politics all play a part.

5 This author does not agree at all with Moeyes' little explained, but curious conclusion that the General Headquarters (AHK) functioned well during the May Days, but that the troops in the field failed (p. 474). Moeyes and Amersfoort/Kamphuis (pp. 405-407) are wrong on this point. War is chaos, and he who controls the chaos best is often the winner. However, to state, as Amersfoort does, that the conduct of affairs by Winkelman and the GHQ went well is to do serious violence to reality. This book will elaborate on the reason for disagreeing with these historians. It is not up to the author to blame the GHQ or the OLZ (without the temptations of hindsight bias), but what Amersfoort states in his chapter 'Proof of the Sum' is historically seen indefensible. In addition, Amersfoort used sources selectively. Captain Somers' statements and the PEC interrogations make it clear that the GHQ was divided and had to deal with subcultures, as we shall see. Perhaps Winkelman's curious decision to have all battle reports and logbooks destroyed at the time of capitulation contributed to the appearance that 'all was right' at the GHQ. But it was not.

6 The starting point of this self-oriented positioning is probably 1839, when the secession of the Southern Netherlands (Belgium and Luxemburg) was formalised and the remaining Netherlands was no longer a territorial player of importance within Europe. When the British - who had been the initiators of 'the Low Countries' with the Southern Netherlands as a buffer against France - refused to support the Netherlands in its rejection of Belgian secession and the French, of course, supported the Belgians in doing so, the Netherlands found itself without a coalition or ally. It was the beginning of a period in which the German-Dutch bond, which was already close on a regional level, had to become closer or stronger on a national level.

7 Weapons development between the beginning of the 19th century and the state of affairs in 1899 had been incredible, from snaphaunce gun (the French equivalent was '*fusil*'), a muzzle-loading gun, to the repeating rifle with unitary cartridge; the introduction of rapid-fire weapons such as the *Gatling* and *Maxim*. From iron muzzle-loaded guns to fast-firing steel breech-loaders. From the thick clouds of smoke from unstable black powder to the almost smokeless but much more stable powder and picric acid; from earthen and brick walls to reinforced concrete. From artillery with a 'range within the line of sight' (direct fire) to artillery that delivered heavy

8   shells 'far beyond the line of sight' (indirect fire). Motorisation of vehicles and ships, steel ships and armour. And obviously the added third dimension (air planes) since 1914.

8   The Netherlands has a strong tradition of arming after a war and not before. This was not only the case at well-known moments like 1672 or 1795, but also at more recent periods like 1870, 1914 and 1940. The same tendency is present today. Each time from the premise that there would be enough time for (quick) recovery. Only in 1672 was this the case, but in other cases the Netherlands was too late. Incidentally, it seems that Winkelman was inspired precisely by the events of 1672, when the country had to retreat to the (later) Fortress Holland and succeeded in turning the odds there. Incidentally, in 1672, the administrators responsible were lynched. An analogy that fortunately for those responsible in 1940 did not extend to that time ...!

9   In 1867, the Netherlands was threatened with war with Prussia for some time, when Otto von Bismarck claimed the former Duchy of Limburg in the German Union. A new treaty in London arranged for it to become part of the Netherlands.

10   However, the investments in defence at that time should be interpreted in a different way from today. The weak armed forces of the past often cost 5% or more of GNP. In 2018-2019, the Netherlands spent 1% net on the armed forces. When one considers that France during the interwar period periodically spent up to approximately 30%-35% of GNP on defence, one will understand that in the days before the Second World War such investments were many times higher than today. The current investment in a decent military force should be around 3-4% GNP.

11   The constitutional monarch Queen Wilhelmina and a select group of experts systematically agitated against the weak national defence and argued that only a well-guarded neutrality commanded the respect of a potential antagonist. Many plans to (re)invest in the country's defence remained intentions, which fell by the wayside in favour of more 'necessary' spending purposes. The analogy with today is apt, although in those days there were far more needs to be met than today.

12   The German Empire was also called the *Zweites Reich* (second empire). The *Dritte Reich* (third empire) is known as Hitler's (1933-1945), the *Erste Reich* (first empire) was the Holy Roman Empire (962-1806). Few people realise that both the First and Second (German) empires were ended by the French. The First by Napoleon, the Second by the Treaty of Versailles following the armistice at Compiègne in 1918. Incidentally, the Second Reich came into being after Prussia defeated the French in 1871, after the latter had tried to block a growing German empire.

13   *"Towards a learning economy: investing in the earning model of the Netherlands"*, WRR Report, 2013, p.58. From 1900 to 1972, the Netherlands had a considerable trade deficit. It therefore imported much more than it exported.

14 The hitherto 'empty' third dimension was not only to be filled with aircraft, but these had to be fought from the air and from the ground as well. The latter required separate weapon systems, contrary to what was originally thought. The whole thing meant extra costs or an investment at the expense of existing people and resources. The aviation department was established in 1913. Dedicated anti-aircraft equipment was not created until 1917.

15 In those days, with more than 6 million inhabitants, 1 million evacuees was an unimaginably large number. For that matter, the longest staying Belgians were treated less and less well and these refugees were partly to blame for the great scarcity during the war.

16 Apart from the perhaps arbitrary manner in which the Netherlands had 'obtained' South and Central Limburg (then the Duchy of Limburg, which would exist until 1867) and Zeeuws-Vlaanderen (Dutch Flanders) in 1839 in implementation of the Treaty of London, the fact that these areas were not Belgian was particularly complicating for the Belgian defence. South- and Central-Limburg with the Meuse running through would have been an ideal preliminary defence for Belgium, but for the Netherlands it was an indefensible appendix due to its lack of depth. Dutch Flanders, which did not even border on the rest of Dutch territory, had only been acquired by the Netherlands in order to control access to the Scheldt river, which meant that sea-trade in Antwerp was constantly under a tight Dutch rein. Both matters were subjects in which Belgium had been objectively severely disadvantaged by the Treaty of London, the effects of which had been felt during the First World War but of course also felt economically in peacetime where Dutch Flanders was concerned.

17 This is a reference to an ideological spectrum in which terms such as national socialism, fascism, right-wing conservatism, (etc.) find their place.

18 For geographical reasons, Belgium was even more helpless than the Netherlands without alliance in its defence. Germany and France needed the Belgian 'space' to launch a major manoeuvre against the other. Belgium would therefore almost certainly be involved in a new conflict between these European superpowers. For the Netherlands, there still seemed to be a chance for neutrality, albeit a very small one.

19 *Hogere Krijgsschool* (HKS). This was the Dutch higher education (Staff School) for talented professional officers who, after successfully completing the training, could then join the general staff. The latter, however, was not automatic. The general staff itself determined whether a successful student was admitted. In that case, he was awarded a Golden Sun symbol on his uniform. If, despite successful completion of the course, a student was not admitted to the general staff, he would be awarded a Silver Sun symbol.

20 Bizarrely, France has basically never been a real maritime superpower, especially when compared to British, Dutch or Spanish maritime history. In the First World War, the French navy was not a leading force either. However, it was apparently believed that everything French was leading, which was

20 an unfounded opinion that prevailed nonetheless. Admiral J.T. Furstner, for example, had graduated from the French higher naval academy in 1928. In May 1940 and thereafter (he evacuated from the homeland before the capitulation act) he was the highest Dutch naval commander.
21 Many people do not realise that most terms within the army have a French (or Latin) etymology. Ranks, units, organisation and weapons largely have a French origin. Partly this was already the case before 1795, but after that it became firmly established.
22 Among others, the later Minister Dijxhoorn, who received his higher military education partly in Paris, would intensively occupy himself with the rewriting of army regulations and would incorporate his French-oriented theory in them.
23 The Belgians, French and British all considered similar scenarios, which presumably were also partly known to the German intelligence services. The Germans, in turn, had serious fears about British use of Dutch territory, even without permission from the Netherlands.
24 Ultimately, during the neutrality period, the Netherlands would take some action against all violations if they could identify who was doing it. This was in the form of active defence, interception attempts and in a diplomatic sense. However, the Netherlands was very cautious in this respect and was sometimes not even aware of a given violation.
25 The Dutch intelligence service GS-III, whose First Lieutenant D. Klop acted as facilitator, and the British Secret Intelligence Service (forerunner of MI.6), of which Major R.H. Stevens and Captain S. P. Best were involved. The German operation was led by SS-*Sturmbannführer* W. Schellenberg, executed by SS-*Sturmbannführer* A.H. Naujocks who had also been involved in the Polish incident at Gleiwitz. The Dutch secret service only provided support, they did not lead the game. That did not matter to the Germans. They considered facilitation already an un-neutral act. Strictly speaking, they were right about that, of course.
26 The establishment still exists.
27 There was serious criticism of the action from the Dutch security service (especially the reserve Colonel H. Koot, cryptology specialist of the first hour, and Captain Somer of GS-IIIA) in advance. They did not trust the scenario and the German side of the matter seemed implausible and suspected a spy game being played. The British insisted on going ahead anyway. However, it was a plot set up by the Germans precisely to have a *casus belli* against the Netherlands by showing that the UK and the Netherlands were colluding.
28 Under the direction of the SS, the German secret service had fabricated a *casus belli* with '*Operation Himmler*' on 31 August 1939 in order to legitimise the invasion of Poland under international law. A pretended Polish raid on the German radio tower at Gleiwitz was actually carried out by an SD commando disguised as a Polish military.

29 However, Major-General Van Oorschot (1875-1952) was to leave for London on 12 May 1940, together with Lieutenant-Colonel J.G.W. Zegers, as a liaison mission. Curiously, Zegers was soon dismissed by Dijxhoorn and interned there because of vague British allegations of pro-German sympathies. No evidence of German sympathies was ever found but he was released in September 1944. He was never formally discharged.

30 Lieutenant-General H.A.C. Fabius (1878-1957) had retired in 1936 (as Major-General) and was reactivated for this position. He had been the last commander of the Light Brigade (the later Light Division) before it was taken over in 1936 by then-Colonel H.F.M. van Voorst tot Voorst – the Chief-of-Staff of the army in May 1940. Fabius had previously performed intelligence work and had been the first commander of GS-III in 1913, but had left GS-III shortly afterwards and never performed intelligence work again. Fabius and his close associate Major J.G.M. Van de Plassche (Head of GS-IIIA) were both very sceptical of Major Sas, the Dutch attaché in Berlin who had an excellent contact with the German Colonel Oster of the *Abwehr*. On 9 May 1940 both did not believe Sas when he reported that the German invasion was imminent, much to the chagrin of other officers at GS-III, especially Captains Olifiers and Somer who both did believe Sas.

31 *Major* Helmuth Reinberger (7th *Flieger Division* but liaison officer to *Fliegerführer* 220) and *Major* Erich Hoenmanns (airfield commander Münster Loddenheide).

32 '*The German Fallschirmtruppe 1936-1941*' (K.H. Golla, 2013: pp. 77-79) Many sources misleadingly state that they were 'the plans' for the invasion, but this is false. However, the content of the notes and instructions gave clear indications of intentions and elements regarding the planned airborne operations in Belgium, so that a good strategist could extract much from the plans.

33 There were in fact three main scenarios for German airborne landings in the West. One in the west of Belgium, one behind the Meuse-defences in Belgium and the third was the landing on the southern front of Fortress Holland. The component of the Hague was later added to the latter. In all scenarios the landing at fortress Eben-Emael as an independent operation was a fixed component. The plan in question included elements of airborne landings at Namur and Dinant, as well as the 6th Army's thrust across the Meuse that was to be supported.

34 The Belgians kept the originals.

35 In the meantime, on 13 January, the Netherlands received warnings from its attaché in Berlin of an imminent German invasion. This was cancelled because of the incident. This cancellation led to the casting of aspersions on Sas' source, although it had been completely reliable. A German plan to attack on 17 January had existed. Major Van de Plassche (GS-IIIA) and General Reijnders did not take Sas' warning seriously so that hardly any measures were taken.

36 Van Waesberghe', p. 174.
37 In particular, Dutch Foreign Minister Van Kleffens was constantly pretending to believe in miracles and remained blind and deaf to things that seemed inevitable to others. This made him seem like a master diplomat, but in the long run he was hardly taken seriously abroad. It also led to the fact that in the Netherlands on 10 May 1940 the war came as a complete surprise to almost everyone. This is a classic case of reality denial by the national administration.
38 Lieutenant-General Van den Bergen – Chief-of-staff of the Belgian army – had border barriers removed to allow French troops access to the country. Leopold III – the monarch and Commander-in-Chief of the Belgian armed forces – was furious because this seemed to break Belgium's (political) neutrality. The borders were quickly closed again and Van den Bergen was dismissed. On 31 January, Lieutenant-General Michels took his place. Thus, the Netherlands and Belgium both had some form of simultaneous discontinuity in their army command, although the Belgian one was of limited significance.
39 A striking overview of the ammunition supply can be found in the archive of the *"Staatsbedrijf der Arillerie Inrichtingen"* (the State Arsenal, NIMH 409-539005), as well as in the appendix of the book *"Beknopt overzicht van de krijgsverrichtingen der Koninklijke Landmacht 10-19 mei 1940"* (D.A. van Hilten, Section Military History, MinDef, 1947). By the way – the parallel with today is particularly striking. The current armed forces also have a pressing shortage of ammunition for all weapon systems, even more significant in relative terms than in 1940. The building up and maintenance of a good war stock fall easy prey to austerity measure in all times and places, but it is probably the most dangerous shortage for an armed force, especially because the need for accelerated stockpiling is almost always accompanied by international tension and therefore international overheating of the market, resulting in shortages and delays so that ammunition cannot be delivered on time, period.
40 The youngest enlistments also included volunteers, who came in addition to the regular enlistments. Also, the already enlarged enlistment of 1940 was accelerated.
41 *"Het Staatsbedrijf der Artillerie Inrichtingen - een uitgebreide beschouwing van het bedrijf dat in de roerige jaren 1935-1945 de spil was van de Nederlandse wapen- en munitieproductie"*, A.M.A. Goossens, 2006-2007. See http://www.grebbeberg.nl/uploads/downloads/nederlandse_wapenindustrie.pdf
42 Although not so relevant for this discussion, it must be said that in 1939, the economic dependency of the Netherlands on the import of strategic (semi-finished) products was still high. This also applied to civilian strategic items such as fuel and food. In terms of industrialisation, the Netherlands had advanced rapidly in the period 1920-1940, but the scale was still so limited that rapid mass production hardly took place. This was of impor-

43 The standard rifle and all carbines as well as the light machine gun (with the exception of some in the cavalry and ML) fired the full metal jacket cartridge 6.5 mm x 53.5R. This was an exotic ammunition that was not used in any other European armed forces, so a large-scale crisis purchase abroad was out of the question.

tance as a Grand Strategic argument for a (medium) long term strategy but hardly for the short term strategy that was in mind in 1939/1940.

44 A limited number of non 7.9 mm converted *Vickers* M.18 machine guns used the 7.7 mm cartridge.

45 (Van Hilten) There were in January 1940 a total of 105,000,000 No.1 cartridges (6.5 mm x 53.5R) and 65,000,000 No.23 cartridges (7.9 x 57R mm). This meant that for each of the 240,000 men in the regular army in theory 437 rounds were available. The fact that equal distribution did not exist and that the 8,000 light machine guns required a considerable amount of ammunition, makes it clear that in practice the Field Army had only three full ammunition rations of 120 rounds per infantryman in stock, including those that had already been issued. Sector-by-sector redistribution meant that this could be increased locally, but there was little buffer in the ammunition stocks elsewhere.

46 [*"Nederlandse Vuurwapens", leger- en luchtvaartafdeling*, G. de Vries/ B.J. Martens, pp. 254 ff.] There was an assault hand grenade No.3 – a tin blast grenade – and an iron defensive hand grenade No.1 that fragmented. Of both types, 340,000 and 240,000 respectively were in stock at the start of mobilisation, and a production order for 207,000 and 257,000 respectively had been placed with the AI during mobilisation. Due to concentration in the Field Army, a reasonable initial stock could still be delivered, but it was clearly insufficient for a war.

47 (Van Hilten) The January 1940 count gave for the 7-veld field-gun 2,025 shells per gun, for the 10-veld field-gun 2,500 and for the 12 cm howitzers a total of 1,455 per gun. Consider that an average fire-mission required 50 grenades per gun. A total of 2,025 shells was therefore sufficient for 40 such fire-missions.

48 (Van Hilten). The measurement in January 1940 gave for mortar ammunition a stock of 820 shells per mortar. For the modern *Böhler* 4,7 cm anti-tank-gun (PAG), there were 400 shells per gun, almost all of those of the armour-piercing type.

49 Both powder in powder form and in mixture form (or in chemical compositions) are subject to quality deterioration. This does not benefit the reliability of ignition and deflagration, so that the calculated range of projectiles becomes unreliable. Many shells and casings had to be cleaned to remove oxidation.

50 Although in January 1940, there were 1,035 shells per *Vickers* 7.5-tl air-artillery gun (Van Hilten), an important part of this was home-made by the AI and proved to be only in part successful. This ammunition was pyrotech-

nical in nature, which means that it worked with complicated mechanically set fuses based on time, which were adjusted with the aid of a semi-automated fire-directional calculator. The timer devices with which the AI worked turned out to be unsuitable, so that many munitions failed to detonate. This had already been observed during the period of neutrality but could only be partially remedied. In addition to the obvious lack of effect of non-exploding shells, this led to rumours of sabotage.

51 (Van Hilten). For the 2 cm *Scotti*, which was also delivered – and of which a delivery to the AI even took place during the May Days because an Italian truck had been under way when the war broke out – much less ammunition was available. Most of the fielded *Scotti's* - or 2tl no.2 - had only a few hundred rounds available.

52 (NIMH 409-539005) This 5% is an approximation of what the AI could produce in continuous shifts with the available tools and raw materials. For most of the raw materials, there was a maximum stock for three months of normal daily production. This stock could therefore be halved for continuous production. A simple extrapolation shows that a maximum of approximately two days of war consumption could be produced before the essential raw materials would be exhausted.

53 It has to be said that the engine technology of those days always pushed the limits of the possibilities and every air force had the problem that large parts of the fleet were grounded for maintenance. The Netherlands, however, had virtually nothing in terms of replacement reserves, which, given the need for them, reduced the operational life of the army air force to one week of war (not counting losses).

54 Of the approximately 135 aircraft that would become operational during the May Days, about half were of the fairly modern *Fokker* types G-1 and D-XXI fighters and the T-V bomber, as well as the *Douglas* 8N strategic recce/light bomber. The recce/light bomber *Fokker* C-X was already dated, the remaining aircraft were very dated. It would have made little difference to the army air force if it had been made stronger in the twenties. The ageing of aircraft was accelerated by the rapid development of technology so that a prototype was often already outdated before it came into production. Anyone who realises that the Netherlands has been flying the F-16 since the early 1980s (although it has had midlife updates) and is now – while in transition to the F-35 – flying an aircraft that is more than 40 years old in terms of airframe and design, realises that in the 1930s, when obsolescence occurred approximately every few years, things moved very quickly. All air forces suffered this fate at the time.

55 The eastern land border was as the crow flies 300 km long, the southern 210 km.

56 In 1944 and 1945, Germany occupied the great *Festung Holland (Fortress Holland)* with fewer troops than the Netherlands did in May 1940, but the allies paid a huge price everywhere to make even the smallest progress. The

West was deliberately ignored by the allies, knowing the enormous losses that the conquest of the waterland would demand. The dramatic operations around the Scheldt estuary (Operations Switchback, Vitality and Infatuate) had been a beckoning prospect, although the operation was vital to allow access to the port of Antwerp.

57 The Netherlands had relatively (outside the Scandinavian countries) the smallest mobilisation force, but the best paid militia in north-western Europe. Both conscripts and professional soldiers were well paid and accommodated. Much budget went to this. In terms of numbers, however, it was a pitifully poor performance. The Belgians, with 10% less population than the Netherlands, had an armed forces strength of over 600,000 men (who, by the way, were very poorly paid and housed). Of these, approximately 500,000 were directly available, the remainder were in the form of secondary reserves or auxiliary troops. That number was twice as many as in the Netherlands. France and Germany also had (relatively) several times more available people under arms.

58 There was still a considerable contingent of barely trained soldiers available in the form of the *Landstorm* corps (territorial reserve). A couple of thousand of these were activated, but about 50,000 men were not. In addition, in large cities there were considerable numbers of Civil Guards, some of which were not uniformed. These were at the orders of the mayor for order control, and usually equipped with army standard *Steyr* M95 rifles and FN pistols. Such militias were not counted in the Netherlands but the availability of a unit like the inactivated *Landstorm* formation of 50,000 men is usually included in Belgian and French total counts.

59 Moreover, the premise of such a firing plan was defensive combat.

60 To put it in perspective, some of the regular foot-infantry spent the first few months practising exclusively at local militia stations and then came to the barracks for service within their unit for only the last few weeks. This part of the militia was poorly trained by any standards. The motorized or mobile infantry and other mounted/motorized arms were significantly longer and better trained.

61 "*Die Deutschen Infanterie-Divisionen*", W. Haupt, 1991. This work concerned all untracked, non-motorised units. The lion's share of the reserve divisions consisted of such soldiers. It should be noted that the high *Landwehr* (=born 1894-1904) contingents in the 3rd and 4th *Welle* also had a history in (para)military units or even the Imperial Army before 1919. The 3e *Welle* had 42% *Landwehr* contingent, the 4e *Welle* 24%. The remaining soldiers had received their initial training in the period 1933-1939 (birth years 1914-1920) and had therefore usually been pre-trained for only three months.

62 The Germans used the term *Welle* (literally: wave) – in full '*Aufstellungswelle*' – for a mobilisation levy/group. Because a *Welle* also had an organisation attached to it, it immediately indicated a class. Regimental numbers indicate

the *Welle* with the initial number (328.IR was from the 3rd *Welle*). The *Erste Welle* (1ˢᵗ Wave) contained active soldiers and hardly any reservists. The organisation of the *Erste Welle* divisions was reflected in the organisational structure of the *Dritte Welle* (3rd Wave). The *Zweite Welle* (2nd Wave) divisions were half active, half reservist. The organisation of this was more or less mirrored in the *Vierte Welle*. From the *Fünfte Welle* (5th Wave) *onwards*, this was abandoned and each *Welle* got its own organisation. In May 1940, so many had come up that the *Zehnte* (10th Wave) was in the depots. There were 141 infantry divisions and *Landschütz* divisions and 10 tank divisions active or in formation in May-June 1940.

63 In May 1940, about 5,000,000 men were under arms or otherwise militarised (including about 500,000 men *Bautruppen, RAD* and other paramilitary organisations). There were about 3.25 million soldiers deployed within *Das Heer* (army) and another half million older *Landwehr* or newly emerged recruits. The *Kriegsmarine* (approx. 60,000 men) and *Luftwaffe* (approx. 450,000 men) were also enlisted from these figures.

64 PEC 1C, 13094. For the PEC, even the Commander of the Field Army (CV), General Van Voorst tot Voorst, could be caught in this misleading picture. He presented the Commission with a very skewed picture of the age ratios.

65 Of all the belligerents, the Netherlands enlisted the fewest recruits. During the mobilisation, even the 1924 batch (born in 1904) and in April 1940 the 1925 batch (born in 1905) were discharged from service (although many remained enlisted voluntarily). In all other countries, enlistments up to and including the year of birth 1900 or even earlier (Germany and France) were mobilised. In the French army, in the Type B divisions, Lieutenants were well into their forties. In the Netherlands, Lieutenants in their late thirties were considered old. The average age of the four regular infantry divisions deployed by the Germans against the Netherlands – the 207th, 227th, 254th and 256ᵗʰ – was about 27-28 years.

66 The number of heavy and light machine guns as well as 8 cm mortars was on the same level. Sub-machine guns were not yet available in most 3rd and 4th *Welle* divisions. They were in the SS and airborne troops though, and quite many too, so the impression was created from that.

67 We should not credit the myth that the Germans had only talent and that mediocrity and underachievement were non-existent. There was plenty to complain about on the German side (albeit from a higher point of departure ...) and after the Polish campaign and the *Westfeldzug* many commanders were transferred or dismissed from combat positions, others promoted after proven abilities. There were also policy failures on the German side, even within the Dutch theatre. The 227.ID, for example, underperformed in Holland. *Major* Einstmann, battalion commander of MG.Btl.15 operating under the command of 254.ID, was later relieved of his position after demonstrated weak tactical leadership at Hatert. He was to have no further

frontal duties and spent the rest of the war as an instructor.

68   By 'German quality' is meant the effectiveness and operational development of the fast concentrated attack manoeuvres, the in-depth reconnaissance ('in force'), the qualities of the vanguards and the 'joint' factor (cooperation of land and air forces). However, the Polish campaign, even more than the *Westfeldzug*, was also an example of 'a lot that didn't go well' within the German army. Even the vanguard still had a lot to learn, but the reserve units in particular showed that they had very limited training. Many lessons were also learned in command. To the outside world, however, an image emerged of a rapid German campaign with a great deal of motorisation, mechanisation and tactical air support. This image seems to have largely passed the Netherlands by.

69   Major Sas joined a battlefield tour organised by the OKH (German Army Command) in September 1939 and was of course presented with a selective picture which he nevertheless sent to the AHK with an analysis. (PEC 1C, Best, 15530 ff.) Typical in this light is that when a Dutch KLM pilot observed the German airborne landing near Oslo on 9 April 1940 because his plane was parked there, a report by this pilot was not considered interesting by the GHQ. It was the Minister of Defence and later the Commander Air Defence, Lieutenant-General P.W. Best, who insisted on measures such as more troops shielding airfields and placing obstacles on the national highways so that no landing could take place on them; in addition, machine gun posts were places on these national highways too.

70   Reijnders and the previous CV, Lieutenant-General Roëll, adhered to the doctrine of the German school. Especially among the older senior officers, who had been active before World War I, there was a greater tendency towards a German orientation than a French one. Reijnders already foresaw in 1935 that Germany would soon be more powerful than the Franco-Belgian defence. However, the younger staff officers were of a pro-French doctrine and upbringing and overestimated French potential and operational procedures.

71   It seems that the idea that the French would be able and willing to deploy troops north of the large Dutch rivers (e.g. in the Fortress) was mainly the wish of Winkelman and Chief-of-Staff Van Voorst tot Voorst, but scepticism about the realisation of this idea was prevalent. Reijnders was (more) realistic about this, expected the French only in the south and foresaw that the French would not be able to develop sufficiently fast, which made a strong preliminary defence in Brabant necessary. Reijnders, although underestimating the French speed, was closer to being right.

72   Winkelman had little more to do with the military after his retirement in 1934, perhaps out of disappointment at his unwanted retirement. Even before that, however, he seems to have been more of an implementer than a strategist. This impression arises when an analysis is made of the man's comings and goings. This assessment was supported by some of Winkelman's

contemporaries, such as the previous CV, Lieutenant-General W. Roëll, who had been in charge of both Reijnders and Winkelman in earlier stages of their careers (PEC 1C, 1911): "*I certainly put General Reijnders as a troop leader and a tactician above General Winkelman. General Winkelman was a splendid law maker but a great tactician and strategist he was not, in my opinion. He never was. He is someone of a perfectly sound character and a brilliant lawmaker of extraordinary ability. He was also very good as an organiser. But he did not have the tactical knack in the first place. He never had that and he never will*".

73   Remarkably enough, the CV, Lieutenant-General J.J.G. van Voorst tot Voorst, who was a strong advocate of the Grebbe-line, was still of the opinion that manoeuvring power was present before mobilisation and even thought that – in the round of fighting after the initial invasion – Field Army units could act (counter-)offensively from the Grebbe-line in the direction of Germany! He was alone in this opinion, but there were many objections within the general staff to fix the Field Army entirely as would be the case under Winkelman. This seems to have been a constant point of dispute between the pessimists and the optimists within the general staff.

74   As a result, the bulk of the operational reserves consisted of position troops concentrated in independent battalions behind the main line.

75   Which argument would gain even more strength if the battle were first fought in isolation and only then joined. This would mean that only Dutch ammunition would be fired across the entire front.

76   The danger of enemy air dominance was not underestimated, perhaps even overestimated. In many respects it appears that the superiority (in time supremacy) of the enemy air force was considered so great that (larger) movements during the day were ruled out, at least if there was a choice. This was partly the reason why Dijxhoorn did not allow the same divisions to defend first the Grebbe-line and afterwards the eastern front of the Fortress. He considered the move from the Grebbe-line to the Fortress under German air supremacy irresponsible.

77   It must be said that this last aspect in particular was probably less known to the Dutch military leadership. The French air force - *l'Armee de l'Air* - had long been a neglected child. Moreover, conceptually it was still a WWI air force, which the Netherlands had copied flawlessly. The French air force had only few capable attack planes, most were still in delivery or on order when the invasion occurred. In May 1940 it was still largely a reconnaissance and fighter fleet. Since the mid-thirties, they had started to invest in a modern air force and eventually – too late – in attack planes. The French industry did not succeed in producing enough good planes, so they also bought from the US and even from the Dutch maker *Koolhoven* (FK-58). This led to a very mixed force. It was decided to concentrate a large part of the air force in the south so that it would not be lost in the first phase of the battle. Thus the reality was that the large French north-eastern field army had to

make do with scanty air support. The British BAFF (British Air-Forces in France) provided several hundred light bombers and *Hurricanes* in support of the BEF and the French field army. The strategy of both France and the UK was to hold back a significant proportion of units for the later stages of the battle. The Netherlands presumably knew little or nothing about this. On the other hand – the Netherlands could not assume for its *Grand Strategy* that the allies would provide significant air support, although the RAF would still fly an impressive number of sorties over particularly the West of Holland during the May Days.

78 Denmark had a symbolic military force, which had only been alerted a few hours before the invasion and which, moreover, consisted partly of recruits. The whole force was not stronger than about 14,000 men with a very small army air force. The navy was a coastal navy of modest size. Denmark capitulated six hours after the German invasion.

79 It is sometimes said that the Netherlands should have followed the Danish example, but this is based on hindsight and usually not free from an anti-militaristic motivation. The Netherlands may not have had a large military force, but it was still substantial and serious enough to resist German aggression, especially in cooperation with allies. Denmark did not have this, had a strategically unfavourable location and, moreover, no chance of direct allied support. The two cases are not therefore comparable on fundamental elements of *Grand Strategy*, even if for other reasons one would consider the option of direct capitulation the best.

80 On 15 May 1940 an army capitulation (with extension to the province of Zeeland on the 17th) was concluded in which the Dutch army on land and in the coastal waters surrendered, but it was explicitly stipulated that other parts of the armed forces outside this territory were excluded. Furthermore, the administration of the occupied Dutch territory was transferred to the (then) occupying power, but the government did not capitulate. There are legal nuances to the legitimacy of a defunct government, but the fact is that the monarch and the Minister of Colonies remained free and could thus continue to govern the Dutch overseas territories as a sovereign and legitimised government.

81 That the Netherlands realised that only allied support would help it in the East-Indian Archipelago was due to its maritime component. Whereas the navy hardly mattered for the defence of the homeland, for the archipelago it was the most important element in the *Grand Strategy*, in combination with the arguments of the vastness of the archipelago and the size and (fire) power of the Japanese navy. For a small country, the Netherlands had a relatively large navy (it has been said: 'Of all the small states, the Netherlands had the largest navy'), but there was not a single large surface unit to be found within it, although there was a relatively large submarine fleet. The construction of three battle cruisers was in the planning stages in 1940 (completion foreseen in 1944), but that still would not have brought the Netherlands defence independence.

82 'Brongers', p. 61, 'Reijnders', pp.19/20. Reijnders reasoned that whether or not to occupy Brabant and South-Limburg with (lighter) troops, that a too frivolous or even absent defence of those parts of the country would lead to a similar Belgian claim to that experienced in 1919 and that, after an unconvincing Dutch effort, such a claim might succeed.

83 Reijnders was not an outspoken advocate of neutrality, and certainly not the methodical neutralism that the government stood for. He only saw advantage in neutrality as long as it was credible, but believed that if circumstances would overtake this continued unilateral policy of neutrality, an alliance would have to be sought even prior to a *casus belli*. In a memorandum of 2 February 1935 to the then Minister of Defence Deckers, Reijnders stated: "*I will leave open the question whether the neutral position of the Netherlands under all circumstances would be in the true interest of our people (...)*".

84 'Brongers', p. 61; also 'Reijnders', pp. 19/20.

85 In reality, the devastating bombardment of Rotterdam added an element that had not been so concretely contemplated beforehand, although Warsaw had borne this fate in September 1939 and Guernica (1937) had already endured a symbolically magnified destruction from the air although the latter had clearly been tactical and not so large scale as history makes us believe. Large scale carpet bombing was a new phenomenon of warfare. Only in retrospect can this be seen as obvious. It seemed illogical to destroy or heavily damage a country that was to be conquered. Great destruction by ground-based artillery combined with aerial bombardment was certainly taken into account, especially around the main positions.

86 The Dutch assumed that for many weeks, even up to three months, it would be possible to defend the Fortress more or less alone. Remarkably, the Dutch command never seems to have considered the inexorable obstacle that the ammunition supply imposed.

87 Izaak Herman Reijnders (1879-1966). Before the war, the 'ij' was often written as 'y'. Here, an 'ij' is used unless families kept the 'y' after the war. This was the case, for example, with General Seyffardt, who died during the war.

88 H.A. Seyffardt (1872-1943) came from conservative descent and was highly regarded as a General and former Chief-of-Staff. However, he was very nationalistic and would eventually after his pension associate himself with National-Socialist ideas before the war, which he continued after the German occupation. During the war, he allowed himself to be used by the *Waffen* SS to recruit members for its Dutch section. He was assassinated on 5 February 1943 by the Dutch underground.

89 The highest military-administrative function, nonetheless in peacetime *ex eaquo* to the Commander of the Field Army (CV) and the Commander of the Navy. Only in the event of a Supreme Commander being appointed in times of crisis or war would there be a truly unified leadership of the armed forces. It should be borne in mind that the Chief-of-Staff could only have

an equal relationship with the CV, so that the latter could allow himself to think, act and communicate differently within the framework of his function. It seems logical that this could result in a division of opinions when preparing a battle plan. Nevertheless, this artificial construction was maintained. Remarkably enough, after the appointment of Reijnders as OLZ in August 1939, various authorities would still go beyond the OLZ and seek an independent judgement of the CV. Both the Queen and the Minister of Defence would be guilty of this.

90 The memorandum is from 2 February 1935 [letter 'Chef Generale Staf no. 1P']. Also 'Brongers', pp. 21-24.

91 Mr. Dr. L.N. Deckers (1883-1978). He was a member of the Rooms-Katholieke Staatspartij (Roman Catholic State Party), which became the KVP in 1945.

92 France and Belgium had a joint military arrangement from 1920 to 1936. On 6 March 1936, this was denounced and limited to general staff consultations. Later that year, Belgium unilaterally terminated it and declared its independence.

93 This refers to an attack without prior concentration and tension build-up, in which the German troops could just cross the border from an innocent-looking exercise or a quick march from the barracks. The Netherlands was not adequately protected against this. In 1934 and 1935 this was prominently under discussion in the general staff and would lead in the period 1936-1938 to measures such as heavy casemates at the bridges across the IJssel and Meuse (and some connected canals and tributaries) and stationing of Police Troops at these locations. Also, a pre-mobilisation (so called 'BOUV') was designed, mobilising about one-third of the militia to be concentrated along the border and the IJssel and Meuse region, so that external security could be guaranteed. Afterwards, a general mobilisation could take place behind this screen. The whole set of concentrations and measures was called Strategic Security.

94 Outside the navy, and until 1938 (after which the yearly levy was gradually growing to almost double that figure) the Dutch army had approximately 8,000 professional soldiers (1,200 officers, 6,000 NCO's and around 750 corporals and cadets) and an annual militia of up to maximum 19,500 men. The latter was divided over a spring and an autumn levy. There was a transition period during each winter when only a few hundred militiamen were under arms, because for foot-infantry (regular ranks, non-NCO) the first exercise was only 5.5 months. It meant that no more than a contingent of about 10,000 militia would always be available for the national defence. Depending of the time of year of an invasion, that militia would not be fully trained either. With this, one could in no way conduct a promising defence.

95 This also included the army air force, as there was no independent air force. Requests made for anti-tank rifles, anti-tank guns, armoured cars,

anti-aircraft artillery and field artillery were to be partially granted, often not meeting the requested volumes though. Requests for light and medium tanks were entirely rejected. Meanwhile (June 1937 to August 1939), the Minister of Defence was the former professional soldier Dr. J.J.C. van Dijk (1871-1954). He was a fervent advocate of a stronger armed force. During the war, from 1 April 1943 until the end of the war, he was held prisoner by the Germans, first as a hostage and later as a political prisoner.

96 Part of the unrealised need was due to a slow ordering process, lack of (timely) delivery or lack of availability of the weapon systems ordered or to be ordered. From 1936 onwards, the arms industry was heavily overloaded internationally. Moreover, the complex Dutch requirements slowed down the ordering process considerably.

97 A.Q.H. Dijxhoorn (1889-1953). From 1 November 1935 to May 1937, he worked at the Division IIB (Organisation Department), which was located at the Ministry of Defence itself. After a short intermezzo, in the period 1 February 1938 to 10 August 1939, he even became Head of Department IIB, soon appointed to the rank of Lieutenant-Colonel, and q.q. First Advisor to the Minister. From 10 August 1939 he himself was appointed Minister of Defence until his resignation on 12 June 1941 in London. Reactivated as a soldier and promoted he was posted as Major-General and Dutch representative to the *Combined Chiefs of Staff* in Washington until October 1944, then briefly attached to Field-Marshal Montgomery's staff and several other short-lived posts. From 9 May 1945 until 1 November 1945 acting Chief of General Staff and afterwards promoted to Lieutenant-General and member of the High Military Court (until his death on 22 January 1953).

98 Dijxhoorn concluded this from the experiences of the German (Pz. Kpfw. I) and Russian light tanks (T-26 - a Russian version of the *Vickers* Light Tank) in Spain in 1936 and 1937. These lightly armoured tanks – effectively armoured cars on tracks – were indeed easily pierced by armour-piercing weapons. However, by the mid-thirties, there had been widespread experimentation with medium and heavy tanks and much was published about mass tank deployment. Moreover, Dijxhoorn had been schooled (in particular in France) in the doctrine of 'manoeuvre warfare', on which, incidentally, he had his own view. Nevertheless, he did not see sufficient use in Dutch circumstances for light tanks. His negative advice on the purchase of tanks (following a meeting between the Minister, Chief-of-Staff and CV on 25 March 1938) was followed by Minister Van Dijk. Dijxhoorn scored negative points with Reijnders and the CV for this. At the end of 1939, he would adjust his opinion, but by then it was too late. Dijxhoorn was also at the basis of the still very dated Infantry Regulations (1934/1935) in which fire plans were declared sacred and systematicity was all-important. He was therefore a conservative and a firm believer in systematic action and dictated and centralized command (*Befehlstaktik*). From 1939 onwards, this would prove to be an essentially crippled principle in the face of the Ger-

	man manoeuvre warfare and the doctrine of mission command (*Auftragstaktik*).
99	The German conclusion after the Polish campaign was largely the same as Dijxhoorn's, although this had long been known in German circles. After all, the light tanks Pz.Kpfw. I and II had never been meant as '*Kampfwagen*' but as training (Type I) and reconnaissance tanks (Type II). Only the Types III (16 tons, break-out tank) and IV (20 tons, infantry support tank) were meant as real '*Kampfwagen*'. Because of the lack of sufficient tanks of the latter types, many tank companies with Type's I and II had been deployed in Poland, resulting in great losses.
100	There were at least two occasions in May 1940 when armoured Dutch action could have made a big difference to the outcome of a manoeuvre or action. The first was on 10 May in the evening during the attempt to retake the bridge at Alblasserdam. Armoured cars would have been able to break through immediately upon the risen opportunity. The second was on the Island of Dordrecht against the light German troops there. In both instances this could have had significant consequences for the German airborne corridor. The retaking of AFB Waalhaven by Dutch troops or the retaking of the Moerdijk bridges would have been extremely detrimental to the German strategy. It should also be considered that with a considerable contingent of Dutch tanks available, German operational plans could have turned out differently.
101	Often only the Reijnders-Dijxhoorn relationship is mentioned, but it is certain that Reijnders had troubled relations with both (successive) commanders of the Field Army (W. Roëll and J.J.G. van Voorst tot Voorst) regarding strategic issues, although certainly the first one preferred him to Winkelman. It is tempting to conclude that Reijnders possessed a rather unyielding personality, even in peer-to-peer matters.
102	(PEC 1C, 13101) CV Lieutenant-General J.J.G. van Voorst tot Voorst, who was present at the discussion of the 'tank proposal', seems to have taken this point more seriously than Reijnders. This is logical because armoured manoeuvring units would have been a welcome addition for the Field Army and would be predominately procured for the Field Army to begin with.
103	In 2022 Tobias van Gent (MSc) published an autobiography on Dijxhoorn ("*De minister en de majesteit*", ISBN 9789024446780). Van Gent was kind enough to give the author insight into his research resulting from personal documents of Dijxhoorn. These documents show for instance that during a conflict in 1936 between Field Army commander W. Roëll (who was in favour of German doctrine) and Dijxhoorn (as the author of the amended Infantry Regulations) – in which Roëll reproached Dijxhoorn for being too much in favour of the rigid French command dictum while giving more initiative to subordinate (field) commander was considered more useful and desirable to Roëll – Dijxhoorn received full support from Reijnders.

Roëll proved in many respects to be correct with regard to his vision of a modern armed force and the future conflict, and also a General who sought the *Auftragstaktik* principle. Reijnders and Roëll were not friends and crossed swords on all kinds of issues, so that sentiment may also have played a role here when Reijnders fully backed Dijxhoorn. At the end of February 1936, after receiving a reprimand from Reijnders, Roëll wrote the following words: "*I praise every officer, however, who has the courage to deviate from a tactical regulation when this appears useful or necessary on good grounds. I praise every initiative and I crave it, as our army was very weak in this respect, yes, even in very high ranks it still is here and there...*". However, Roëll would state before the PEC that he considered Reijnders an excellent troop commander and attributed to him far greater tactical ingenuity than to Winkelman.

104   The cabinets tumbled over each other with unsolvable problems. On 29 June 1939, the 4th Cabinet of Colijn (Colijn IV) fell, after which Colijn V took office at the end of July 1939. This Cabinet formally fell on 4 August 1939, after which the 2nd Cabinet De Geer took office on 10 August. This cabinet would serve out the period of mobilisation and the May Days, but would perish in London on 2 September 1940.

105   This created tension because a Lieutenant-Colonel of the general staff suddenly became the superior of a Lieutenant-General. The otherwise not very martial government attached importance to an expert acting as minister in times of tension, but in doing so they also took a risk of (improper) interventions by the government in strategic and even tactical matters.

106   Apart from Reijnders' own brochures, the instruction is discussed in the PEC interrogations and the other known post-war publications on the subject. Among others: Amersfoort/Kamphuis (chapters 1 and 3), Brongers, Van Gent and Moeyes.

107   Moeyes concludes (pp. 426, 427) that the neutrality policy was in fact abandoned. This conclusion seems rather formalistic. Moeyes again reasons remarkably rigidly on this point in a subsequent phrase when he views Winkelman's actions as follows (p. 473): "*Winkelman took his decision in a way that was completely incompatible with Dutch neutral status*". This on the basis of the clandestine efforts for coordination with Belgian and French authorities in February 1940. Moeyes neglects to add the necessary nuances to this conclusion. Moreover, he is inconsistent in his work in the definition of what this neutral status entailed and what it stood for under international law. Making contingency plans is, certainly in principle, not a violation of neutrality.

108   In Seyffardt's time, the general staff worked out many concentrations that were colour-coded, with Concentration Blue indicating a (counter)concentration based on German aggression.

109   Reijnders had asked the then Captain of the general staff J.J.C.P. Wilson to examine whether the suitability if concentration of an army corps for

the defence of the Peel region still corresponded to the terrain advantages it offered. The Peel-region was originally known for its peat, swamp and forest density and the lack of infrastructure. Peat extraction and new infrastructure had changed this during the twenties and thirties. Wilson had studied the Peel concentration as part of his promotional research during his staff education. It was therefore hardly surprising that he recommended the Peel concentration to be maintained albeit 'with some modifications'. This set the final tone for the construction of the position and the construction of an elaborate anti-tank ditch (later called the Peel Canal). Within the general staff the Peel-concentration was a divisive subject, that only a part of the general staff officers supported, but another part preferred the Orange-line (*Oranje stelling*) between Den Bosch and Tilburg, while other members wanted to conduct the defence exclusively on the borders of Fortress Holland.

110 The positioning in fixed positions raised the fundamental question whether there was still a Field Army (manoeuvre force) when it was tied to positions everywhere. Field Army commanders W. Roëll and (from 1937) J.J.G. van Voorst tot Voorst opposed this fixation of the Field Army and saw it as hopelessly defensive and an abuse of their manoeuvre forces. In theory, they were right, but the army and its leaders (officers) trained according the text books of the general staff had been educated only in defensive warfare and were hardly tactically trained. The premise had been that one could not adequately train reserve officers for battle. This doctrine was supported when the book "*Vers l'armée de métier*" ('Towards a professional army') by Lieutenant-Colonel Charles de Gaulle became known in the Netherlands in 1934. Just like today, De Gaulle's premise was that a modern military had become such a tactical complicated instrument and the complexity of manoeuvre so great that only professional soldiers could fulfil this profession. The Finns and especially of course the Germans and later the Soviet Union and the US would prove the invalidity of this reasoning five years later, but it was eagerly accepted by the elitist general staffs of north-western Europe, including the Dutch. It echoes, moreover, in our time, where it is assumed that conscripts could not master the essentials of the ordinary military profession because of the complexity of the manoeuvre and the personal mission, but once again recent wars, including the (current) war in Ukraine, invalidate this theory.

111 The strategic security measures included trenches (and the first casemate construction) along the IJssel- and Maas-lines, trenches in the Peel-region and emplacements along Fortress Holland and coastal fronts.

112 It was also considered that preparing trenches would reveal where the Dutch army planned to conduct its defence.

113 Brongers' (uncritical) biography of General Reijnders mainly defends the General's policy in his disputes with the government after his appointment as OLZ, but ignores the vulnerability in his own policy. His remarkable lack

of urgency in construction of defence structures could have led to a disastrous result if a German invasion had occurred at any time in 1939. Along the great rivers, except for bridges, no casemates would have been built, no positions would have been dug in the projected Field Army positions and no clearing of the field of fire would have taken place. This criticism also applies to the CV, who after all had equal responsibility with the Chief-of-Staff. Before mobilization, the construction of positions was considered to be a revelation of military plans, after mobilization the lack of a unified (military) policy was the reason that positions were tardily constructed.

114 One might think that the policy of neutrality would have dictated that clear positions would have to be taken on all sides. If the intended positions had been built before the autumn of 1939, this would have damaged the policy of neutrality.

115 Reijnders. Chapter IV 'The military policy'.

116 One encounters in many historical writings the erroneous reasoning that the mobilisation of 280,000 men (some mistakenly speak of 300,000 men) was remarkably well executed. That was an exaggeration. With the large numbers already in the training depots and the extensive pre-mobilisation of April 1939 (which was maintained), there were already about 80,000 men under arms and the military infrastructure was already well prepared. In August 1939, therefore, there were "only" 200,000 more men to be mobilised. This was also done in two phases with 50,000 men (mostly officers and NCO's) as quartermasters and 150,000 men a couple of days later. The fact that the mobilisation and especially the concentration went well afterwards was without doubt a credit to the army command.

117 It was not until 19 April 1940 that a State of Siege ("*Staat van beleg*", martial law) was proclaimed, and even then with some restrictions.

118 It would be going too far to explain all that is involved here, but in short it came down to the fact that the armed forces were not given extraordinary powers to control civilian activities (as would normally be the case with the State of Siege). As a result, parts of the defence line area remained accessible to everyone and civilian necessity continued to prevail over military necessity. All kinds of management and emergency measures were thus withheld from the OLZ and countless administrative laws and regulations as well as civilian budgetary responsibility remained wholly or partially intact. This seriously hampered the preparations of the armed forces in the field.

119 There were four echelons along the main route of the enemy coming from the east: (i) the delaying frontier echelon, (ii) the outer defences behind the great rivers, (iii) the extended defences on the line 'Grebbe-line / Peel-Raam-line' and (iv) the echelon in the main defence on the fronts of Fortress Holland.

120 Reijnders and the minister also had differences of opinion regarding declaring the State of Siege, press censorship and mobilisation clubs (unions for militia), but that was in fact secondary. The core of all the problems lay in

121 the divergent strategic visions, which greatly obstructed all kinds of related matters such as resources for position building and daily policy.

121 The minister also allowed it to be whispered by spread of the Cabinet, some of them known as anti-military, that the death of (many) soldiers on behalf of allied defence in Brabant, which was seen as a side show from the governmental point of view, would not be tolerated in Holland. Moreover, Dijxhoorn's vision diverged strongly from what the general staff had developed and accepted during the thirties as Concentration Blue, of which a considerable concentration of the Field Army in Brabant was a prominent part.

122 The choice that Winkelman would later make was also in accordance with the neutrality principles, because he decided - not without receiving criticism - to withdraw the troops only after the beginning of hostilities. Winkelman thus aimed at respecting the neutrality requirements and not letting the Germans know that the defence of Brabant would only be symbolic. He succeeded.

123 Dijxhoorn initiated these visits with the CV and the commanders of the 2nd and 4th Army Corps in order to check whether retreat orders had been worked out for the Field Army from the Grebbe-line to the eastern front of the Fortress. In addition, he wanted to know how the three Generals viewed the principle of retreating over such a long distance and continuing the defence on the east front with the same units after this manoeuvre.

124 This concerned the Crown-meeting of 30 December 1939 at which the Queen, the Prime Minister, the Ministers of Defence and Foreign Affairs and General Reijnders discussed the state of affairs. Reijnders, who heard about this visit for the first time, which was an enormous *faux-pas*, was humiliated and was moreover used by the Queen in an extremely dubious way by giving the General a sneer that his subordinates saw things better than he did. Dijxhoorn thus probably forfeited any possibility of constructive cooperation with the OLZ. Nor did this incident improve the relationship between the CV and the OLZ. Dijxhoorn knew the Generals' diverging views from his time as a head of Division IIB.

125 It is going too far to give an exposé on the premeditation with which Dijxhoorn demolished the reputation of General Reijnders between September 1939 and January 1940. The mosaic of sources and the nature of events that support this conclusion is overwhelming. Without suspecting General Reijnders of being faultless or of having remarkable diplomatic talents, he certainly deserves the respect that he put up with the treatment by this Minister of Defence for so long and, moreover, at the time of the events, did not make a public outcry about it. Although many people within the group also criticised certain decisions by Reijnders, almost every General in his time was in awe of his ability to cope with the Minister of Defence. It is also certain that Prime Minister De Geer, who eventually lost confidence in the OLZ, fended off requests from Dijxhoorn to replace the OLZ in

December and early January. Dijxhoorn's premeditated demolition of the OLZ's reputation was aimed at manipulating the Prime Minister and the Queen. Wilhelmina also played a dubious role in this. Her conduct was far from shrewd. By her actions, she proved not to be above the parties but to be a party herself, yet without any genuine knowledge on the subject.

126 Apart from personal motivations of those involved, it should be noted that before the appointment of an OLZ (i.e. before September 1939) direct military etiquette communication with, for example, the CV was not a breach of etiquette because in that phase, curiously enough, the Navy and Field Army had commanders who functioned on the same level to the Chief-of-Staff.

127 This seems a contradiction – after all, the Peel-Raam-line and Grebbe-line were in Reijnders' strategy connected as a front – but it is not. (PEC 1C, 1400) The CV was in favour of an Orange-line in the variant of a diagonal between Den Bosch and Goirle (south of Tilburg near the Belgian border). This line was shorter than the Peel-Raam-line and connected the intermediate defence north of the Meuse with the defence below, so that the intermediate defence did not have an open right flank. Moreover, the Orange-line was synchronized with Belgian-French wishes and had a better coverage from the air. Van Voorst, however, only had become a supporter of this option during mobilisation.

128 Reijnders had two border infantry battalions and the Light Division to dynamically defend the border sector against significant enemy penetrations. However, this was to cover a gap between Weert and Goirle, south of Tilburg (a 45 km stretch). It was also clear to Reijnders that this was a liability, but his objective was only to do this as long as no allies had deployed in his rear. In other words, his aim was a firm forward defence.

129 Reijnders did have field explorations carried out into the Oranje-line in 1939, among others by General Fabius.

130 A more nuanced approach would probably be to say that Reijnders had made the *a priori* mistake of allowing Wilson to examine 'his' Peel concentration and to underestimate his coloured opinion of it. This led to the fixation of the Peel-Raam-line from 1939 onwards. However, the Peel concentration without Belgian support was vulnerable. That was a widely supported consensus within the general staff, where the Peel-defence, except for Wilson, had almost exclusively opponents. But it was Reijnders who was in command. He received no extra funding for a new position further back. Because he did stand for a war in alliance – and had the majority of the general staff behind him – his hands and feet were effectively tied. He had to stay on the Peel and compensate the gap by positioning the Light Division and two border battalions along the southern border. As we will see, not without reason, Reijnders assumed that he could count on allied support, for a retreat partly secured by the French, within a few days after the beginning of hostilities. The French would probably have given

131   that support in the sector before Tilburg if the Netherlands still had held the Peel-Raam-line and wanted to move out in a controlled manner. That premise was plausible and not at all as disastrous as many critics claimed.

131. On 30 January 1940, Reijnders was summoned by De Geer, who informed him that if the OLZ would remain, the Minister of Defence would resign. As De Geer wished to retain the minister, Reijnders was requested to submit his resignation to the Queen. He submitted his reasoned resignation in writing on 31 January, but never received an answer from the Queen, who in doing so again went beyond the bounds of etiquette but also demonstrated that she was not lacking in despotism. Reijnders' later attitude during the war – his absolute refusal to do anything for Queen and Fatherland – had everything to do with this unfortunate state of affairs. And one can sympathise with him. On 5 February, Reijnders heard informally that his dismissal had been effected and he did not receive the honours that would normally have been due to him. It had therefore become an 'affair' in the literal sense.

132. Henri Gerard Winkelman (1876-1952). Born in Maastricht, sworn in as a Second Lieutenant in 1896 after completing the KMA (Royal Military Academy). Graduated the HKS (General Staff School) and was subsequently appointed to the general staff. Passed through various staff positions and commands, including that of divisional commander. In 1934, he was on the short list to succeed Chief-of-Staff Lieutenant-General Seyffardt, but he was outmanoeuvred by Reijnders. He was requested to retire that same year as a Lieutenant-General. In 1939 reactivated and appointed the commander of the Utrecht-Soesterberg Air Defence District.

133. "*Generaal H.G. Winkelman - standvastig strijder*",2006, T. Middelkoop, pp. 94/95, an edited reprint of the book first published in 2002 by the same author with the subtitle '*A soldier does his duty*'.

134. His Chief-of-staff, Major-General H.F.M. van Voorst tot Voorst – a younger brother of the CV – stood firmly behind this policy and did not show any new insight during his PEC-hearings in 1948 either (1C, 15688, 15689; 15701 et seq.). Thus, this liberal policy was deliberate and predetermined.

135. An interesting work on the pleasures of "*Auftragstaktik*" (Mission Command) has recently been published "*The German Way of War: a lesson in Tactical Management*" by Jaap Jan Brouwer (2021), ISBN-10 1526790378.

136. It will be dealt with in more detail. Some examples are between 9 May 20.00 hrs and 10 May in the morning (i) the failure to alarm the troops inside Fortress Holland (except for the coastal and air defences), (ii) the execution of demolition of bridges and road-obstructions by the Field Army on the southern border whereas it should be easily accessible by fast allied units coming to the aid of the Netherlands and (iii) the fact that Winkelman allowed part of his close staff to openly doubt the German invasion during the night and therefore to neglect their duties during the evening and the night.

137 In Belgium, General Van den Bergen had to step down as chief of the Army Staff in favour of Lieutenant-General Michiels on 31 January 1940. In Belgium, however, there was continuity because there was only a single replacement and not of both the Chief-of-Staff of the army and the military advisor of the Commander-in-Chief (Belgium had the sovereign as Commander-in-Chief with an advisor who actually ran things for the sovereign), Major-General Van Overstraeten. The blunder made by Van den Bergen left the decision-makers in Belgium with few other choices. Although secretly Belgium constantly explored and maintained the scenario of a joint allied defence, formally it was neutral. That neutralism was seriously infringed by Van den Bergen's untimely act.

138 Although such a transition process is logical and none of the Generals is to blame, it is a fact that by choosing an already long-retired General as OLZ and a Chief-of-Staff who had previously been 'only' a divisional commander, the transition was longer and more complex than if one of the already functioning subcommanders had been selected.

139 Both generals did not seem to be 'kindred spirits', but the performance of one during the May Days and the post-war brochures of the other would certainly later bring the relationship to a frigid level. There must have also been some emotion in knowing that both had been candidates for the position of Chief-of-Staff in 1934, which of course made the relief in February 1940 all the more emotionally charged.

140 It is unknown how intensive the transfer process really was, but there was at the most a transfer of several days between the chiefs and only one single hour between the supreme commanders (e.g. PEC 1C 15655-15657 Van Voorst; PEC 1C 15768 - 15770 Winkelman). Winkelman's biographer, among others, reproached Reijnders for this (*"Generaal H.G. Winkelman - standvastig strijder"* 2006, T. Middelkoop, pp. 94/95). Reijnders was accused of not handing over the contents of the safe and not have said anything about sealed envelopes with the (possible) allies to be turned over to the allies in case of war to inform the general staffs of those countries about the Dutch strategy and requests. The last charge was untrue but above all irrelevant because the envelopes were replaced with new ones with new content by the end of March 1940. However, the very limited transition of the command does not seem to have taken place at the instigation of the departing generals. Neither Reijnders nor Winkelman seem to have felt the need to go through an extensive transition. This transition should have been directed by the Minister, but it was not. Moreover, it was up to the intelligence service and the heads of sections at the GHQ to actively inform the new leadership, although the new leadership itself should have pursued this process. Winkelman himself and the incumbent staff are to be blamed that during the transition so much information seems to have remained undiscussed. In defence of the Generals, however, it should also be noted that in such a position so much information comes to them that they can

hardly be aware of what is missing. It is precisely for this reason that the section heads seem to be responsible for the poor information transfer. This again shows that the conclusion drawn by Herman Amersfoort and Moeyes that the GHQ functioned well is incorrect.

141 Particularly concerning the intelligence available to the GHQ, much of the information available to the previous OLZ apparently did not reach the new Supreme Commander. Winkelman certainly claimed before the PEC that he lacked much information about the German troop concentrations east of the Dutch border, while General Fabius (head of intelligence) claimed to have assumed that both OLZs would have exchanged this with each other (PEC 1C, 4813 et seq.). Fabius and his direct subordinate, the head of GS-IIIA Major Van der Plassche, are seriously guilty of making this assumption about such weighty information. Also, both newly appointed Generals seem to have had little current information and knowledge about the state of affairs in Brabant. On the other hand, their actions show a certain degree of disinterest in the positions they did not consider as main defences. A reproach can be made here, certainly to the Chief-of-Staff who was responsible for this.

142 See also the chapiter concerning frequently used terms and abbreviations. The 'heart' of the country is somewhat misleading as a concept. The term concerned the provinces of North and South Holland and the west of the province Utrecht. This geographic area was referred to as "Vesting Holland" (Fortress Holland) and lay behind and/or above the "Nieuwe Hollandse Waterlinie" (New Dutch Water-line).

143 It was normal strategic process to concentrate forces in the desired area and not to risk having to redeploy under enemy pressure and likewise not to disperse troops too much either. In the Reijnders' period as Supreme Commander, however, no choice had yet been made between the Grebbe-line or the eastern front of the Fortress, so both were occupied. Winkelman made the choice for the Grebbe-line but this had the inevitable consequence that if it was broken through the eastern front would still have to be defended by the same troops. The distinction between the policies of the two supreme commanders in this matter has been repeatedly explained. In fact they intended the same thing, but Winkelman sold his concept better to the minister and the weakness was in the rear, along the eastern front of the Fortress. On 14 May 1940, the inundations were still insufficiently high and the eastern front had not been reinforced and had no prior occupation of forces.

144 In all fairness, it must be said that during his interview with Dijxhoorn before being appointed the new Supreme Commander, Winkelman almost certainly indicated that he wished to conduct the defence on the eastern front of the Fortress. During the first weeks of his appointment, however, he quickly – not the least due to advice from the CV – changed his mind and decided that the Grebbe-line would have to become the first line of

firm resistance. In the first instance there was complete agreement between Dijxhoorn and Winkelman, because the former did not like the Peel-Raam-line and wanted to concentrate the main force directly on the Fortress with only outposts outside the Fortress. After Winkelman's rapid change of mind, there remained – before mid-March – less difference between two views of the succeeding supreme commanders.

145 Ambitious plans for the further 'fortification' of the defence lines and fronts of the Fortress had already been submitted to Winkelman. However, no money was made available for heavy reinforcement of both the Grebbe-line and the east front. After Winkelman's choice of the Grebbe-line, work on the eastern front (which had already been halted due to the winter weather) was not resumed.

146 The choice was left open whether the eastern front of the Fortress or the Grebbe-line was the main position on the central front.

147 In fact it is more accurate to say that the southern part of the province of Zeeland was included, that is Walcheren, Zuid-Beveland and Zeeuws-Vlaanderen (Dutch Flanders). The more northern parts did not matter and were hardly occupied by troops. On Walcheren and Zuid-Beveland two thin defence-lines (the Bath-line west of Woensdrecht, the Zanddijk-line in the heart of Zuid-Beveland, near the canal Wemeldinge – Hansweert) were constructed to defend against a land attack. This is the same region where in 1944 the large-scale allied operations Infatuate and Switchback took place.

148 The Molotov-Ribbentrop Pact was of 24 August 1939 (Russian time). It was a non-aggression pact between Germany and the Soviet Union, which also included collusion on the partition of Poland after a German invasion. The treaty achieved what Germany had failed to do in 1914, namely pacifying Russia in order to free its hands for the Polish campaign and the Western Front. For Western strategists, it was a warning sign.

149 The main lines were known in the Hague, some details too. The actual '*Blitzkrieg*' element (as operational doctrine) was probably insufficiently understood in the Hague. The military attachés in Berlin were offered the opportunity of an organised 'battlefield tour' to Poland at the end of September 1939. Major Sas attended (PEC 1C, 4362) and on 28 September 1939 he submitted a report to the OLZ about his findings and his knowledge from his contacts with the *Abwehr Oberst* Oster. It is almost certain that Dijxhoorn was informed about this as well. The CV indicates that he studied the manoeuvre to take Lwow (Lemberg, Lvov) and stated that he had learned from it (PEC 1C, 13169). This manoeuvre was in principle also typical of the modus operandi of the Germans in the south of the Netherlands in May 1940, with the aggressive deep penetration of motorised units ahead of the main force achieving considerable success. The Poles, however, would put up tougher resistance, slowing down the German manoeuvre and ending up in a classic siege of Warsaw. In Holland this was in fact the case at Rotterdam.

150 Zeeland was considered important only in view of British interests. It was considered unwise to offend the British and not to defend the Westerschelde (Scheldt estuary giving access to Antwerp) properly, partly because of the fear of a renewed Belgian annexation claim (after the next war) if it was not defended. In the end, the French were also committed to this and to such an extent that even in 1939, the French had developed plans to land on Walcheren, both by sea and with airborne troops and paratroopers. These plans were even so aggressive that they could be carried out without explicit Dutch prior approval. This fell under the *Hypothesis Escaut* (Scheldt), one of the prominent French defence strategies. From these pre-war French considerations eventually emerged that in May 1940 a French division was sent to Walcheren, preceded by a motorised brigade. See also 'Van Gent', pg. 145 ff.

151 It is sometimes suggested that the change of supreme command seriously hampered the construction of positions during the period November 1939 - March 1940. The reality (KNMI database - Dutch Royal National Meteorological institute) is that the winter of 1939/1940 was extremely harsh. In 1942, a report on that winter of 1939/1940 stated that there had not been such a severe winter since 1829/1830. The winter had no less than 62 ice days (temperature below zero for 24 hours). During the period from mid-December to March 1940, the night temperature was constantly around -10°C or lower (mid-January to mid-February even -20°C was approached) and the daytime temperature hardly ever rose above freezing temperature. As a result, digging in the ground was impossible and a lot of energy went into ice saws and extra patrols due to the frozen state of strategic inundations for the Grebbe-line and rivers.

152 In May 1940, there were still 22 border battalions, 14 of which were on the eastern border and the light defences behind it. These units had 19 professional Captains or Majors as battalion-commanders and only three were led by reserve officers. Many more professional officers led companies in these battalions. The 17 reserve border companies that were formed during the mobilisation (6 of which were on the eastern border or the defences behind it) were mainly commanded by reserve Captains. Only 2 professional Captains were involved.

153 From the point of view of strategic security, there was every reason to have the border troops led by professional officers. The external security was intended to slow down the enemy sufficiently to enable the Field Army to mobilise and concentrate quickly in the hinterland. With mobilisation and concentration – especially in the Winkelman phase, when all troops were tied to positions – the need for professional officers in those border units disappeared. However, the Field Army and the GHQ failed in their search for professional officers – and that search was intensive – for units in the main defence.

154 The French would become furious when they crossed the Belgian-Dutch border on 10 and 11 May 1940 and found the roads blocked and the bridg-

es blown up. The three Dutch border battalions along the southern border had carried out all planned demolition when instructed to do so by the staff of the 3rd Army Corps (PEC 1C, 15868, 15869 Winkelman). Winkelman claimed in his testimony before the PEC that he had not realised that such an instruction existed, which was implausible because it concerned strategic demolition for which the prerogative lay exclusively with the OLZ himself (PEC 1C, 4397-4403, Kroon, chief of staff 3rd AC). The idea was that the Germans might appear on the southern border near Breda before the Belgians because the Belgians hardly defended the region known as the Kempen, the bordering region with the Netherlands. Although this idea can be defended in principle, one should have asked oneself what damage the destruction would do to the Germans, and in case the French would be there first, what hindrance it would be for them. Things were thought out badly and the idea of isolation was emphasized.

155 Major (shortly before the invasion promoted to Lieutenant-Colonel) of the General Staff J.J.C.P. Wilson (head of operations section, GHQ) – originally of the Engineers Corps – was seen as the spiritual father of the 'Peel Concentration', later the Peel-Raam-line. It was his doctrine and he was constantly involved in it throughout his career and was the ambassador of this Field Army position in the south of the country.

156 It is sometimes claimed that Winkelman, who – because of his previous military career – in the mid thirties had been hired by Philips corporation after his retirement to set up the company evacuation plans, came into the picture as a successor of Reijnders thanks to mediation by the Philips board. No proof of this has been found as yet. However, it is a fact that the Philips management was not only a tier 1 partner of GS-III in the field of information and intelligence, but cabinet members also had open relations with this multinational. It is by no means a negligible hypothesis that Winkelman came into the picture with Dijxhoorn or one of the other cabinet members as a result of a formal or informal tip from Philips. Philips corporation, because of the fear for destruction of its complex (at Eindhoven), may not have been in favour of a prolonged defence in the east of Brabant. On the other hand, it seems not very likely that Winkelman would have made the interests of Philips greater than those of the national defence. Winkelman seems to have been a person of integrity.

157 Chief-of-Staff Major-General H.F.M. van Voorst tot Voorst had been both commander of the Light Brigade and briefly (ad interim) of the 3rd Army Corps. He must have known the Peel concentration and its challenges quite well. He showed himself to be an even greater sceptic than Winkelman before the PEC. It is likely that he influenced Winkelman.

158 In May 1940 the Grebbe-line was insufficiently strengthened and developed at some locations. In addition, it had long been concluded – from the time of Reijnders – that the defence line needed much more 'fortification'. However, the 'Beton Plan' (lit.: 'Concrete Plan', a highly ambitious plan for

many hundreds of ferro-concrete structured pill-boxes of high grade within the main defence sectors) was only approved by the government in the first week of May 1940. Its implementation would have strengthened the positions considerably. However, at the time of Winkelman's findings, the position was weaker (in terms of development) than the Peel-Raam-line. Winkelman's objections could have been improved by further expansion of the latter position and the troops that were rather hopeless in the Maas-line could have been moved to the Peel-Raam-line. The argument about the quality of the position (besides its vulnerable flank) was largely arbitrary because it applied to all positions of the Field Army.

159 The connecting trenches between the lines were essential for the effectiveness of the French defensive concept, which was apparently not recognised in the Netherlands.

160 The French concept was based on a strong front line (front echelon) with deep trench systems and a high absorption capacity so that many troops and tactical reserves could tenaciously defend a sector. Connecting trenches not only provided cross-connections to the rear stop line – the second line – but also provided flank protection in the event of a local breach by the enemy. In this way it was possible to seal off the rear line and react from the stop line – which also had a fairly large absorption capacity – and restore the front line situation. The third line (rear line) was there for operational reserves and the recovery of retreated troops. In addition, there were the sector headquarters and supply units. Much of this had not been adopted by the Dutch. The Dutch Field Army and planning engineers had slimmed down the French concept and abandoned many virtues for the sake of time and lacking funds. The German system was similar to the French system but their trench-systems had considerably more depth, much more interconnecting trenches and the trenches itself contained extensive underground works. All these aspects were ignored in the Dutch trenches.

161 The front line was almost everywhere a simple cordon arrangement with hardly any absorption capacity behind the front trench. Only where old fortifications were embedded in the front line was there sometimes depth to a line. There were few field of fire overlaps from permanent fortifications. This meant that in many locations a battalion was stretched across 1 km of front line or more. Only at a few vulnerable points such as the Grebbeberg, for example, was there a front width of about 500 m for a battalion, but this still only led to 1.5 soldiers per linear metre of line. That was modest for a line whose logistic support from the rear was uncovered.

162 In their fixed and thin positions the border battalions were of little use. Even the planned demolition and obstruction plan carried out had long since countered by the Germans because it was so obvious. After the concentration of the Field Army, only patrols with small units would have been useful – as the Belgians did – but in no way was that a good reason for placing many battalions in border positions.

163 Winkelman had already reduced these troops to some extent in the outer defences in favour of the main positions. In this he made an improvement on his predecessor. However, he did not follow through, which is remarkable considering his chosen strategy and the position of his Chief-of-Staff (who apparently had already proposed this in 1939, see PEC 1C, 15748). When one sees how many troops were sacrificed in this way along the eastern border up to and including the IJssel- and Maas-line and finally Limburg and Brabant to symbolic battles, then this can be blamed on Winkelman and associates. Here we are concerned with 5 battalions in the three northern provinces (of which 4 near the border), 6 border battalions between Emmen and Nijmegen, 5 battalions in the IJssel-line, 4 battalions in the intermediate defence (Arnhem-Malden), 9 battalions in the Maas-line up to Roermond and 5 battalions in central and southern Limburg. There were thus 34 battalions in border positions and thin preliminary defences which were in fact all written off. With the sacrifice of the Peel-Raam-line and its rear guard another 16 battalions were added. The sacrifice of 50 battalions for delaying action is problematic concerning a Supreme Commander who maintains a strategy involving a concentration of resources. After all, this number of 50 battalions was equivalent to 16 infantry regiments (of 2,250 men each). They could have been used for the main defence or could have occupied the Peel-Raam-line and the southern border. However, it should be noted that at least part of those battalions in all scenarios (such as the symbolic occupation of South Limburg) would have had to perform certain security and demolition tasks, as well as delaying actions at road-junctions. Presumably, however, it would have been more effective to do this with independent companies rather than battalions. It must be clear, however, that the OLZ could have taken at least half the units thus sacrificed to the rear without affecting the result along the frontier or immediately behind it in the slightest, to the profit of the main defence further back.

164 Reijnders also rejected the Orange-line as the only defence in Brabant because he thought it did not rest on natural obstacles and would be weak, especially in the north. He had, however, commissioned research into this line as a second or third line of defence. The position, if shortened across Geertruidenberg – there were several possible variants – could find natural strength and a strong tank obstacle behind the Wilhelmina Canal and the (Meuse river arm called) Amer. That was the position the Belgians and French were looking for. The disadvantage was the lack of cover from observation in many western sectors, which made the area open and bare. Reijnders did not receive additional funds for it and therefore opted for the already prepared Peel position.

165 That would be a compromise between the Peel-Raam-line and the (imaginary) Orange-line near Tilburg. This indicates that Winkelman may have been prepared to a certain compromise. The Zuid-Willemsvaart had become an explored and slightly prepared but undeveloped fallback position

for the Peel-Raam-line. One of its major disadvantages was that on certain locations its high eastern bank made it quite unsuitable for effective defence.

166   Moeyes calls this on p. 473 very clinically *"utterly incompatible (...) with Dutch neutral status"*.

167   Support came from the Ministers Dijxhoorn and Van Kleffens. The Secretary-General of Foreign Affairs, A.M. Snouck Hurgronje (1882-1951), disagreed with this demarche and stated that it violated the principles of neutrality. During the war, he would effectively keep the Dutch administrative apparatus running for the occupier, but resigned in July 1941 when it all became too much for him. A far-reaching proposal was added by Winkelman. If the French would commit to linking up with the Peel-Raam-line, Winkelman would be prepared to place a second army corps there (PEC 1C, 23757 Van Voorst Evekink). If the Belgians were to support the line, the Chief-of-Staff said that they could hold out for 10 days in the Peel-Raam-line (PEC 1C, 23759 Van Voorst Evekink).

168   Van Voorst Evekink was in fact an attaché in Brussels and Paris but had a deputy in Belgium, Captain P.L.G. Doorman, who maintained contact with the Belgians. However, many contacts were made through the Belgian attaché in the Hague, Colonel Van Diepenrijckx.

169   The French called their strategic scenarios *"Hypothèse(s)"*. This term is also used here.

170   *Hypothèse l'Escaut* (The Scheldt) was the other prominent scenario, but it was superseded in 1939 by the Dyle Plan. That Scheldt Plan (after the river De Schelde) envisaged a more modest allied advance up to Zeeuws Vlaanderen (Dutch Flanders), with the river Scheldt forming the easternmost front.

171   This was also called the Gembloux Plateau or Gembloux Gap. See also *"La Grande Illusion - Belgian and Dutch strategy facing Germany, 1919- May 1940"* by J.A. Gunsburg (2014).

172   Such barricades – like the Dutch ones along the border – were virtually worthless without being actively defended. The *Cointet* elements were numerous and eagerly used by the Germans in the Atlantic Wall where they would cause the Allies considerable trouble in many locations in 1944. The Germans were very adept at interweaving these passive elements with others (such as land and anti-personnel mines of all kinds) to create a strong system.

173   The British Expeditionary Force (BEF) in France under *General* Lord Gort consisted essentially of British professional soldiers and exclusively motorised units with some slightly mechanised components. Later the BEF was enlarged with a few classical (reserve) infantry divisions and some divisions that contained large formations of recruits, of which also troops behind the Maginot Line or elsewhere in forming in the rear echelons in France. The main part was formed by 10 infantry divisions and a tank brigade with in

174 total about 250,000 men who were brought under the command of the 1st French Army Group. In May 1940, the BEF was expanded even more, so that the strength increased considerably.

174 The Belgian defence was obviously more challenging as it had to be run almost without natural obstacles in the north. However, Belgium had as its main defence, a system of existing and modernised fortifications around major cities such as Antwerp, Ghent, Namur and Wavre, as well as new positions under construction, including the *Réduit National* in French *Stelling van Antwerpen* in Dutch (National Redoubt) which linked various locations in western Belgium around Antwerp.

175 Van Gent, pp. 162/163. The personal instructions no. 10 and 11. These instructions focused on the execution of the Dyle manoeuvre with the addition that the French 7th Army under General Giraud north of the BEF would occupy the position between Antwerp and Breda with a preliminary defence near Tilburg and Turnhout. The latter formed the *Hypothèse* Breda. See also *"La Grande Illusion - Belgian and Dutch strategy facing Germany, 1919 - May 1940"* by J.A. Gunsburg (2014), pp. 629 & 641.

176 The Dyle-basis was already known before, as discussed in the *"Stafwerk - inleiding en algemeen overzicht"*, pp. 47, 48. However, very concretely, between 29 March and 5 April 1940, Van Voorst Evekink had several contacts with the GQG, among others with Colonels Jean M.G. de Mierry (souschef Intelligence) and Jean P.L.M. Petibon (adjutant to Gamelin) as well as Gamelin himself. Here, the decision of March 1940 is explained with the development of the Dyle Plan and the Breda variant (PEC 1c 23759, 23760; see also *"La Grande Illusion - Belgian and Dutch strategy facing Germany, 1919 - May 1940"* by J.A. Gunsburg (2014), p. 629). Moreover, in the morning of 10 May 1940, the final French plans were passed on by the attaché to the Dutch head of operations Wilson (PEC 1C, 2006) and almost certainly had already been reported to the GHQ by the French attaché in the Hague. Gamelin then also had a telephone conversion with the OLZ himself on 10 May 1940.

177 The strategy of the Dyle manoeuvre also included a French occupation of Walcheren and Zuid-Beveland as well as of Dutch Flanders. This component gained even more weight in the expansion to the *Hypothèse* Breda, because then a connection between that component and the French occupation of the sector Roosendaal -Tilburg was created. Reconnaissance units (deployed as light advance guards) finally made that connection.

178 Generalissimo Gamelin was also solitary in his conviction that the Breda variant was the strategy to be pursued. He had to 'sell' it internally to his senior subordinates, Generals Georges (commander north-eastern theatre of operations) and Billotte (commander 1st Army Group: 1st, 7th and 9th Army), who were both opposed (see also: *"La Grande Illusion - Belgian and Dutch strategy facing Germany, 1919 - May 1940"* by J.A. Gunsburg (2014), pp. 640/641). Gamelin received their acquiescence by providing additional

troops to the 7th Army, including the very strong 1st DLM (mechanised division). General Georges thought it irresponsible to remove the 7th Army from the Pas-de-Calais as a strategic reserve and move it north. The reserve would be missed and the 7th Army could be cut off. In the end he was completely right. Billotte would not live to see this though, because after an inter-allied meeting he would be killed following a car-accident near Ypres on 23 May 1940.

179 Although there is no evidence that the Netherlands always had a line with the French general staff (and officially this was also denied), this periodic coordination suggests that the Netherlands was aware of the dynamics in the French decision-making process. This coordination probably took place verbally, to prevent evidence from pointing back to the Netherlands in case of German espionage. Dutch officers abroad were also systematically dressed in civilian clothes and meetings were often held at unsuspicious locations.

180 "*Stafwerk - inleiding en algemeen overzicht*", pp. 47, 48. As early as 26 November 1939 – when the November alarm was still reverberating – Gamelin had pointed out via the French military attaché in the Netherlands that the Netherlands would have to take defensive measures on or behind the line of Geertuidenberg - Mark-canal - river Mark (Breda region) and widen and deepen this small river. This and a report by Van Voorst Evekink of the same period about a French concentration at the Scheldt already foreshadowed Gamelin's Breda and Scheldt plan. The Netherlands did not act on this. General Reijnders ignored the French proposals.

181 PEC 1C, 23759 Van Voorst Evekink. General H.F.M. van Voorst tot Voorst hoped and had some faith until March 1940 that the Belgians would link-up after all.

182 "Van Waesberghe, p. 180: *"(...), attaché Diepenrijckx inspected the Peel-Raamstelling for three days in civilian clothes. His report, intended for Van Overstraeten, was truly damning, but the Dutch did not accept the adjustments proposed by Belgium. So the 'gap' simply remained and this was dramatic according to the King's military advisor.*" Moeyes, as mentioned earlier, identifies this Belgian inspection as completely incompatible with Dutch neutrality (p.473).

183 That too was an anti-allied act. The Belgians did prepare positions for the allies, although they too were behind schedule and the quality left much to be desired. The Netherlands did nothing, did not provide a liaison structure, nor was any form of quartering considered. The Netherlands had really adopted an 'all or nothing' mentality and it had become 'nothing'. Nonetheless the Dutch had many expectations of the allies. It is not known whether Winkelman applied for funds to build a position in this area. The same applies to his predecessor. Without that information, no judgement can be made as to whether they knowingly did nothing or whether they did not reject it in principle but lacked the capability to do what was requested.

184 The French, in particular, would point this out to the Dutch very clearly and would make their great displeasure known to Dutch officers during their shared captivity as POW's. Dutch sources often report this displeasure on the part of the French, but in fact these claims by the French seem understandable and justified and the same would apply to Belgian reproaches to the Netherlands. One also sometimes reads in the Netherlands that the Belgians had done little to develop the Dyle main position for the French and British units. However, the Belgians had done much more than the Dutch who – literally – had done nothing despite the knowledge that French troops would come to West-Brabant and Zeeland and had expressly requested some preparations.

185 H. Amersfoort, in 'Amersfoort/Kamphuis' (p. 405 ff.), remarkably concludes otherwise, albeit without substantiation. He states that the GHQ functioned well on the main points.

186 The Afsluitdijk (a 30 km long causeway) formed the entrance to North Holland and ultimately the northern front of Fortress of Holland.

187 The intermediate defence system refers in the first instance to the continuation of the main defence line between the Grebbe-line and the Peel-Raamline (the river area between the Rhine and the Meuse), and later to the connection of the Grebbe-line to the southern front of Fortress Holland.

188 This aspect was curious, because under Reijnders this would have been unacceptable to Minister Dijxhoorn and the Field Army itself. Under Winkelman, however, with his choice for the Grebbe-line, the eastern front was the obvious alternative (fallback position and last line of defence) after defeat on the Grebbe front. It shows once again the convoluted nature of the dispute between Reijnders and Dijxhoorn on this issue.

189 (PEC 1C, 1481,1483 H.F.M. van Voorst tot Voorst): [Chairman]: *"Did you think it likely that the Grebbelinie would last a week, maybe longer?* [Van Voorst tot Voorst]: *"Yes, I had thought that the Grebbelinie would hold out for some time."* [Chairman]: *"... Did you expect that somehow the heart of the country would be able to hold out for quite some time?"* [van Voorst tot Voorst] *"Yes, I was optimistic, certainly expected to be able to hold out until we could get help from our allies. That they would not come, we did not know."*

190 Reijnders: *"The OLZ explains that it would probably only be necessary to go back after three weeks of fighting at the Grebbelinie ..."*. (PEC 1C, 1432), H.F.M. van Voorst tot Voorst (Chief-of-Staff) *"quite some time"* ... *"Had certainly expected to hold out until we could get help from our allies"*. (PEC 1C, 1481, 1483), J.J.G. van Voorst tot Voorst (Commander Field Army) even thought of possible counter attacks from the Grebbe-line (PEC 1C, 1391, 1392), MoD Dijxhoorn: " (...) *I had hoped for longer than 5 days, maybe a couple of weeks* (...)" (PEC 1C, 588). Winkelman made no concrete statements about it, but thought he could hold out for a longer time in the Grebbe-line and had as an alternative scenario the eastern front of the Fortress. Remarkable is that biographer Teo Middelkoop in *"Generaal H.G.*

Winkelman - standvastig strijder", (p. 103), stated that Winkelman thought he could hold out for a week in the Grebbe-line, but does not give a source for this. Also his assertion (p. 106) that the expectation was that the army would be able to hold out for about three weeks remains undocumented. The sources indicate that people were diffuse about it. Moreover, the sources used were probably more modest in their estimation than they had been before the invasion, because all source data date from after the war, from PEC interrogations and brochures. The limited ammunition supply does not seem to have been an important limitation for any of the decision makers, although this fact was absolutely critical. The real limiting effects were apparently not recognised at the highest level. At lower levels the rationing of ammunition was known and felt.

191 Van Voorst Evekink stated before the PEC (1C, 23724 ff.) that Winkelman's request to the French to ship four divisions to Fortress Holland was 'absurd'. Moreover, he indicated (PEC 1C, 23725) that he had discussed this matter directly at the GHQ with Chief-of-Staff Van Voorst tot Voorst. Apparently without effect, because the request remained and the General declared that he believed in it until war broke out. The French, of course, ignored it. Winkelman probably knew that this request would not be followed up and the possibility must not be excluded that these sealed envelopes with requests also had a political charge, namely that an OLZ could hide behind this (rejected) request afterwards. On the other hand, the Netherlands was not the only country that seriously overestimated the military power and strength of the French.

192 The French could not spare these troops and had a problem forming an adequate army reserve themselves. Gamelin had made assurances about the latter to his subordinates Generals Georges and Doumenc after the strategic reserve (7th Army) had been diverted to the active occupation of the Dyle-Breda sector (see also: *"La Grande Illusion - Belgian and Dutch strategy facing Germany, 1919 - May 1940"* by J.A. Gunsburg (2014), pp. 641, 642) a new fast GQG reserve was not (yet) in place, which facilitated the German breakout from the Meuse sector.

193 A major problem was that the small-calibre ammunition for the Dutch rifle/carbine and light machine gun (6.5 mm x 53.5R) was not in use by any ally. Many other weapon systems also required typical indigenous production, as the Netherlands converted many weapons-systems to own needs and circumstances. Only for the *Vickers* anti-aircraft guns could a basic shell be purchased (a pyrotechnical ignition was already much more complex) and for the *Vickers* 15 cm howitzer (Hw 15 lang 15) and the few *Vickers* machine guns that had not been drilled up from 7.7 mm to 7.9 mm, the UK was a logical source. It was also known in advance that the British would not be able or willing to supply anything, as what they could supply was reserved for their own forces. Despite the fact that the Dutch army air force flew on very different octane levels of fuel than the British, the latter

were asked for squadrons of fighters. However, they would have run out of fuel and sufficient air bases were also lacking. The Belgians, who were a major potential supplier, would have been faced, in addition to priority for their own needs, with the fact that all their factories were in the east and thus under direct German threat.

194   If every step of a strategy had been validated against the requirements – of strategy as to feasibility, usefulness and necessity – Winkelman would logically never have been able to arrive at his final strategic plan.

195   It must be said that the Chief-of-Staff and his brother, the CV, for example, did not consider these issues at all given their belief in weeks of resistance by the Dutch army. Ideas about a rather long resistance had no basis.

196   He probably asked the question in a slanted way. From statements of his Chief-of-Staff it appeared that both Generals assumed that they could hold out for some weeks in Fortress Holland until allied help would arrive (PEC 1C, 1481-1483). This premise was not only devoid of realism with regard to the limitations of the *Grand Strategy*, but it was apparently assumed that allies would 'just' come and take over the defence of the entire Fortress, while the Netherlands had only withdrawn itself into isolation before! For the Entente the Netherlands was not a very important issue. Preliminary investigations by the Navy (concerning the UK) and by attaches had long since shown that no help could be reckoned with. The expectations of substantial allied assistance was based on fantasies of Generals Winkelman and Van Voorst tot Voorst themselves. The facts and the information received pointed out the unreasonableness of those expectations.

197   There was a very clear aversion to 'needless losses' within the government, but also among some senior officers. General Reijnders at one point argued to the government that waging war simply meant that people would be killed. It was objected to him that the deaths of people in Brabant contributed little or nothing to Dutch interests and therefore those losses should not be allowed to mount up. It was like serving meat to a convinced vegetarian. The government reaction was unrealistic, but typical of the surrealistic national administration of those days.

198   The Netherlands did not promise any cooperation to the French, British and Belgian diplomats and military who sought contact with the Netherlands. In turn, the other parties tried to ascertain from the Netherlands what it would do in case it was attacked, something that the Netherlands remained very shy about until shortly before May 1940.

199   Undoubtedly such a case of an invasion confined to the southeast – the only one in which a withdrawal of the main force from Brabant might have been defensible – would still see Winkelman continue (even accelerate) his strategy when on 10 May 1940 the German attack turned out to be country-wide, so that it is certain that as an influence on his strategy this did not appear to be a consideration for him.

200 The plans had already been tested in a war-game during a staff exercise on 15 March 1940 and the secret instructions were given to the CV on 30 March. At that time, there was still a very slight chance that the execution of the withdrawal from Brabant could be reconsidered as a consequence of (awaited) French reassurance. The commander of the Peel-division had already been informed of the plans at this time.

201 According to Wilson, the sealed information letters for the attaché's in Paris, Brussels and London (to be handed over to the high commands in these countries after an outbreak of hostilities) were written by the end of March, which, together with the simultaneous instruction to the commander of the Peel-Division, makes it clear that Winkelman had made up his mind and that the meeting of 5 April was only a formality. This is also evident from Van Voorst Evekink's statement to the PEC (1C, 23722).

202 This was the case both militarily and diplomatically. Foreign Minister Van Kleffens also adopted an arrogant and undiplomatic attitude abroad. The Netherlands behaved like a beautiful princess for whose hand the European princes would have to fight, but in reality the Netherlands was anything but the beautiful bride. See also Van Waesberghe's "*De Belgisch-Nederlands verhoudingen en het gevaar van een Duitse aanval op de Lage Landen*" (1995).

203 It is possible that the then Major Wilson was also at the meeting on 5 April 1940. Winkelman (PEC 1C, 1294, 1295), H.F.M. Van Voorst tot Voorst and Van Voorst Evekink (PEC 1C, 23737) do not remember the presence of the head of the operations section at this meeting, but the latter claims to have been present (PEC 1C, 2001, 2002).

204 The former *Hotel Royal* – it was to serve as an *Ortskommandantur* for the occupying forces during the occupation – but it was also known as Villa Mignot. It has since been demolished. Delegations entered secretly through the back garden and back door, and the police kept an eye on the surrounding streets. Closing off the streets would have attracted too much attention.

205 Although remarkably little publicity is given to this 5th April 1940 in historical books, Winkelman and his small staff did not only consult Van Voorst Evekink that day, but also a Belgian delegation led by the Belgian attaché Colonel Van Diepenrijckx. The next day this delegation, accompanied by Dutch Captain Van Boven, made another inspection of the Peel-Raam-line (PEC 1C, 2002).

206 PEC 1C, 16341 et seq.

207 The Peel-Division was an unofficial collective name for an irregular and several times changed formation of strategic security forces in the north of Limburg and the east of Brabant. The meeting took place at the Peel-Division headquarters in Eindhoven.

208 PEC 1C, 4397. The then chief of staff of the 3rd Army Corps, Major of the general staff A.G.J.M.F. van der Kroon, testified before the PEC on the announcement of the new strategy, that he and his commander, Major-General A.A. Van Nijnatten (1880-1948) – who suffered a stroke in 1946 and

died in August 1948 so that he could never be heard by the PEC – were 'flabbergasted and devastated' by the new instruction. And Kroon went on to say "... *and we also assumed that this would also eliminate a certain element, which in case the enemy invaded, would still give the possibility of a connection with the Belgians. If there remains nothing or very little, it is not possible; if there is sufficient reserve, it is always possible to use it, either on the wing for a connection with the Belgians or in other places*".

209 The Light Division had until Winter 1940 been referred to as the Light Brigade. In the meantime, however, it had been equipped with second regiments of infantry cyclists and hussar motorcyclists (still partially in forming). In addition, the artillery had been motorised so that the unit was fully mobile by 1 May 1940. However, the army command had stripped it of the two squadrons of armoured cars and of the 1st *Regiment Huzaren Motorrijders* (regiment of hussar motorcyclists), all of which were already concentrated within Fortress Holland. Furthermore, the motorized 6-veld battery had been detached from the division in favour of the middle section of the Peel-Raam-line.

210 Which took place on 9 April 1940.

211 Brigade G was formed under the reactivated Major-General G. Dames (1879-1955). This brigade had six battalions of infantry from reserve regiments and was concentrated in the assembly area for the Waal-Linge-line. It was unreal that a retired Colonel, promoted to General, was used to command this temporary brigade (which was to be absorbed after the withdrawal of the 3rd Army Corps) while the Peel-Division had to make do with a Colonel. This too was a curious case in terms of inimitable policy from the General Headquarters.

212 The BOUV-mobilisation was a pre-mobilisation that formed part of the Strategic Security. These units had already been mobilised in April 1939 and had remained under arms since then and concentrated along the border region and the most forward defences as well as in the Peel-Raam-line.

213 The territorial commanders of Friesland (north-eastern provinces), Zuid-Limburg, Zeeland and Den Helder (which was Fortress Den Helder) fell directly under the OLZ. Only the TBO (commander Overijssel) resorted under the CV. The secret order meant that the territorial commander Brabant (TBB) would also again resort under the OLZ after the first day of war.

214 The whole consisted of six Field Army battalions (II-2.RI, I-3.RI, I-6.RI, I-13.RI, III-14.RI, II-17.RI), four border battalions (2.GB, 4.GB, 15.GB, 17.GB) and twelve battalions of the BOUV-units (26.RI minus I-26.RI, 27.RI, II-29.RI, 30.RI and 41.RI). In addition, GBJ (border battalion of the *Jagers* Regiment) was added to man the southern border and the east of the Wilhelmina Canal. One regiment of outdated 8.4 cm *Krupp* field artillery (20.RA) was formed and added to the Peel-Raam-line defences, its three battalions divided over the left, central and right flank. Modern artil-

lery and most anti-tank guns were removed from the Maas-line and partly from the Peel-Raam-line in favour of the main force in Fortress Holland. Two pioneer battalions were available to the whole. The divisional staff was in fact more of the scale of a regimental staff and division troops and trains were minimal.

215 In the pre-war Dutch army, a division was commanded by a Colonel and an army corps by a Major-General. The Dutch army only had two regular General ranks: Major-General and Lieutenant-General. The only full General was the appointed Commander-in-Chief, a function that did not exist in peace time.

216 NIMH 409-521001. Report of January 1941.

217 Schmidt was given no further instruction on how to organise the delaying defence such that the matter was left to him to decide. In the army of the day, there was no provision for holding isolated positions for all-around defence ('hedgehog positions') to cover a retreat or effectively slow down an enemy advance. Thus a retreat from one line to another required preparations and – ideally – existing minimum occupations on such lines. However, this could not be organised under secrecy – or so it was believed. It is known, incidentally, that Minister Dijxhoorn had a personal preference for defending Brabant by setting up 'hedgehog positions' in order to slow down the enemy. He saw no utility in linear defences which he considered outdated. Dijxhoorn was probably right in theory but found no support for this. Moreover, this tactic required extensive schooling of officers. This training and the elaboration of this concept were lacking. Incidentally, Colonel Schmidt stated after the war (NIMH 409-521001, handwritten letter 22 January 1951; PEC 1C, 4962) that he also aspired to this method of delayed defences and the application of 'hedgehog positions'. There is no evidence of any form of implementation though, because the Colonel continued to give orders for a linear defence, what was probably the right thing to do in the given circumstances of prepared defences.

218 The controlled delaying retreat had by now become commonplace in military doctrine (the 'Combat Manual' and 'Infantry Regulations'), but it had become a doctrine in flux due to motorisation and mechanisation. In 1939, Captain of the general staff H.R.M. Calmeijer (who until August 1939 was a student at the German staf-officer course for division officers) wrote an article on this subject in the Military Spectator *"Het vertragende gevecht – een vergelijkende beschouwing tusschen de Nederlandsche en de Duitsche strijdwijze"* *("The controlled delaying retreat - a comparison between the Dutch and German field-doctrine")*.

219 In those days, many of the middle- and upper-class still spoke good French and, moreover, during the interwar period, much of the orientation of the general staff was toward French ideas, which had brought a lot of French jargon into the armed forces. The formation of an adequate liaison staff with French-speaking officers would have been logical in view of the fact

that the French arrival in the Netherlands was confirmed. It would not only have give a better impression of the Dutch and support the Dutch case, but it would also have relieved the already overburdened small staff of the Peel-Division. The same would have been true for the leadership of such a staff by a (reserve) General. The liaison staff should have been big enough to attach at least two or three officers from it to the French Army Corps that was scheduled to operate in the Dutch/Belgian sector in the Breda area.

220 Promotion to the General ranks was the prerogative of the government. This was done by Royal Decree, which in those days was not a mere formality.

221 Schmidt would have to deal with at least one French General (Brigadier-General F. Picard, commander of 1.DLM) while a second (Brigadier-General L.E.E. Monniot) would be in Etten-Leur (10 km west of Breda) as commander of the vanguard of 25.DIM. Moreover, Schmidt encountered at least two French Colonels, whom he did not dominate in rank. Certainly in French eyes a Dutch Colonel as the highest ranking military officer carried little authority, although on the French side this probably proved again how little value the Netherlands attached to an alliance with the French. Therefore, this qualifies as yet another error of judgement of the army command in this matter.

222 The major airborne landings in the west of the Netherlands immediately put Winkelman's 'Alamo' scenario at risk. Moreover, in the morning of 10 May 1940, the French (by means of Gamelin himself) reconfirmed that they would move formations of the 7th Army towards the Netherlands. The Moerdijk bridges had fallen into German hands, which meant that the door was open on the south front of the Fortress – especially if the corridor remained weakly defended. Thus there were three prominent reasons to put up a firm defence in Brabant. Winkelman, however, would cite the second reason (the French arrival) in order to justify his elimination of the other two reasons, as will become clear in dealing with the hot strategy.

223 The defence of Fortress-Holland had not been in order under Reijnders either, so this was certainly not only Winkelman's fault. Yet, under Reijnders it would have had the firm defence by the Field Army formations in front of it probably rendering ample time to reinforce the south front of the Fortress. Under Winkelman that assurance of adequate prior defence was obviously removed.

224 In principle, the western front (the coastal defence), southern front and eastern front were occupied under Reijnders. The northern front (except for the Afsluitdijk fortifications) was not, while the eastern front would lose its safety occupation under Winkelman, with the exception of the south-eastern front. Winkelman would reinforce the thinly occupied south-front by doubling its forces in April 1940.

225 In spite of many misconceptions about the higher Dutch regiments and deviating from what applied to other armies, there was only a modest dis-

tinction between the lower-numbered regiment (the first 24) and the higher-numbered infantry regiment (from 25th RI onwards). The Fortress Army formations had less motorisation, one third fewer machine guns and the units were about 10% smaller. Some also lacked anti-tank guns or mortars. The main difference between the Field Army and the Fortress Army was organisational. The former lacked brigade, division and corps structures, staffs and troops, so that the difference in effectiveness was mainly found in the combat support and higher echelons. This was partly compensated within the Fortress with outdated artillery and taskforce commands.

226 In the Netherlands, the older artillery pieces were '*staal*' (steel) guns. First, 108 pieces of 8-*staal* (8.4 cm *Krupp* light field artillery) were brought out of mothballs in the early spring of 1940 to compensate at least partially for the shortage of firepower in the outer defences. These had been introduced in 1880 and with the introduction of the 7-veld from 1904 onwards, they were removed from the force. Secondly, the cumbersome steel artillery of 12-*lang-staal* (144 pieces) and 15-*lang-staal* (36 pieces), respectively 12.5 cm and 15 cm cannons, were used as fortification artillery. These had been introduced in the 1870s and 1880s. The 12-*lang-staal* remained (modified) in the armament after the First World War, but the 15-*lang-staal* had long been stored in the arsenals until three battalions were reactivated during the mobilisation due to the hampered delivery of ordered modern artillery. Of the more than 800 pieces of artillery available (all army artillery from calibre 7.5 cm and up; excluding coastal artillery, anti-aircraft artillery and 6-veld), this ageing 'only' concerned 280 pieces, exactly one third of the used arsenal. Although artillery in the era in question aged much faster than today, it is good to remember that the well-known NATO 155 mm howitzer M109 dates from 1963 and is still the standard (albeit modified) howitzer within the United States armed forces more than 50 years later, and will remain so for the foreseeable future.

227 The artillery, together with the lack of a genuine strategic air force, would be a major Achilles' heel of Germany for the duration of the Second World War. In May 1940, the arsenal of the Germans was still considerable by keeping a relatively large contingent of older guns (such as the FK.16 and the sFH.13, the latter also possessed by the Netherlands) in the divisional artillery, but as the war progressed, the quantity of artillery in relation to the needs became increasingly strained. Also the quality of the German artillery was not exceptionally good. The lack of any form of mechanised medium- and long-range artillery in May 1940 was a shortcoming that would never be made up for and ensured that Germany was completely outclassed in terms of artillery by the middle of the war. When the *Luftwaffe* also disappeared as tactical support, the relative strength of these weapons on the German side fell dramatically in comparison to the early years.

228 The '*Persoonlijke Aanwijzing voor den CV van een aanval uit het oosten, 30 maart 1940*' (' The Personal Instruction for the C-Field Army in case of

an attack from the east, 30 March 1940') dictated the instruction for the shift of the units occupying the east-front of the Fortress to the south- and south-eastern front in case of an imminent (or actual) attack from the east. It also contained instructions for the two Border Infantry Battalions in the sector Breda – Bergen op Zoom to withdraw back into the Fortress after planned demolitions along the border regions would have been executed.

229 Jan van Andel (1877-1972). A General of noble descent who, as a person was very amiable and warm, which was not often said of chief officers in this era. Van Andel had retired from the military in May 1937 after previously being promoted to the rank of Lieutenant-General in November 1936. He was reactivated after the mobilisation to take command of the Fortress Army. This was later to become the Fortress Holland command. Initially, this was not much more than depots, training facilities, barracks and security positions with the coast as their essential protection. During a defensive war, the Fortress would eventually become the domain of the Field Army, supported by the Fortress Army. Already during the mobilisation and concentration of the army the importance of the Fortress fronts grew and security positions were occupied on most of its fronts. Winkelman's strategy made it a much more prominent post already during the mobilisation. Van Andel was only once asked to testify before the PEC and that session was remarkably short. Had the PEC really wanted to study military policy, it would have had every reason to question this General about his policy. This did not happen, perhaps partly because the General's memory appeared to be very poor; he was barely able to give a sensible answer to the committee. On the other hand, the military inexperienced PEC did not seem to have recognised the weight of the decision-making process with this commander and his staff. Van Andel is therefore one of the least known key players of the May Days of 1940. The question is to what extent this senior officer in May 1940 was up to his task. His policy during the May Days was weak, emotional and seemed devoid of tactical and operational insights. Staff members later testified that the General broke down and sobbed at his desk several times during the May Days. Another prominent military leader from whom such stories were known was the French General Billotte, who could not hold back his tears sometimes. Nothing human need be alien to a General, of course.

230 The southern front was very poorly protected and fortified with the exception of the wide Meuse estuary which, with its powerful currents and tides, would be a considerable obstacle if the bridges over the Meuse were blown up. There were four heavy casemates defending the Moerdijk bridges and a row of concrete shelter-casemates along the dikes was the only reinforced protection for the allocated infantry groups. There were no reinforced weapon positions at all on the northern side apart from the four aforementioned heavy constructions. Moreover, practically no trenches had been constructed. As the polder landscape made this ex-

tremely difficult in any case, a quick construction after the arrival of the reinforcements was impossible. Efforts were made though. On 10 May 1940, field fortifications had been constructed in the Moerdijk bridgehead but finished concrete casemates were scarce still. On the northern side, group trenches had been constructed but artillery and many other projected infantry concentrations were still completely free of prepared hide-outs. (PEC 1C, 1953-1961, Wilson) The construction of the defence lines was organised in a very complex way, with many authorities having a say in things. There was the central Field Reinforcement Construction office that fell under the General Staff Section V (Engineers) that had oversight over main defences. Furthermore, the construction of trenches and fortifications was an operational responsibility of local commanders, but only outside the Fortress the head of operations at the GHQ was responsible. Inside the Fortress, this was the C-VH staff section led by Colonel Van Dooden, centrally and specifically on the southern front by Major of the general staff J. Govers. For the Field Army it was also the engineers-section of the staff. Thus there were many organs involved with fortification and there was no integrated representation.

231 The maritime names in the Netherlands are inimitable. The Maas (Meuse) changes its name three times between Bergen aan de Maas and the Haringvliet, into which it eventually flows before it reached open sea. From the Maas to the Bergsche Maas (in fact a canalised extension of the dammed original Maas at Bergen) to Geertruidenberg where it is called the Amer and then changes to the Hollandsch Diep. The Nieuwe Maas (New Meuse) in Rotterdam has in fact nothing to do anymore with the current Maas. The Nieuwe Maas is nowadays a continuation of the Lek, which in turn is a continuation of the Nederrijn (Lower Rhine). The Oude Maas (Old Meuse), however, is connected to the original course of the natural Meuse, although this is no longer evident from the current maritime map, because it dates from the time when the Hoekse Waard was still largely a water-covered area.

232 Only the Moerdijk bridges offered good access to Fortress Holland because of their location and accessibility. The other bridges were not very relevant because the fronts of the Fortress would in fact be behind the Upper Merwede and Linge rivers and after those there was still no easy access to the Fortress. The route over the Moerdijk was the only one at that time that was well connected to the west.

233 An infantry company and an independent machine gun company were stationed here, supplemented with a section of 6-veld. In the village of Moerdijk a section of pontoon engineers was stationed with some ships. Their task was to maintain a ferry service after the eventual destruction of the bridges. Finally, a battery of heavy anti-aircraft guns (with on 10 May only two working 7,5 cm *Vickers* pieces) and three platoons with anti-aircraft machine-guns were positioned here.

234   The barrier fence, that could have been lowered onto the roadbed at a location some 150 m from the southern abutment, and would have been a real obstacle for the Germans had not been lowered either.

235   These shortcomings call into question Winkelman's reputation of excellence in armed forces logistics. In fact, on the southern front none of the fundamental logistic elements were fulfilled. There were no positions of any kind, field hospitals were small-scale and only locally prepared for dozens rather than hundreds of patients; ammunition depots were completely absent, telephone- and telegraph-connections were lacking (just before the May Days one single good connection to Puttershoek – where the headquarters of Group Kil was situated – became available) and every form of accommodation, shelter, supply or forage for reserves and (to be expected) Field Army troops was lacking.

236   To put this into perspective, other armies – the French, for example, at corps level – still used pigeons and did so throughout the war, including the allies who landed on the continent in June 1944. The scene from the famous film '*The Longest Day*', in which pigeons are released from a British landing beach, was factual. Homing pigeons remained a tried and tested tool.

237   The *Dekkingsdetachement Willemsdorp* (DDW, or Defence Detachment Willemsdorp) originated from regular infantry but was supplemented with soldiers of the *Vrijwillige Landstorm* (Territorial Reserve) who lived near their post. DDW was part of the strategic reserve and had been activated and present almost continuously since the autumn-alarm in 1938 (due to the German threat of Czechoslovakia). The position also had a police troop platoon, which had been based on this site since late 1936 in the special barracks building (which still exists today). These Police Troops occupied the heavy bunkers and performed the permanent civil and military security-service around the bridges. A group of railway-engineers was added for a longer period and also a group of maritime engineers that patrolled the waters-ways around the bridges on a couple of sloops armed with MG's. The DDW comprised a total of about 120 men under a Captain. Later on, a group of machine gunners was added as reinforcements for the casemate machine guns and three platoons of heavy machine guns against air targets were deployed on both sides of the bridges. In April 1940 an additional company of infantry and a platoon of heavy MG's was added for coastal protection. Their encampment was in the barracks camp at Willemsdorp and three farms north of it. They were meant to occupy the positions along the Kil-entrance and the south side of the Island of Dordrecht. In the Moerdijk bridgehead, south of the bridges, came a detachment consisting of a company of infantry, a full MG company (12 heavy MG's) and a section of 6-veld infantry guns. This detachment was commanded by a Captain and his small staff from a CP in the village of Moerdijk. They formed the security force that had to occupy the southern bridgehead until a border

infantry battalion (6.GB) would take this position over. 6.GB also had four pieces of PAG (*Böhler* 4.7 cm antitank guns) which could be deployed in the position and for which semi-permanent positions had been prepared.

238 For the record, however, it should be noted that improvisations were usually restrictions or short-sighted improvisations. These included more liberal leave arrangements, less rigid discipline or – as in this case – more focus on peacetime reality of an unexpected ammunition accident than on the wartime reality that security forces should have access to live ammunition quickly.

239 The head of Section IIIA was Major J.G.M. van de Plassche (1888-1961). This officer, who would end up in London and finish his military career as a Major-General after the war, appears in several sources as a schemer, not very constructive and showed remarkable villainous qualities during the PEC hearings. He was no friend of Major Sas, attaché in Berlin. Sas, by the time of the hearings a Major-General, was killed in a plane-crash in Scotland in October 1948. In 1939-1940, Van de Plassche missed few opportunities to discredit Sas, both by slandering his person and by not taking his information seriously. Sas' reputation was actively damaged by this conduct. Van de Plassche was also known for his lack of sophistication and respect for other intelligence officers, and he regularly appeared to make major errors of judgement, which called into question his suitability for the job (foreign intelligence). He was also a known leak from the GHQ to Minister of Defence Dijxhoorn and discredited General Reijnders by sharing instructions with the Minister that were not intended for him (PEC 1C 31744). Van de Plassche was also no friend of the new army command and found it necessary to demonstrate in the evening of 9 May 1940 that he did not expect an invasion – in spite of the instructions that had come from the OLZ and Chief-of-Staff to take this very seriously. Van de Plassche decided to go to a restaurant with the French military attaché where he enjoyed alcoholic beverages in stead of either manning his desk and telephone on the GHQ or taking the rest that was prescribed by the army command for all not on duty.

240 Evert van Dijk (1893-1986). Former Fleet-Air-Arm (MLD) pilot and employed by KLM since 1925. He was the first Dutchman to fly across the Atlantic to the US in 1930. He was at the airport near Oslo in the evening of 8 April 1940 and during the following night. From the airport quarter, he observed the German airborne landing which took place here in the morning of 9 April 1940. Van Dijk's DC-3 returned to Schiphol on 16 April 1940. Afterwards, he reported his observations. On 10 May 1940, Van Dijk was in Naples (Italy). Van Dijk later experienced the Japanese attack on the Dutch East-Indies, but managed to escape from there to the UK. There, he would fly on the KLM service Bristol-Lisbon. In 1947, he retired as a pilot.

241 PEC 1C, 15528, 15532 (Lt-Gen. P.W. Best); PEC 1C, 19228-19930 (Dijxhoorn). Winkelman denied having been against the proposed addition-

al roadblocks. He did not oppose them, but also showed little interest in them.

242 Especially the occupation of the AFB's Waalhaven, Schiphol, Valkenburg and Ypenburg. Instead of a company of security troops they received a battalion of infantry. In addition, at Schiphol and Ypenburg, each half a squadron (6 off) of armoured cars M.36 of the 1st Armoured Car Squadron (type *Landsverk* L181) with a platoon of motor hussars. At Waalhaven two heavy machine gun carriers *Carden-Loyd*. Other (auxiliary) airfields got for the first time – or got more – security troops. (PEC 1C, 15511).

243 PEC 1C, 15804, 15805.

244 The proposals of the Minister and General Best came to fruition in the fabrication of concrete obstructions that could be placed on roads. On 10 May 1940, these were still only theory. In the meantime, vehicles and other types of mobile barriers had been placed on roads as improvisation until the permanent solution was in place. This was a matter brought to fruition by the Ministry of Waterways and Public Works, although largely military vehicles were made available by the Military Transport and Traffic Service.

245 Captain Jan Marginus Somer (1899-1979). He was a KNIL (Royal Dutch East-Indies Army) officer who returned to the Netherlands in 1928 to serve as a teacher at the KMA (Royal Military Academy). He was one of the first who immediately went underground and set up the first international pilot escape lines. In March 1942, he left the Netherlands himself and reached England in January 1943 via long detours. There he was promoted in the rank of Major and second-in-command of the Intelligence Bureau. In this role he discovered the infamous *Englandspiel*, a large German spy-game that still has an enigmatic ring to it and that costed dozens of British and Dutch spies their lives. In 1948, he became the director of the Central Military Intelligence in the Dutch East Indies, which was, by its very nature, disbanded in 1949. He left the service as a Colonel.

246 The Dutch general staff officers looked down on KNIL (Royal Dutch East-Indies Army) officers, or at least there always seems to have been a kind of rivalry between them. However, it is remarkable that KNIL-soldiers who had been activated in the Netherlands (many pensioners were called back into active service during mobilisation), both officers and NCO's, often performed excellently. They seem to have been more resistant than their Dutch counterparts to the realities of war. KNIL non-commissioned officers often turned out to be much better than Dutch NCO's. They had much more authority and were better educated; many of them actually had field experience or even combat experience in the Dutch East-Indies.

247 The relationship of trust that Sas had with the German Colonel Oster attracted much commentary in later historical works. International publications usually refer to multiple sources that were feeding the allies but in fact it was only the *Abwehr*, of which a couple of leaks were active though. Oster informed at least two sources frequently, Sas in particular, but he also

cooperated with the Americans. Because Sas was also in contact with other attachés, like the Belgian Colonel Goethals, a chain of information emerged that led to several nations being fed primarily by Oster/Sas. ('*Spies of the Pope: Pius XII's Vatican plot against Hitler*', M. Riebling, 2015) Admiral Canaris, Oster's chief at the *Abwehr*, had a frequent contact with Pope Pius XII (Eugenio Pacelli). The flamboyant Josef Müller, a Bavarian lawyer with political leanings, was used as an intermediary. Müller was also controlled by Oster.

248 Under earlier leave restrictions, certain leaves had still been permitted. On 7 May 1940, no leave at all was authorized. This was a sign of real concern to many.

249 This decision depended (with the exception of the border battalions along the Belgian border that fell under the CV) on Lieutenant-General Van Andel, but before that it had been Winkelman's decision not to bring Fortress Holland (with the noted exceptions) to the highest degree of combat readiness. This policy would bring many initial German successes and many Dutch casualties.

250 For example, many units of the air defence and strategic security as well as regionally encamped regiments were quartered, also with NCO's and officers living or lodging in the immediate vicinity. Not infrequently, officers simply spent the night at home or at external private quarters. The army commanders permitted this, because it saved costs. Ammunition depots were also kept closed and there was no ammunition distributed except in guard units and security detachments. Certainly preparatory measures, such as the installation of detonating cords at objects to be destroyed, were not carried out (although it is certain that this consequence had been considered). Certain leaves were allowed in such a status. There was no prescribed evening assembly and even parties or movies were allowed. All these side-effects would have been keenly felt by knowledgeable commanders. This is where Winkelman's detachment from the reality in the field came into play.

251 General Reijnders thought that the OLZ and the Chief-of-Staff should prescribe the alarm centrally and not leave this to subordinate commanders. The author is convinced that this would have been the correct policy. It was irresponsible to leave anything to chance in an armed force with so many subordinate commanders with own local interests. Winkelman's policy in this area, however, fitted in with his choices not to strictly discipline the GHQ and to spend the night at home like the Chief-of-Staff. There was an obvious lack of war realism in his policy, but at least Winkelman was consistent in it.

252 J.J.C.P. Wilson says in his book "*Vijf oorlogsdagen en hun twintigjarige voorgeschiedenis*" (1960) ("Five days of war and their twenty years of history") on p. 83: "*I can still hear General Winkelman say: 'Surely the threat now comes so clearly from the east that it would be foolish to alert the troops on the southern*

front'. Then (...) it turned out (...) that because of the General's decision no detonators would be placed [to the demolition charges - AG] *at the bridges near Moerdijk, near Keizersveer, near Heusden and near Hedel. I reported this personally to the Chief-of-Staff of the Army and together we informed the Commander-in-Chief. General Winkelman smiled kindly and said almost word for word: 'So, my compliments that you have discovered this, but I knew it. Over those bridges the Light Division and the III Army Corps must withdraw and I want at all costs to prevent them from going up prematurely because of nervousness or otherwise".*

253 "*De Tweede Wereldoorlog*", Luc de Vos (2nd edition, 2004), p. 64; "De Fabribeckers", pp. 86, 147, 149. See also "*The German Fallschirmtruppe 1936-1941*", Karl-Heinz Golla, 2013 revised edition, p. 124.

254 (PEC 1C, 4810) According to General Fabius, the relations in the intelligence section were quite troubled. He had his hands full. Much has been written about the last night before the war. It is said that Van de Plassche was in his 'usual pub' in the evening of 9 May 1940, but that was not so. He had dinner with the French military attaché at restaurant Trocadéro (Lange Poten, The Hague). According to the testimonies of Captains Olifiers and Somer, after returning to the AHK, when the first alarm message from Sas had come in, he had '*eaten and drunk rather heavily*'. Afterwards, he would have behaved unashamedly towards the Captains and remained completely disbelieving, despite a clear second warning by phone from Sas – his cynicism somewhat supported by his superior, General Fabius. Van de Plassche believed that the Germans would not allow telephone calls over the open network (over which Sas called) if things were really serious. Consequently, Van de Plassche reportedly returned to the restaurant. Be that as it may, he appeared at the GHQ again afterwards and had a meeting with the OLZ and the Chief-of-Staff. Van de Plassche's testimony about this episode (PEC 1C, 4486 et seq.) is unclear and with the appearance of 'recovery afterwards'. Virtually everyone involved criticises his attitude and judgement so this criticism seems convincing.

255 In the evening, Lieutenant-Colonel Wilson arrived at section III and was informed by Captain Römer about Sas' message and the analysis made by the three Captains at GS-III. According to the Captain, the Lieutenant-Colonel then said literally "*Another nervous patient! You are raising the alarm and rushing things along! I don't believe a word of it. Did you follow my strategy lessons? If I had known you were going to act like this, I would never have given you a pass. These messages are false and I believe it is a diversionary tactic. They are not going to announce a strategic invasion in advance!*" Meanwhile, Captains Somer and Olifiers had left the room in disbelief. Olifiers even burnt his pocketbook with secret notes in anticipation of what was coming, Somer was very frustrated by the behaviour of Van de Plassche and Wilson.

256 Including PEC 1C, 15687 (Van Voorst), PEC 1C, 18930 (Winkelman).

257 The Lange Voorhout itself was put on standby before midnight by the De-

tachment of Police Troops which was assigned to the AHK as staff protection. A number of machine guns and an anti-tank gun were then positioned on the Lange Voorhout.

258 This meant that except for the troops within Fortress Holland that did not belong to the western front, the air defence or the strategic security, the armed forces had to be in the highest degree of combat readiness on 10 May 1940 at 03.00 hours Dutch time. For the eastern and western border units, the readiness applied immediately and permission was also given to carry out part of the demolition at the eastern border already. A number of measures were left to the sub-commanders themselves. The C-VH, for example, had the freedom to put his Fortress on full alert, but chose to follow his Supreme Commander, who had made exceptions to this on several occasions before. Explicitly forbidden was the installation of detonators on the demolition charges at the bridges of Hedel, Heusden, Keizersveer and Moerdijk. The retreat of the troops had to take place over these bridges and they were not to be destroyed prematurely. They remained explicitly under authority of the OLZ.

259 PEC 1C, 18928-18930.

260 PEC 1C, 18928, 18948. Winkelman defended his decision in an unfortunate and unreflective manner before the PEC, who (in this instance) asked the right questions. Winkelman showed that he was largely immune to self-criticism. Many years later he had apparently still not developed any insights that deviated from his curious decision-making before and during the war days.

261 The Supreme Commander and his Chief-of-Staff put remarkably little pressure on the staff and allowed a lot of freedom of choice. Winkelman and Van Voorst radiated calm and deliberation – as several staff members testified – but this could also have been the case without the implied message that they were not that worried, that things would turn out all right. It is difficult to condemn them for this behaviour, but it seems tempting to conclude from other perils at the GHQ that the GHQ needed stricter leadership and instruction. In any case, the absence of OLZ and Chief-of-Staff during that night seems an unwise choice and an underestimation of the situation.

262 Both Generals showed remarkably little insight and self-reflection during the PEC hearings. In the face of most of the criticism the OLZ defended himself by claiming that that was reasoning after the fact, but on no matter of importance did he seem to have developed a clearer insight. He would have done just about everything the same way again. Whether this was feigned self-conviction, vanity or actual lack of insight we will never know. Herman van Voorst tot Voorst also reaffirmed his correct handling and behaviour in the period before the invasion.

263 A number of demolition orders could only be given by the OLZ or Chief-of-Staff. These included the destruction of the bridges over the Meuse where

	no detonators had yet been attached to the charges (Moerdijk, Keizersveer, Heusden and Hedel).
264	The Generals maintained after the war that faced with the same situation, they would have acted again the same way. PEC 1C 15703-15705 (Van Voorst), PEC 1C 7686-7687, 15816, 18928 (Winkelman).
265	PEC 1C, 15711. Van Voorst tot Voorst himself estimates he arrived at about 04:30 hours. The German invasion started at 03:55 hours. Since the OLZ passed the Chief-of-Staff by car on the Benoordenhoutseweg, the OLZ himself probably arrived about a couple of minutes earlier. The distance from Benoordenhoutseweg at Jan van Nassaustraat (where the Chief-of-Staff lived) to the GHQ location at Lange Voorhout was less than a kilometre via Houtweg and the Vos in Tuinstraat. Notably on the Malieveld, next to the Benoordenhoutseweg, anti-aircraft guns had been set up and were in full action when the Generals passed. This typifies the risk that both men took. It is certain from a preserved telegram that it was not until 04:40 hours that the OLZ gave the order to 'destroy' the Meuse bridges (*"Stafwerk - Limburg/Noord-Brabant"*, p. 193). That was exactly 45 minutes after the formal German attack, but almost two hours after the first serious reports of enemy action and massive airspace penetrations.
266	One could argue that in this first phase of an invasion one is primarily the target of a surfeit of information and one must mainly wait and analyse. However, it is precisely this overload of information that puts enormous pressure on the commander to filter out the main trends in good time. That is why commanders must be ready from the start and not begin such an operation with a two-hour delay.
267	A mysterious phenomenon that was never clarified was that in the evening of 9 May extraordinary leave (for family funerals) was suddenly permitted again. Winkelman and his Chief-of-Staff both claim that this measure did not come from them (PEC 1C, 15677, 15785), but this order led to much confusion and to a lowering of guard. The leave notice, for example, led the detachment at Willemsdorp to show the local commander the courtesy of allowing NCO's to sleep at home in Dordrecht instead of at the camp near the bridge.
268	(*"De Tweede Wereldoorlog"*, Luc de Vos (2nd edition, 2004), pp. 72, 73; "The Fabribeckers", pp. 153, 154, 159). At Eben Emael, which was reached by the first gliders with German troops at 03:50 Dutch time, and at the *"Dekkingsstelling"* (covering position), although the alarm was raised shortly after midnight, the Germans were not expected to arrive until after they had crossed the southern part of Limburg, so that the readiness process was slow and far from completed when the battle began at 04:00. The many alerts in the months before had made the troops cynical about the threat and the command did not act against this mentality. See also *"The German Fallschirmtruppe 1936-1941"*, Karl-Heinz Golla, 2013 revised edition, pp. 125,126.

269 This had many adverse side effects. The motorised French infantry units were mostly motorised with external transport units – usually equipped with civilian transport vehicles such as requisitioned taxis, buses and trucks. These then took them from A to B, after which these divisions became foot infantry again albeit that staff and support units were largely motorised. 25.DIM, for example, which was to arrive in Holland, was in large part externally motorised by city buses. These external units only became available when they had been alerted and moved towards towards their infantry units. The fact that Gamelin did not provide the necessary alerting led to the first externally motorised units not moving until around 13:00 on 10 May. Some forward cavalry units were also designated to act directly in the Ardennes region in south-east Belgium and Luxembourg. They had to be able to leave immediately to outmanoeuvre the Germans.

270 Luxembourg was, like the other Low Countries, a neutral state. It had no genuine armed forces, just a small formation of around 700 volunteers, a combined military and gendarme corps. The defence of Luxembourg was ensured by France, although it was only formally requested to do so by a request in a sealed envelop that would be opened upon the outbreak of hostilities. The country had constructed an extensive security line (Schuster-line) along the German border which was mainly a long-stretched obstruction-line with numerous positions from where activities or breaches could be reported by radio and telephone. This system also served the French intelligence. The French had planned for a couple of cavalry units of the 3rd Army to advance into Luxembourg and seize a number of strategic key-point, execute demolition and thus slow the anticipated German advance through this region.

271 It was not only in the Netherlands that the German special forces carried out *Brandenburger* (and related) commando actions. They were also carried out in Belgium and Luxembourg. In the latter country, in combination with Gamelin's tardy response, they were decisive for the successful German capture of some road-junctions that the French cavalry had targeted too.

272 From May 1, 1909 until May 16, 1940, the Netherlands used Amsterdam time. This was 20 minutes ahead of standard time (called UTC today). This meant that at 12:00 in the Netherlands it was 11:40 in London and 12:40 in Berlin (UTC+1). Because in Germany, France and the United Kingdom summer time was in force on 10 May 1940 and the Netherlands had not set summer time, the differences became even more significant. Therefore, the Germans were 1:40 ahead of the Netherlands while the Belgians, French and the UK were 40 minutes ahead. On 16 May 1940, Germany introduced German time on the occupied territory. This was maintained after the war.

273 For the bridges across the Meuse, apart from the four that were considered extremely strategic for the retreat of the 3rd Army Corps and the Light Division, C-3.AC, C-Peel-Division and the local bridge commander had

a role in the destruction. The first two could (on orders from above or on the basis of an acute danger) order 'demolition' and it had to be carried out immediately. The bridge commanders themselves had the strict instruction that upon visible actual appearance of the enemy, demolition had to be initiated immediately. This regulation has been decisive for timely destruction at a number of bridges.

274 The Germans deliberately violated the law of war by attempting to capture important bridges and infrastructural interchanges in the Netherlands, Belgium and Luxembourg, usually (in the Netherlands) with commandos disguised as Dutch, Polish or (captured) German soldiers or civil servants, before the actual state of war had even commenced. The '*Bau-Lehr-Bataillon zur besonderen Verwendung 800*', originally from Brandenburg and therefore nicknamed the '*Brandenburger*', was specially constructed to carry out this kind of commando raids. In case of the *Brandenburger*, it consisted of regular soldiers and specially recruited foreign civilians, but there were other units and branches executing covert operations. These raids were requested and set up by the *Abwehr*, the SS and the regular army. A weak and unsuccessful contemporary excuse was that all of this would fall under the heading of 'stratagem' and would therefore be permitted under the Laws of War on Land (LWR: *jus ad bellum* and *jus in bello*). However, such conduct was absolutely not a stratagem. A stratagem was (for instance) to hide a troop of regular armed soldiers in a ship's hold and to hope that they would not be discovered (an action attempted by 254.ID near Nijmegen). However, disguising soldiers in Dutch uniforms or otherwise deceptively dressing them was in explicit contravention of the land war provisions which stipulated that members of the armed forces taking part in the battle had to be uniquely identifiable as such. Many *Brandenburger* also expected that capture would be met with summary execution. There is an indication that this was done once by troops of 11.GB, at Neer, west of Nijmegen. For the rest, captured *Brandenburger* were treated as prisoners of war in the Netherlands.

275 The exact time of the raid is not clear, but it was very shortly before the official invasion time. Therefore, a "Destruction" order given from the Hague would not have provided a timely remedy. Prior to the raid time, the pickets at Gennep station had already been captured. Although properly and timely warned by the station picket of the local MP-post, lack of local leadership and policy at the guard posts at the bridge caused indecision about how to handle the group of people (Germans in disguise) appearing in front of the bridge, what caused insufficient readiness on the east side of the bridge. As a result, the assault command was able to easily take-out this guard and get inside the barricade fence, make it across the bridge onto the west side and thus continue the raid. When the Germans were held at gun point and searched on the west side – with as result that weapons and hand-grenades were found on them – the bridge commander still remained unsuspicious. Even when a train appeared on the German side he still refused to order

the destruction of the bridge and trusted the train to be a legitimate transport, notwithstanding that it was clearly an odd model and timing. When the train crossed the bridge its crew quickly jumped off and captured the stunned guards. The local commander was a Police Troop NCO, who had not been up to the task and failed to act when he still was in position to do so. This caused the bridge to fall into German hands.

276 Across the Juliana Canal in central and southern Limburg, as many as five (Roosteren, Obbicht, Berg, Urmond and Stein) of the eleven bridges were captured intact. Immediately to the west, however, the Meuse was still a major obstacle so that these bridge losses mattered little. Also in the northern provinces at a few locations a local drawbridge fell intact into German hands. These events did not matter at all to the main front in the Netherlands. The only captured bridge that had any significance – mainly because of the Dutch reaction to its capture – was the one at Gennep.

277 The Dutch success had a number of negative consequences for the Germans. The first was a delay, particularly in South Limburg, in linking-up with the Eben-Emael bridgehead. The second was the delayed deployment of the two tank divisions (3rd and 4th PD) and a motorized division (20. ID) on the west side of the Meuse. This was something to which the OKH attached great importance because they feared Belgo-French counterattacks before sufficiently powerful units west of the Meuse had deployed. Thirdly, much pontoon bridging material was needed which was sorely missed in the later stages of the battle in Holland and Belgium. During the May Days OKH and OKW were very busy with these issues. Only in hindsight would they conclude that it had made little difference.

278 Partly because of the unrealistic attention the PEC paid to this incident, its operational value to the Germans was considered greater than it really was. (Freiburg archive, Ba/Ma RH46-720 XXVI.AK Pi.Rgt.413) The reality is that the Germans gained very little from it operationally. The bridge at Gennep was a narrow, single-lane railway bridge that was impossible for motorized vehicles to cross without wooden duckboards and planks filling in the spaces between and adjacent to the rails, and the high embankments had substantial ramps. Although a platoon of Pz.Kpfw.I (light tanks) and infantry on bicycles used the bridge on the morning of 10 May without these modifications, the light tanks damaged the track and embankment to such an extent that its use as such was immediately terminated. This also caused the train with timber from *Festungsbaubatailion* 220 not to be able to reach the far western side of the bridge to offload the timber. It had to be offloaded on a less convenient spot what caused engineers to hand-carry the timber in-situ. The train had arrived in a timely manner but it took the pioneers until the afternoon of 11 May before the bridge could be used by mounted or motorised equipment. This had also to do with the fact that the bridge was used by at least three German infantry battalions to cross the river whilst the engineers were constructing the timber structures. Poor

traffic planning then caused the bridge to be hardly used until the 12th of May. By then, the 9th *Panzer Division* and most of the the motorized SS-V *Division* had already crossed the river via the two pontoon bridges at Mook and Gennep. The German follow-up operation at Mill – where the armoured train and following troop-train with a battalion of infantry ended up on 10 May 1940 – failed largely. The German battalion was offloaded to the rear of the Peel-Raam-line at Mill but when the armoured train returned it derailed as a consequence of exploded charges under the tracks that had meanwhile been placed by the Dutch. It was only when troops were brought in over the pontoon and railway bridge at Gennep in the evening of 10 May to launch the attack near Mill, preceded by an intensive *Luftwaffe* bombardment, that the Germans broke through at Mill. There was therefore little operational advantage for the Germans. Any logistic advantage in the follow-up operations was only after 12 May. The early success at Gennep and penetration of the Peel defences at Mill did provoke Winkelman to speed up the evacuation of forces out of Brabant. That may have prevented that substantial Dutch units were cut off during their retreat into the Fortress by German formations.

279   The raid on Eben Emael can be interpreted much more at the tactical scale whose operational effectiveness was already known. Small-scale parachute landings and even airborne landings, for example, were already part of the options available to the French. In Denmark and Norway such actions had already been observed from the German side. However, landing paratroopers along a chain of bridges within a vast fortified area, as happened in the Netherlands, and depositing a large concentration of airborne troops around a strategic town, was a novelty that suddenly confronted the Dutch army command with an active front across the full breadth of the country (from Groningen to South Limburg) and a vertical perimeter within Fortress Holland itself.

280   There were no elaborate theoretical studies written about this in the Netherlands. It is noteworthy, however, that in the Soviet-Union this knowledge was already available and in 1932 an inspection tour of already constructed parts of the Maginot Line, accompanied by French staff officers, elicited the comment from Soviet representatives that a German airborne landing behind the Maginot Line would threaten the entire line. The French had brushed this aside, but it shows that the insights were there. Incidentally – the Germans themselves had also drawn inspiration from the Soviet Union with whom there had been close cooperation during the earlier interwar period.

281   A salient detail is that Major-General Carstens had become commander of this army corps after his resignation as army chief of staff.

282   NIMH 409-479004, chief of staff VH, Lieutenant-Colonel W. Thomson. It concerned the 2nd Battalion of the *Regiment Jagers* (Rifle Guards Regiment), which in the end (after a countermand) was not to be directed to

Rotterdam but to Hook of Holland to intervene there, because (unintentionally) a large concentration of mis-dropped airborne troops had landed there and this was seen as an even greater threat.

283 *"Stafwerk - Operatiën Veldleger"*, p. 39.
284 The documents found entered the archives as the 'Sponeck papers'.
285 NIMH 409-479004, chief of staff VH, Lieutenant-Colonel W. Thomson.
286 The French military attaché was *Lieutenant-Colonel* Roger M.J. De Mascureau. *Rear-Admiral* G.L.C. Dickens was naval attaché from the UK. He would continuously serve as liaison between the Dutch Navy and the *Royal Navy* during the May Days. The military attaché for the UK was Lieutenant-Colonel W.L. Gibson.
287 The exact time and content of this conversation is lost. Gamelin mentions nothing about promises to the Netherlands regarding Moerdijk in his memoirs that even contain no reference to any conversation with Winkelman on May 10th, only on the 11th and 12th. It is however almost certain that both generalissimo's spoke to each other on the first day of the invasion and that Gamelin mistakenly attached another date to this conversation. The conversation on the 10th took place somewhere around 10.00-11.30 hours according to Dutch sources. After the briefing of the French attaché and the conversation with Gamelin there was no longer any uncertainty for Winkelman that French formations would come to West-Brabant. The requests for four divisions for the Fortress Holland was dismissed and so were requests to the French for assistance as far east as the Peel-defences. The French attaché did – at least according to Lerecouvreux in '*l'Armee Giraud en Hollande*' (1951) p. 281 – not received instructions from Gamelin during a short informative conversation between these two French officers before Winkelman came on the line (See also "*La Grande Illusion - Belgian and Dutch strategy facing Germany, 1919- May 1940*" by J.A. Gunsburg (2014), p. 648.).
288 In spite of the myth that the Military Aviation (abbreviated ML in Dutch) was largely destroyed on the ground – which in reality happened to only a limited number of operational aircraft – many aircraft were lost in the next phase, during the first hours of the invasion. This was partly due to losses in air-to-air combat but also as a consequence of the loss of four AFB's (and therefore forced landings on terrain from which take-off was not feasible). The Dutch air force used a tactic of free hunting where the *Fokker* D-XXI fighters flew (initially) in formations of three aircraft, but later, like the *Fokker* G-1 twin-engine fighter, often individually. This led to dispertion and thus to systematic enemy supremacy. The flying qualities of the equipment and pilots were usually not the problem. The Dutch pilots were actually quite skilled and the modern part of the equipment was usually well able to cope with the German adversaries. The fighter-force achieved and maintained a positive balance in aerial combat with adversaries during the May Days.

289 Van Voorst Evekink went to the GQG in the morning and delivered the sealed envelope with instructions and requests for help. The French immediately indicated that they had no troops available to send to the Dutch Fortress. The Dutch were requested to send a liaison team to Antwerp to join the 7th Army staff and also to receive and escort the four-officer strong French liaison mission to the Hague, which was led by General Mittelhauser. See also *"La Grande Illusion - Belgian and Dutch strategy facing Germany, 1919- May 1940"* by J.A. Gunsburg (2014), p. 648.

290 Apart from the fact that the RAF with its policy of limited liability on the continent refused to commit forces in Holland and that the Dutch bases were too exposed, the British aircraft used fuel with octane rating 100 (the ML with octane rating 90) and used a different calibre of weapons (7.7 mm instead of the continental 7.9 mm).

291 Winkelman's plan was to retreat to the Fortress with the scarce resources and wait for relief there. The fact that this allied force was not intended to reach as far as Fortress Holland entirely destroyed his strategic plan.

292 (*"The Battle of France - then an now"*, Peter D. Cornwell, 2008, hereinafter "Cornwell"; *"Verliesregister 1939-1945 - alle militaire vliegtuigverliezen in Nederland tijdens de Tweede Wereldoorlog, 1940"* Dutch Ministry of Defence 2008 hereinafter "Aircraft losses"). AFB Ypenburg was attacked twice. Once by *Blenheim's* of the 40th Squadron (four aircraft lost, see also "Cornwell" pp 174, 184 and "Aircraft losses" p. 22) and once by *Hurricanes* of the 32nd Squadron A-Flight (no losses). AFB Waalhaven was attacked twice by *Blenheim* formations during the day on May 10, once by fighters (600th Squadron, five lost; see also "Cornwell" pp. 175, 184 and "Aircraft losses" p. 22) and once by light bombers (15th Squadron). The last attack was successful, leaving 8 Ju-52 of the *Luftwaffe* destroyed and some personnel and troops dead. During the night AFB Waalhaven was attacked seven times by a total of 36 *Wellingtons* in successive raids by one or two flights of three aircraft at a time from the 9th, 37th, 38th, 75th (ANZAC), 99th, 115th and 149th Squadrons (see also "Cornwell" p. 175). One of these flights dropped the bombs on the north of Rotterdam by mistake. On 12 May AFB Waalhaven was attacked by nine *Swordfish* and six *Beaufighters* of the Fleet Air Arm (815th Squadron; see also "Cornwell", p. 243). Each of them dropped two 225 kg bombs. The British dropped in total no less than 65 tons of bombs on and around Waalhaven. Dutch *Fokker* T-V bombers and *Fokker* C-X light attack airplanes also managed to drop bombs on Waalhaven so that in total around 68 tons were dropped by the allied countries. For comparison – the large bombardment on Rotterdam of 14 May by *Gruppe* Lackner and Höhne's *Kette* of KG.54 on the city of Rotterdam dropped about 65 tons (about 32 tons were dropped elsewhere).

293 A time-fuse with delay was deliberately used to produce (in this instance) more of a 'plowing-effect'. The Germans therefore thought it was 7.5 cm artillery firing because the detonation was muffled by the ground. However,

this led to cratering of the landing strips and that was the intention.

294　On 10 May, Dutch prisoners of war were employed to repair field damage and remove wreckage from the field. This was discontinued when the artillery bombardment began.

295　There was a great shortage of ammunition on the German side on 12 May. On 11 May, mortar shells were already on restriction; on 12 May, they were out of ammunition in some locations, particularly the 7.5 cm howitzers and mortars. The Germans had to drop many supplies to supply the operations. On 11 May, however, the soft landing drop containers ('*Behalter*') were finished, so only the rigid supply containers ('*Bomben*') could be dropped with *Heinkel* He-111. These were not very effective so much of the contents was lost. The limited number of available parachutes made this process vulnerable as well. The Dutch side seems not to have realised that the Germans could only use AFB Waalhaven sparingly.

296　The airfield was particularly used by courier services and a reconnaissance squadron for Student himself. This squadron, however, was almost completely destroyed after two days of war. Liaison aircraft, mostly of the light types like the *Fieseler* Fi-156 *Storch* and *Messerschmitt* Bf-108 *Taifun*, continued to use the airfield.

297　Carl Philipp Gottfried (von) Clausewitz (1780-1831) – usually paraphrased only by his original surname without the later acquired 'von' – was a well-known strategist and war philosopher, known to all general staff officers. His axiom that in wartime the general staff is confronted with a deluge of messages, most of them contradictory or false and almost all of them uncertain, was well-known. Nevertheless, what happened on 10 May 1940 was never practised, not even by proximity. This was partly because in war games the Dutch army practised classic war scenarios and – obviously simulating the opponent – never applied modern German strategies and tactics. Few serving soldiers could be blamed for this fact. Dealing with chaos also depended on character and basic qualities and not just thorough training. The chaos of countless and relentless messages in all shapes, sizes and grades of reliability generates a confusion that was addressed by Clausewitz and became internationally known as '*the fog of war*'. Clausewitz concluded that war is chaos and he who manages the chaos best, usually wins.

298　There were attacks in the north by the German 1st *Kavallerie Division*, opposite the IJssel by the 10th Army Corps (two infantry divisions, two motorised SS regiments), in the sector Nijmegen - Boxmeer by the 26th AC (two infantry divisions, one motorized SS division and one tank division as well as two infantry divisions of the reserve) and from Venlo to Maastricht almost the entire 6th Army with from north to south 9.AC, 11.AC, 4.AC and 27.AC. Of these four, only the last one was partly intended to squeeze through between Maastricht and Liège. The four corps' first line of attack between the Venlo-Maastricht sector was no less than eleven infantry divisions (most of them of the best classes) and two tank divisions strong. Of all these divisions, however, only two would be significant to the operation in Brabant (30.ID and 56.ID), the rest would immediately push through Limburg into Belgium. Furthermore, there was an airborne corps with about 12,500 personnel to be deployed from the air-lifted part of the 22nd *Infanterie Division* (with reserves of IR.72 of 46.ID) and the small 7th *Flieger Division*, the latter in fact only comprising five battalions of paratroopers with some light support.

299   Limited scale tactical para-troop actions around airfields, which could be followed by airborne landings, were expected. Especially the Commander Air Defences General Best had foreseen this and requested measures to be taken. Winkelman followed his lead. Large air-landings, which for example Dijxhoorn and Best had seen as a possibility, Winkelman did not see as a serious risk, as is also evident from the measures after 9 April 1940 which were proposed and carried out by the Minister and General Best. Para-troop actions around strategic points other than airfields were not foreseen, as is also evident from the construction and single-sighted layout of the fortified bridgeheads near strategic bridges. The Dutch were especially surprised by the scale of the German operation. Also para-troop actions behind the concentrations of the Field Army or behind the Meuse – both seriously considered by the Germans – seem not to have been considered as possible attack scenarios.

300   Rotterdam, being a large harbour and central logistical point, was a bulk hub for the armed forces containing huge magazines and storages. Combat formations were scarce though, it had only one garrisoned infantry battalion and about 150 combat-ready marines. The remaining military personnel in the city – no less than some 6,000 men – were mostly depot-troops and trainees of the engineer-corps, navy and the army air-force, as well as a very large contingent of services and logistics intendants units. Around 11:30 on 10 May, the staff and staff support of 11.RI were assigned with its 3rd Battalion, a coy of 4,7 cm AT-guns and a coy of 8,1 cm mortars, as well as the battalions IV-10.RI and IV.15.RI. Both were battalions without a heavy machine-gun coy. IV-15.RI did have a section of AT-guns as an extra. Later the three battalions III-21.RI, II-25.RI and II-32.RI were designated. The first regiment arrived in the night of 10 to 11 May and its commander, Lieutenant-Colonel Leeser, took over infantry command in the city. C-20. RI and the also designated battalion III-16.RI were halfway re-directed to Leiden, where a smaller-scale German air-landing had taken place on the nearby AFB Valkenburg. Also a battery of four modern *Bofors* 10-veld guns, that was positioned in the Grebbe-line, was requested, but having already arrived in Rotterdam it was cancelled and returned to the Grebbe-line on the morning of 13 May. All these units were taken off of the balance of the Field Army and only a part could do useful work in Rotterdam and Leiden.

301   NIMH 409-479004, chief of staff VH, Lieutenant-Colonel W. Thomson: This concerned the battalions of 31.RI that also came from the formerly occupied eastern front.

302   Only about 1,000 Germans held the Nieuwe Maas front until 13 May when the ground-component troops of 26.AC joined up with them. The river front was mainly occupied by troops of the battalion III./IR.16 on the central river island (Noordereiland) and immediate surroundings and a company of IR.72 (Charlois, the southwest of Rotterdam) and some individual mortar and AT-gun sections. The rest were positioned elsewhere within the corridor or concentrated as reserves far outside Rotterdam. About 30 men of III./IR.16 and 20 airbornes of III./FJR.1 (*Fallschirmjäger*) occupied the only German position on the northern river side, in the Bank building near the traffic bridge.

303   In the end, around 11,000 men were actually dropped off inside the Fortress divided over the Hague, Rotterdam, Dordrecht and Moerdijk positions. Particularly around the Hague the German losses would mount up, including around 1,500 POW's of which the majority would be shipped to the UK before the Dutch capitulation on May 15th. At AFB Waalhaven personnel and material was flown in until 12 May. A battalion of 46.ID (I./IR.72) landed there as well. They were a tactical reserve attached to Student's Corps.

304   NIMH 409-479004. Actions involving large formations were subject to prior concurrence by the C-VH staff before they could be carried out. The C-VH wished to have troops available and ready in case of renewed German landings.

305   It was thought that the Germans had deliberately landed in a very large area, whereas this was merely a result of the far too optimistic German planning and the effective initial Dutch reaction to the raid. Also, it was apparently expected that the Germans would try to cross the Nieuwe Maas at Rotterdam with airborne troops, while on the German side there was just a 'holding strategy' at that position after the initial attempts to gain a bridgehead on the north side of the river had been denied by Dutch counter attacks.

306   This multiplicity of reports was due to the frequent sighting of parachutes from all directions and the fact that the airdrop of supplies near the airborne concentrations was constantly reported as landed airborne reinforcements.

307   The analogy of the German airborne operation in May 1940 with the allied operation *Market-Garden* in 1944 is striking. Not only the basis of the Moerdijk-Rotterdam sequence of bridges in particular, but also that the Germans had in fact also gone one bridge too far. Only the Dutch failed to block the ground forces connecting at that last link, whereas the Germans succeeded in doing so in Arnhem. However, the salvaging of large chunks of the operational plans in a crashed aircraft in the Hague, is also a striking resemblance.

308   Clausewitz rightly stated that no strategy comes through the first battles unscathed. He was referring to the fact that waging war is not a single action but a complex of continuous interactions (dynamics), i.e. it requires

the commander to make continual adjustments and, if necessary, to adapt or change strategy along the way.

309 "Immediately" is a relative term in this case. Winkelman had only around 06:00-07:00 hours (from the Group Kil via the C-VH) a reasonably reliable picture that the Moerdijk bridges might have been captured by German para-troopers, but confirmation about this did not arise until the afternoon. This perspective is important.

310 The fact that AFB Waalhaven had been taken and was being used by German aircraft was suspected early in the morning of May 10 and confirmed not much later. The loss of three airfields around the Hague (AFB Valkenburg near Leiden, AFB Ypenburg at Rijswijk/Delft and the auxiliary strip at Ockenburg at Loosduinen/the Hague) also became apparent quite soon.

311 The French attaché had already reported this in the early morning and Van Voorst Evekink reported it by telephone to Lieutenant-Colonel Wilson at the AHK between 10:00 and 11:00 (PEC 1C, 2006). It is not known whether Gamelin also reported it, but he probably did. With this it was no longer logical to retreat to the Fortress and wait there for a relief that would not come. Actively joining French and Belgian troops and maintaining the front defences in Brabant suddenly seemed by far the most logical solution.

312 Around 07:00 the telex instruction from the OLZ to the CV was sent. At the same time the great risk of such an evacuation across two large rivers in full daylight suddenly became apparent. Winkelman had distanced himself from this in relation to Reijnders' operational strategy a few months earlier, but he himself would twice apply in his own hot strategy. Those who would argue that this was logical given the developments and that Winkelman was right to try to prevent a northern cutting off of the units, ignore that Winkelman did not have to retreat but built in this risk himself by adhering to his paradigm that everything had to return to the Fortress. By doing so he took exactly the same risks as his predecessor who had been much more realistic and honest about it. He could have – and perhaps should have – reacted by sending the 3rd Army Corps to the Peel-Raam-line and the Light Division – whether as a whole or not – to the sector below Eindhoven for the border protection behind Weert. This would have given the French more space and time to deploy, on the basis of which their retaking of Moerdijk would have been more reasonable and could have been demanded by the Netherlands with more justification.

313 The 2nd Regiment of Motorised Hussars (2.RHM) was still under construction and about 35% under organic strength. This unit was scheduled to use newly procured 2 cm *Solothurn* AT-rifles of which the first batch had been received and in the cavalry depot, but the ammunition was still in delivery with exception of a small stock which had been distributed to the Maastricht legion. Hence the AT-rifles were omitted as also the organic 8 cm mortar section. There were only six of the twelve heavy machine guns and there was a considerable shortage of cadre still. Besides staff and liai-

son group, there were only two squadrons of motorcyclists with nine light machine guns each, half of the heavy machine gun squadron with only six MG's on motorbikes and a squadron of *Böhler* 4,7 AT-guns. The latter two were combined in one support squadron. Nevertheless, this was a powerful unit.

314 The structure of the Light Division was based on the principle of duplication. It even had a second staff. All combat units were included in duplicate: two squadrons of armoured cars, two battalions of field artillery, two regiments (with each three battalions) of bicycle-infantry and two regiments of hussar-motorcyclists. In addition, the infantry-regiments were equipped with tactical pioneer equipment of their own so that they could carry out many technical manoeuvres independently. In this way the division was able to provide two equally strong and well-equipped and supported combat groups. All this was a product of modern understanding of light warfare. The division was therefore on paper by far the most capable of the army and also had the best cadre and many professional personnel at its disposal.

315 NIMH 409-479004, Lieutenant-Colonel W. Thomson. Moreover the OLZ prohibited to attack the Moerdijk bridge with airplanes or artillery. The premise remained retaking Moerdijk and linking-up with French troops, while Winkelman had been informed already in the morning that no French troops would come to the Fortress. This prohibition against destruction of the Moerdijk-bridges remained in force until 12 May midnight. By then, however, the German 9th Tank Division had already reached Moerdijk. After this, C-VH received the order to bombard the traffic-bridge with aerial bombs and both bridges with artillery. From the order one could also deduce that the thought apparently existed that the charges could be hit by artillery. This was not the case with the Moerdijk bridges because, apart from the fact that the charges were barely accessible to artillery shells, they had already been removed by the German para-trooper engineers. Artillery could not have destroyed the bridges kinetically e.g. without the aid of hitting a charge. Even the bombing raid on 13 May with two 300 kg HE-bombs (about 175 kg of net explosive material) would probably only have damaged the superstructure in case of a direct hit. The heavy pillars would hardly have been damaged, which conclusion is supported by the photographic evidence of the only mild damage caused by a 250 kg bomb from a German *Junkers* Ju-88 at the modern fort near Kornwerderzand. Earlier those May Days the C-VH had ordered the ML to bomb the two traffic bridges in Rotterdam. The ML thought they could do this with *Fokker* T-V bombers loaded with 50 kg bombs (apparently lacking expertise). Although all the bombs missed their targets (but did cause collateral damage to German occupied houses), the OLZ got wind of the action and ordered it to be stopped immediately. The bridges had to remain intact! That order too was revoked on 13 May, yet no bombers remained to raid these bridges too.

316 Dutch marines were ordered to recapture the Rotterdam bridges in order for these constructions to be demolished prior to German attempts to cross them. This mission almost succeeded, although boldly executed, but eventually failed due to poor planning by the senior command of the marines.

316 Winkelman, after the armistice announcement, immediately gave the order at the GHQ and elsewhere to destroy the war-diaries and other documentation. He never properly defended this rather bizarre decision – which he would soon come back to and which led to an instruction to commanding officers to write down diaries from memory. The only explanation he gave was that he did not want to inform the Germans in order to harm the allies. The Germans had other things on their minds than to analyse the mistakes of the Dutch armed forces and it is hard to imagine what disadvantages the allies could suffer from destroying Dutch reports, war-dairies and records. Obviously, burning the contents of vaults, destroying genuine secret and sensitive data and reports as well as the GS-III records was only a smart and perfectly logic thing to do.

317 NIMH 409-521001 (L.J. Schmidt) "*I asked the GHQ how the coordination with the French and the Belgians was arranged (11 May at 2.30 a.m.) and received the message from Lieutenant-Colonel Wilson, that this coordination did not exist and it was left to me to establish it.*"

318 The para-troopers had removed the existing charges and ditched them into the Hollandsch Diep. There was still a considerable supply of explosives in the cellar of the casemate next to the road bridge. What happened to it is unknown. It seems likely that if it had been preserved, it would have been destroyed in the event of an imminent French conquest. Bringing in new explosives from the Fortress of Holland was not easy. The lack of a depot on the southern front already led to cumbersome supply of ammunition by boat and barges during the May Days, which took days and was very exposed. If the French had not supplied explosives, it is not unlikely that the bridges would have remained undestroyed and captured by the 9th *Panzer Division*.

319 It is relevant to explain the suggestion that SS formations would likely have been used. They were deployed in Holland because the Germans considered that theatre less important and the OKH still resisted the fighting formations of the SS as undesired (political) assets. Their combat power was considered low and their use during the Poland campaign had not been a great success. Therefore only the fully trained and partially battle-hardened SS-V *Division* and *Leibstandarte* SS 'Adolf Hitler' were given a role in the first phase of the battle. The SS-*Totenkopf Division*, which was deployed later, consisted almost exclusively of poorly trained soldiers. The same applied to the SS-*Polizei Division* that remained in reserve with *Heeresgruppe C*. The 9th *Panzer Division* was wanted back by OKH as a tank reserve, although in reality it was directed into battle again and would even contribute in the final stages of the Dunkirk encirclement.

320 Intelligence for this came in from the Group Kil and Group Spui, sightings from soldiers on the front-line and fugitives crossing the road being the first. A formation of military refugees from the other river-bank, among which an MP of the *Marechaussee* Brigade in Moerdijk, reached by boat the Hoekse Waard island and reported the German airborne landings around Moerdijk. There was no contact with the Dutch position at Willemsdorp and here too, escapees were the source of the intelligence that they had been attacked and had been overrun. In the afternoon of May 10, a contingent of defenders who had been on the western front of bridgehead Moerdijk reached Willemstad and was able to make a proper report on the loss of the bridgehead. The 6th Border Infantry Battalion was already at 06:00 hours instructed by the commanding General of 3.AC to move immediately to Moerdijk and to attack the German paratrooper positions there and retake the traffic bridge. Around 11:00 hours a large part of the battalion crossed the Mark-canal at Terheijden (north of Breda). Shortly afterwards its forward elements made contact with German outposts, that hastily retreated onto the Moerdijk bridgehead. The battalion commander had telephone contact with the commanding General of 3.AC, in which the Major was urged to retake the bridges without further ado. On the question of the Major if he would get support from the Brabant Field Army formations, a resolute 'no' followed; "*You're on your own, get the job done!*".

321 Discussions were general and vague. Officers did not trust the lines of communication. That was certainly true for the French. It is therefore remarkable that Winkelman attached so much weight to this conversation.

322 The French sent Lieutenant-General Eugène Mittelhauser (1873-1949) with three officers (Major Winsback, Captain Henquin and First Lieutenant Pirson) as liaison staff. The intention was that Mittelhauser would soon be replaced by Brigadier-General Georges Lascroux (1885-1956). The latter did not come to pass. The British sent Major-General T. Heywood (1886-1943) with a few subordinates, who arrived on May 10 with HMS Wivern at the Hook of Holland. The Netherlands sent Lieutenant-General J.F. van der Vijver to Paris with the general staff officers Captain W.T. Carp and Captain P.J. de Broekert; to London Major-General J.W. van Oorschot (1875-1952) with Lieutenant-Colonel J.G.W. Zegers (1891-1952) and to Brussels Major-General G.B. Noothoven van Goor (1874-1942) and Captain A.C. de Ruyter van Steveninck (1895-1949). These Dutch delegations would all end up in London after the May Days of 1940. ("*La grande illusion - Belgian and Dutch strategy between the wars*", part II, p. 648, J.A. Gunsburg) Gunsburg refers to Gamelin's Memoirs (*Servir*, 1:99; 3:395) mentioning that also a mission was requested to be sent to the 7th Army HQ. This request is untraceable in Dutch sources and reports. It was already addressed before that no liaison teams were sent to the 7th Army HQ.

323 PEC 1C, 15858, 15859.

324 PEC 1C, 15856, 15857.
325 PEC 1C, 15872.
326 PEC 1C, 15870.
327 The PEC asked the question "*Couldn't the light division have been sent to the Moerdijk in a more decisive manner that first morning? Did you find it strategically absolutely necessary to do so on the north side?*" Moreover, the question may arise, that if speed had been the main consideration, how could the alternative plan of the commander of the Light Division have been sanctioned by the C-VH on 11 May? After all, his plan was cumbersome and could have taken days.
328 PEC 1C, 15873.
329 There was also a collection of artillery at Group Spui on the southern front which, certainly in the early stages and bearing in mind that the French were going to control the other side of Hollandsch Diep opposite this Group, could have been moved to the Oude Maas front (south of the Island IJsselmonde). One artillery battalion would be ordered to do this, only on the third day of the war!
330 Troops were moved across the Nieuwe-Waterweg and a company of infantry had been located near the Pernis crude oil installations until the morning of May 13th, which was to continue securing the BPM-installations (BPM was the Dutch Shell predecessor) until these installations were partly demolished by British engineers and commandos (See also "*XD Operations - Secret British missions denying oil to the Nazis*", C.C.H. Brazier, 2004, ISBN 1-84415-136-0). At this point, troops could have been transferred across the Nieuwe Maas river to the island of IJsselmonde during all combat days, that would not have encountered any opponent, and could have prepared for action against the south of Rotterdam and above all, AFB Waalhaven. The Germans had only a few outposts in this sector until 12 May, later only the company of airborne infantry of 1./IR.72 reinforced with a few mortars, near Hoogvliet (west of the island IJsselmonde). Another such company (6./IR.72) – located at Charlois (SW side of Rotterdam) that worked with patrolling outposts along the Waterweg on the west side of the city – made a tentative reconnaissance against Pernis on 11 May but was repulsed, leaving behind some casualties, and did not show itself again afterwards. Student had a clear holding strategy on his corridor and deployed securing outposts to parry any attack with local concentrations. Everything west of AFB Waalhaven did not matter to Student, except for the fixed passage at Spijkenisse (opposite Hoogvliet) that he had occupied. Dutch passivity confirmed Student in his choices. The poor situational awareness at the staff of C-VH and the confined focus of the military commanders in Rotterdam itself caused this loophole in the German front not to be utilized by the Dutch.
331 This opinion is found in many assessments of the battle. At the time, several senior-officers had already made this claim to the PEC, which is why the

PEC also presented it to the then OLZ and Chief-of-Staff. See also "*The German Fallschirmtruppe 1936-1941*", Karl-Heinz Golla, (2013 rev.), Final comments pp. 308/309.

332 The Light Division would perform poorly at the Noord and in the manoeuvres in and around Dordrecht. Its largely professional leadership failed and across the board. They proved to be extremely sensitive to the uncertainties brought about by 'the fog of war' and went off the rails in numerous areas. There was panic amongst its commanders, questionable executions of alleged traitors in Dordrecht and a strongly backed rumour of treason about Lieutenant-Colonel Mussert (the regional military commander Dordrecht – he was the eldest brother of the leader of the Dutch fascist party NSB). This rumour – which was totally false – would completely paralyse the command in Dordrecht, and eventually cost Mussert his life when he was murdered by a junior officer of the Light Division under suspicion of treason. Meanwhile, in the field, their performance was nothing spectacular – a few individual samples of courage aside, of course.

333 This was the Waal- and Lingestelling. This was a weak spot of the Fortress par excellence that would stand the least chance of a concentrated German attack. On the 13th and 14th units of this parked army corps were deployed to hot spots on the fronts.

334 C-VH failed hopelessly here. He gave the commander of the Light Division virtually no situational information. He did not even receive the crucial information that the Germans had occupied the bridges over the Oude Maas near Dordrecht and that strong German formations were present on the Island of Dordrecht. The divisional commander learned this only when he arrived in Alblasserdam in the evening of 10 May and had to send the battalion, which he had to relinquish to Dordrecht, over the ferry near Papendrecht instead of sending it to the city after the crossing at the Noord via the bridges over the Oude Maas. Moreover, the Light Division was hardly pressed to launch the attack immediately. While the attack had been coordinated with the RAF and with the assisting 3rd Border Infantry Battalion (3.GB) it should have followed the RAF bombing of Waalhaven that night.

335 On the flank this attack from the Hoekse Waard would receive support from 3.GB. This unit had primarily been intended to occupy the Willemstad redoubt south of the Meuse but during the first day of the war it was put at the disposal of the Group Kil. Later, Group Kil was ordered to use the battalion as a flanking unit for the Light Division attack. It had to across the Oude Maas by night, approach AFB Waalhaven from the south and link up with the Light Division and jointly attack the air force base after the scheduled RAF raid. The battalion did not do very well, had an ineffective BC and had a few weak and sluggish company commanders on top of that. It was true that in the early morning of 11 May two companies made it to the north side of the river Oude Maas, but one company went quietly to breakfast (without taking any security measures). The Dutch had been

spotted by a German outpost that called in an airborne formation. The following attack caused quite a number of casualties and abandonment of much gear and weapons, although most of the company made it safely back across the Oude Maas. The other company had been successfully moving in on Barendrecht but quickly fled back to the Hoekse Waard after a civilian had told their commanding officer that the Germans were on their way. This last company would by the way fully recover and prove itself more than capable on 12 and 13 May at Wieldrecht (SW of Dordrecht), were it would stand its ground regardless of heavy casualties.

336 The bridge at Alblasserdam was occupied by a few dozen lightly armed German airborne troops. The commander of the Light Division however thought that a direct attack on that bridge was too risky and decided to wait until the next morning. This decision forfeited a good chance of immediate success. During the night, the now-warned Germans brought in reinforcements including a small company of infantry, a group of pioneers, an anti-tank gun and some light 7.5 cm *Skoda* howitzers.

337 The commander of the Light Division had believed, having lost no more than five men while successfully landing two shore-parties on the enemy side of the river, that crossing the Noord in force was impossible. In reality he had killed realistic chances of success by lack of perseverance and a weak tactical policy. In the end, a *Luftwaffe* interdiction was the cause of the panic among the Dutch formations. This was understandable because the division lacked any proper anti-aircraft defence and in this whole sector there was not a single anti-aircraft gun.

338 One could argue that the C-VH could not have known that the Light Division commander had acted and judged so poorly, but the alternative plan was, from the outset, many times more ambitious. If the magnitude of the ambition of the alternative plan would be laid aside (only for argument sake), certainly the obvious chances of massive *Luftwaffe* interdiction or the to-be-expected defence of German troops defending against one or two more river crosses definitely could not. All in all, the concurrence by General Van Andel of the alternative plan to get to Waalhaven is incomprehensible.

339 This encounter was unnecessary, because on 12 May in the early evening, Ensign Marijs, who had been taken prisoner on the 11th and been held as a POW of the airbornes on the Island of Dordrecht, had been sent back to his own troops with the permission of the commander of the 1st German Parachute Regiment (*Oberst* Bräuer), with the information that the 9th *Panzer Division* had arrived and the German advice to surrender the city. He himself had seen the German scouts with their armoured cars near Tweede Tol, a hamlet within the German corridor on the Island. Other soldiers, including some from Light Division elements, also reported German armoured cars on the highway between Moerdijk and Dordrecht on 12 May (between 18:00 and 19:00 they were actually there). The command of the Light Division re-

fused to believe this and even had Marijs imprisoned for treason. While during the late night German tanks of the *Gruppe Apell* (33.Tank Regiment of 9.PD) came over the Moerdijk bridge, and one tank squadron was retained at Tweede Tol for an action against the Dutch on the Island, the commander of the Light Division gave the go-ahead for an attack on Tweede Tol. Whilst in receipt of these orders, the commander of the Dutch attacking formation was not informed that the German tank division had already arrived, which meant that the anti-tank guns were not positioned in the point formations but pulled along more to the rear. The reason for this was the nature of the landscape. The Island of Dordrecht was in fact 'new land' (polder), well below sea level. It consisted of low grasslands traversed by narrow single track interconnected causeways (dikes) that did not allow for formations other than long single columns. The adjacent meadows allowed light foot-soldiers to move forward, but not heavy equipment or guns. It led in the morning of 13 May in the ensuing encounter battle to heavy losses. A total of about two battalions of the Light Division and a battery of field-artillery were forced into surrender, followed by the retreat of the remains of this battle group over the railway bridge at Sliedrecht off of the Island.

340   Apart from the manoeuvring of the Light Division, only one other major manoeuvre was attempted and that was during the evening and night of 10 May 1940. That was an action in which three battalions started a manoeuvre to retake the coastal sector Valkenburg-Wassenaar and disrupt the German airborne position around the Hague. A clumsily executed movement led to a debacle in the dunes, where one battalion chose a night bivouac without securing the perimeter and suffered a bloody raid with heavy losses and a large part of the battalion taken prisoner. All other actions within the Fortress took place on a small scale afterwards. These were initiated at battalion level or even lower. Only on 14 May did another initiative unfold at a regimental level between Delft and Overschie (a suburb of current Rotterdam), supported by some armoured cars as well. Despite substantial initial success it stalled as a consequence of the major German aerial bombardment of nearby Rotterdam.

341   The Netherlands should ideally have had a liaison mission with the French north-eastern theatre HQ (Georges) or with the 1st French Army Group (Billotte), and perhaps more importantly, with the 7th Army (Giraud). None of these missions were prepared and none were assembled in May 1940 either. That too shows how weak Winkelman was in all that concerned relations with the allies. Had these missions been prepared, the GHQ would have been much better informed. In reality, the Netherlands had no liaison mission during the first days of the war and the information it received was that which came via the GQG and had therefore arrived with a considerable delay.

342   Whoever follows Gamelin's directives (*instruction personnelles*) to his subordinate commanders can see in them the ambition to intervene operationally

(and thus, in principle, go beyond the limits of the agreements between the highest military authorities), but they are mainly written in terms of overall directions and do not often enter into details. Coordination between Gamelin and Georges did take place, of course. When Georges planned to appoint Billotte as allied co-ordinating commander over the French 1st, 2nd, 7th and 9th Armies, the Belgian field army and the BEF in the Dyle position, he consulted Gamelin first on 11 May. He hesitated but finally approved it. According to *Général* Doumenc Billotte got teared-up when he heard of this because he thought that this task was far too heavy ("*La grande illusion - Belgian and Dutch strategy between the wars*", part II, p. 657 and p. 661, J.A. Gunsburg).

343 "*La grande illusion - Belgian and Dutch strategy between the wars*", part II, p. 656, J.A. Gunsburg. He appeared around noon at the office of the military advisor to the Belgian King Leopold, Major-General Van Overstraeten, and showed himself convinced of the chances. However, this was before the retreat order had been given to the Belgian field army and – presumably – before he knew that the Dutch army had already evacuated the Peel-Raam-line.

344 "*L'Armee Giraud en Hollande - 1939/1940*", M. Lerecouvreux (1951), p. 186. Giraud was instructed on 11 May: " *De ne pas s'engager au-delà de Breda, d'où la VII Armée est d'ailleurs en état d'aider les Hollandais à reprendre le pont de Moerdijk, et de reprendre la liaison avec eux* ". This instruction clearly left room for Giraud himself to be the judge of the situation whether it was in the interest of the 7th Army to help the Dutch to retake the Moerdijk bridge or not, after all the instruction said (translated):"... *where the 7th Army in addition is able to help the Dutch to retake the bridge at Moerdijk* ...".

345 There was an additional line behind the Scheldt (l'Escaut).

346 The sector between Eben-Emael and Liège was particularly vulnerable and, if penetrated, would mean a very dangerous implosion of the Belgian forward defence, as described before.

347 This is also an element that Gamelin greatly underestimated, but which his subordinates in the theatre saw as a major risk. It is therefore remarkable how the various parties looked for the most favourable deployment for their own interest in a diverse and inconsistent manner, without really considering the coherence. The Dutch and Belgians with a strategy entirely focused on their respective Fortresses, the French with the mainly political preoccupation that inserting the 7th Army in the north would lead to the connection of Belgian, French and Dutch interests – save Gamelin's secondary considerations that deploying forces on the (own and German) flank would also mean that a German break-out from the Maastricht-Liège Meuse-region into the Gembloux plains would give the Germans food for thought – but in the end it was all in the interest of the quest to keep the battle away from French soil. Thus, the reality was sobering; all three parties would go their separate ways, which in essence highlights the bankruptcy of

the fragile alliance between the countries under attack at the time.

348 As mentioned before, Winkelman had emphatically failed to offer the then remaining Dutch troops a strategic and operational objective after the retreat of the 3rd Army Corps and Light Division would become a fact. Acting according to their own judgement was all that he offered to his subordinate commanders, even after the war had broken out on 10 May. It was already addressed that there should have been a liaison staff in the Breda region, knowing that the French would arrive there. A direct connection could then be made and liaison officers at various levels could be exchanged. In reality in relation to the continental theatre, two small missions, meant exclusively for the Belgian and French General Headquarters, would only be prepared after hostilities had broken out and only then leave the Hague for Brussels and Paris. Those missions would no longer serve any operational purpose due to the shortness of the war in the Netherlands. It is remarkable that Brussels and Paris had not received one or two additional military attachés following the German invasion of Norway and Denmark. Those would have been ideal to function as liaison-quartermasters and, after outbreak of hostilities, without delay join the Belgian and French headquarters in anticipation of the final liaison parties.

349 Around noon the Belgian field army was taken back to the KW-position (Koningshooikt – Wavre line), the Belgian defence line that also formed the basis under the Dyle-plan of the allies and was therefore referred to as the Dyle-line. As early as 10 May, certain units had already received orders to move backwards during the night. The German breakthrough below Maastricht was already feared. Thus, the Belgian 3rd Army Corps in the sector Liege already made position changes to the left side of the river Meuse on 10 May ('De Fabribeckers', p. 222 ff).

350 Desperate attempts by Belgian, French and British assault-planes to remedy German bridge captures between Maastricht and Eben-Emael by the destruction of those all failed while sustaining heavy losses. The aircraft used were totally unsuitable, the bombs much too light and the tactics (often not or barely escorted by fighters) fundamentally wrong. If one or two planes managed to survive the dense German air force shield and reach the target area – the *Luftwaffe* had such an overpowering concentration that it was largely a question of *Air Denial* – the dropped bombs were of no avail. The air forces of the allied countries lost here and elsewhere along the Meuse river a very large part of their tactical capacity because hardly any aircraft returned.

351 Vanguard units had already arrived on 10 May. The light brigade of 1.DLM arrived at Turnhout (Belgium) in the late evening of 10 May and already expanded to Goirle (on Dutch soil) during the night. Two motorized reconnaissance battalions (*Groupe* Lestoquoi and *Groupe* De Beauchesne) arrived with their forward units at Tilburg and Woensdrecht. On the second day of the war part of the heavy brigade of 1.DLM arrived (largely by train) and a

first regiment of infantry of 25.DIM arrived in West-Brabant. 60.DI gradually arrived in Zeeuws-Vlaanderen. One regiment had been sent ahead by ship and troops from this regiment arrived on the island of Walcheren on 11 May. On the third day the main force of 25.DIM had largely arrived. Also the 9th DIM, positioned on Belgian territory behind 1.DLM, had largely arrived in the designated area. The 4th and 21st *Division d'Infanterie* of the 7th Army were not yet in the sector and would only be brought to Antwerp by train in the second phase.

352 This summit meeting was held between the Belgian, British and French commands in a small castle in Casteau near Bergen (Mons, in French). The Belgian sovereign Leopold, Commander-in-Chief of the Belgian army, received there together with his advisor General Van Overstraeten the French Minister of Defence Daladier and the French Generals Georges and Billotte as well as the British General Pownall, Chief-of-Staff of the BEF. There it was concluded that the mutual coordination had to be established to improve cross-army command. Billotte was ordered to coordinate operationally, in addition to his First Army Group and the 7th Army, the Belgian Army and the BEF. The consequences of the Belgian retreat were evaluated and it was decided that the defence of the Dyle position would prevail. It should be borne in mind that the desired duration of the preliminary defence along the Meuse and facing Luxembourg had been calculated in advance to be at least four to five days, which Gamelin considered the minimum time necessary to be able to develop his troops fully behind the main defences. In reality this had become two days in most front sectors. (Frieser, p.166) *"Für einen feindlichen Vorstoss durch die Ardennen kalkulierte das französische Oberkommando mindestens fünf, wahrscheinlich aber neun Tage ein"* ('An enemy offensive through the Ardennes is reckoned by the French army staff to take at least five but probably even up to nine days'). The Germans appeared much faster than only after five days on the Gembloux plain ('Battle of Hannut') and the Meuse sector west of Luxembourg ('Battle for the Meuse at Dinant and Sedan').

353 The knowledge would be obtained at the GHQ at some point on 13 May. Presumably through the French attaché. Curiously, according to Gamelin, he and Winkelman must have had telephone conversations on 11 and 12 May, which have not made the Dutch archives but are marginally addressed in Gamelin's own memoirs 'Servir'. Although Gamelin may have logged the dates wrong, the reproduction of these conversations in his memoirs are interesting enough to share. Gamelin calls the Dutch Supreme Commander erroneously the Chief-of-Staff but referred to Winkelman. Translated the notes in *'Servir'* contain the following (Vol.1, pg.99, on 11 May): " *Given the situation, particularly that of the Belgians, General Giraud should not engage substantially beyond Breda, from where in any case he will be in position to aid the Dutch to retake the bridge at Moerdijk. . . . From a telephone conversation which I have just had with the Dutch chief of staff [sic] , what bothers them*

are the Germans landed in great numbers in the area of Delft heading toward the Hague. It seems to me that it is above all the British aviation which can aid them. I will look into this with the British and General Vuillemin." The first part of the message is reflected in an official instruction by Gamelin on the 11th. The second reference in '*Servir*' was (Vol.3, pg. 395, on 12 May):" *I was able to have two long telephone conversations with the Dutch chief of staff in command [sic], General Vinkelman [sic], emphasizing to him that there are no German forces in the essential region, that is inside the 'Holland' position, other than parachutists [sic]. His regular forces should be able to chase them away or even exterminate them."* There was no mention at all of the changed French strategy or operational plan for the Netherlands and, moreover, not of a promise of retaking Moerdijk – just that Giraud's forces once deployed at Breda would be in position 'to aid' the Dutch at Moerdijk. In other words, the Dutch would make the efforts, the French would aid if in position. A substantially different perspective from Gamelin than Winkelman would make believe the PEC after the war!

354 These were two B-type units, the 60th (Deslaurens) and 68th DI (Beaufrère). The first was under command of the 7th Army. The second was a unit constructed from reserves in January 1940 and belonged to the coastal protection force under French navy command. Of these French troops, approximately 150 would be killed on Dutch soil and approximately 2,000 would be captured by the Germans during their deployment in the Netherlands. General Deslaurens would himself be killed in action on 17 May 1940 at Vlissingen (Flushing). This happened while he personally led the rear-guard in Flushing to protect the retreat of the main force from the harbour. Remarkably enough, the Netherlands never felt the need to award any bravery medals to the French army, despite the fact that the French fought for three full days for West Brabant, Zuid-Beveland and especially Walcheren and made significant sacrifices. In 2012 the author sent a petition to the then Minister of Defence Drs. J.S.J. Hillen to correct this error by awarding a posthumous decoration to General Deslaurens. The request was declined by the Minister to the author in a letter on October 1st 2012 (ref BS2012031041) with the statement that in his opinion a few local monuments were already sufficient … The Dutch Navy was more courteous and would, immediately after the war, award about a dozen gallantry medals to French naval men for their maritime efforts in Zeeland waters in May 1940.

355 On 11 May reconnaissance units of the 6e *Regiment de Cuirassier* (6.RC; part of 1.DLM that was deployed near Turnhout and Goirle) east of Tilburg took some German prisoners. This occurred during a fight between a French recce platoon and a vanguard formation of 9.PD at a small bridge near Moergestel. The prisoners turned out to be from a *Panzer Division*. Also on 11 May, near the Belgian hamlet of Oerle – west of Tongeren – a battle took place between French scouts of 12.RC (part of 3.DLM) and some German tanks of 5./Pz.Rgt.35 (4.PD). Both incidents were unmis-

takable indications of advancing German tank units. In addition, French aerial reconnaissance revealed that the Germans were advancing. ('*l'Oeil de la 7e Armee - le Groupe de reconnaissance I/35 dans la campagne de l'Ouest 1939-1940*', Franck Poiré, 2013, pp. 32-34) Also the air reconnaissance unit of the 7th Army flew a number of individual reconnaissance sorties on 12 May, which included one sortie over Veere - Haamstede - Waalhaven - Dordrecht - Moerdijk - Breda - Woensdrecht and one over Antwerp and Breda – intended for Den Bosch but intercepted by a German Bf-109 and shot down near the border with Belgium. There was also a third sortie flown to Tilburg and finally a fourth to the Turnhout sector. All with French *Potez* 63/11 strategic scout-planes from St. Omer AFB. They collected many verticals (photos) of the areas mentioned according to the aforementioned French source.

356 PEC 1C, 15851. Winkelman claimed – and then suddenly allowed himself the hindsight he always blamed the PEC for – that the position would not last two days in an actual attack. Although in hindsight his reasoning seems very speculative; had the position been occupied as originally planned it might have been able to hold out for more than two days. The German 'flanking operation' at Weert (by a formation of the German 1st independent recce unit 1.AA) was only by light reconnaissance units which had no intention of encirclement but sought the path of least resistance to the west, and lacked the men and resources to sustain a breach. The Light Division could easily have blocked that unit. The attack on the Peel-Raam-line defences, the latter occupied by artillery-regiments and a more than three times larger force than it actually had on 10 May after the implementation of Winkelman's plan, should have been capable of holding off the German infantry divisions (254.ID and 256.ID - both *Vierte Welle* divisions) for several days. There is no reason to think that the Peel-Raam-line would have lasted less time than the concentrated attack on the Grebbe-line, where the defence had held out for three days. The reality was that the line did not fall until the night of 10 to 11 May near Mill. Had the position here been occupied by two artillery-supported regiments of infantry – as originally intended – instead of two battalions without proper fire support, the German attack might have been repulsed or the temporary breach sealed off. For now (after Winkelman's withdrawal) only the forward line (canal position) was occupied while the underlying front- and stop-line had been empty.

357 The French scouts of 6.RC reported in the afternoon of 11 May that the Dutch position at the Zuid-Willems canal (between Den Bosch and Weert) had been broken through and that a major chaotic retreat was underway.

358 The French Major Michon (6.RC – of 1.DLM, coming from Tilburg), who appeared on 11 May with a large reconnaissance unit at Terheijden, had no other assignment than to reconnoitre the status of the Meuse-bridges at Moerdijk and Keizersveer and to estimate the strength of the German bridgehead(s) in order to assess to what extent this could be dangerous

for the French development in the sector. While Michon was in the process of this reconnaissance by having a few armoured car patrols probe the sector – an activity that did not escape the German watchful eyes – suddenly a reconnaissance patrol from 25.DIM arrived to his rear. This was a formation from 5.GRDI, that held position west of Breda, and on its turn reconnoitred the bridges of Moerdijk and Keizersveer because the French liaison mission of General Mittelhauser wanted to proceed to the Hague. Only then the French officers decided on the spot that this was reason to see if the German bridgehead could be broken through. The attempt to do so was thwarted by bombers of the German KG.4. Bombs rained down on the sector chasing of the French and most of the Dutch formations. Mittelhauser had to look for alternatives and found those more to the west. He would finally reach the Hague via the islands of South Holland in the late morning of 14 May (only to have to flee again immediately when Winkelman announced the armistice). After this intended assault on the German para-troopers bridgehead the French would not approach Moerdijk again, nor would they issue any orders to do so.

359 As we've seen Giraud was instructed on 11 May " *De ne pas s'engager au-delà de Breda, d'où la VII Armée est d'ailleurs en état d'aider les Hollandais à reprendre le pont de Moerdijk, et de reprendre la liaison avec eux* ". This instruction – that had come from Gamelin himself ('*Servir'* Vol.1 p. 99) – clearly gave leeway to Giraud to judge the situation himself whether it was in the 7th Army's interest to assist the Dutch retake the Moerdijk Bridge. "*… where the 7th Army is in addition capable of assisting the Dutch to retake the bridge at Moerdijk …*". Giraud at that time most likely had already made up his mind and decided in the French interest. And from a French point of view, it was perfectly understandable not to intervene at Moerdijk at that point of the battle.

360 *Major* Ernst *Freiherr* von Lüttwitz (1898-1942) was the commander of I./Aufkl.*Rgt*.9. He went missing as an *Oberst* during the Soviet Union in 1942 not be recovered. Lüttwitz led the reinforced reconnaissance group of the northern attack group of the 9th *Panzer-Division* under *Oberst* Wilhelm von Apell. They crossed the border near the *Reichswald* early on the morning of 11 May and reached the outer limits of the Moerdijk airborne bridgehead as early as around 15:00 hrs on 12 May, finding an undestroyed secondary bridge near Oosterhout which he could utilize to get his heavier units cross the Mark-canal. Since the French and Dutch had no defence here, the Germans drove on to Moerdijk unchallenged. Around 18:30 in the evening an advance guard of this formation made contact with the German commander of the airborne operation, General Student, who attended a staff meeting of the German troops around Dordrecht. Student knew already beforehand from a radio message that the ground troops were in arrival.

361 The SS-V *Division* was led by the outstanding former army General Paul Hausser. It had three motorised regiments with independent operational

capabilities – the *SS-Standarten 'Der Führer', 'Germania'* and *'Deutschland'*. It included the SS-Artillery Regiment, the SS-Pioneer Battalion and the SS-AA with about 20 armoured vehicles and divisional units. SS *Der Führer* was seconded with one SS-*Artillerie Abteilung* to 10.AC (central front, opposing the Ijssel-line and Grebbe-line) and another SS-*Artillerie Abteilung* was attached to LSSAH Adolf Hitler, also part of 10.AC up to 12 May.

362   General Student had incidental radio contact with units of 26.AC that crossed Brabant. As early as 12 May, a signals-unit of 26.AC near Tilburg managed to establish a permanent long-wave connection with Student. Before that, it was incidental reports. In the morning of 12 May, it was reported that the front units were only a short distance away from Moerdijk. This was the reason for Student to deploy his last reserves and to ensure that from Dordrecht no further threat to the corridor could occur.

363   There was a very good opportunity for Student to eavesdrop on Dutch telephone and radio traffic. There were some interpreters in Student's staff and the corridor occupied by his troops contained the main route of Dutch PTT-connections (PTT was the Dutch agency for '*Post Telegraaf Telefoon*' - or in English - Mail Telegraph Telephone) as well as the connection with England across Zeeland. This route ran along the bridges and was easy to tap. There is no evidence of German wiretapping, nor does it appear from German actions that they were fully aware of the Dutch operation plan, but the possibility cannot be excluded.

364   The Dutch Captain observed units of Colonel De Beauchesne's reconnaissance group and 25.DIM. The former had *Panhard* armoured cars and motorised anti-tank guns, the latter had heavy artillery drawn by half-trucks what would be labelled as mechanized units.

365   Here the term 'train' does not refer to a train running on a railway track but to the contemporary term for a larger column of troops, in this case of mechanized and/or armoured vehicles.

366   There were continuous messages circulating within the Fortress and the Field Army as well as in Brabant from higher commanders that French help was on the way. C-VH and CV were both guilty of feeding this. The fact that the often announced French never appeared led to great frustration. This was a cheap, short term morale booster with a quick and severe cold turkey effect.

367   PEC 2C, 7405 (Minister Dijxhoorn). "*Sunday afternoon the commander in chief (...) came to report. (...) The Germans had advanced through Noord-Brabant and one column moved along the Langstraat. The bridge at Moerdijk was still in enemy hands (...) and the French did not want to comply with the request to recapture this bridge by an attack.* Sunday was 12 May 1940. The quote is from April 1948 and seems (at least to some extent) tainted by hindsight. The 'Langstraat' referred to the area Den Bosch - Waalwijk - Geertruidenberg. One has to consider that during the May Days and after the departure of 6.GB from the sector Moerdijk (11 May), the area north

of the Wilhelmina canal and Mark canal remained completely undefended. The GHQ had no knowledge of this but for a long time it also did not actively search for information from this sector. They counted on French resistance there.

368   NIMH 409-488036, report by Captain J.C.A. Isaäcs (Commander MC-I-39.RI).
369   During the engagements south of Dordrecht and in the city itself, the rumours that French tanks were advancing towards Dordrecht (which were explicitly reported to subordinate commanders by the C-VH himself – the commander of Group Kil, the aids to the regional commander of Dordrecht Lt.-Col. Mussert and the staff of the Light Division all testify to this), led to several incidents with casualties because Dutch soldiers mistook German armour for French.
370   The German Airborne Division was originally the 22nd *Infanterie Division*, from the *Wehrkreis (military district)* Bremen. It was also called the '*Bremen Division*'. It was occupied by many locals and therefore Radio Bremen reported on the arrival of the relief force at Moerdijk.
371   NIMH 409-479004. Lt-Col. Thomson's report, also PEC 2C, 7405. Dijxhoorn states that he had lengthy telephone contact via the now London-based Foreign Minister in the afternoon of 12 May (approx. 16:00).
372   The *Fokker* T-V was an example of the failure of military procurement by the armed forces itself, as well as a minister (Colijn, 1936), who blocked procurement of a ready German bomb-rack system (*Heber*) in favour of a yet-to-be-designed indigenous system. The T-V was a capable aircraft, not inferior to its British contemporaries. There had been a lot of fiddling with the bomb release system, which Colijn had insisted on having made in the Netherlands by the Dutch firm J.B. Van Heijst, and the Ministry of Defence had set unprecedented requirements for the type of bombs it had to be able to deliver (8, 25, 50, 100, 200 and 300 kg). Van Heijst proved unable to meet these requirements. Consequently, besides the two *Heber* racks that were available in May 1940 (which enabled the T-V to deliver up to 4 x 300 kg bombs) all other T-Vs had old racks intended for auxiliary bombers (civil KLM aircraft types F.VIIa, F.IX and F.XII). These could carry only a 400 kg mix of smaller bombs or 2 x 300 kg bombs. See also: '*Fokker T-V luchtkruiser*', by F. Gerdessen et al, 2009; also '*Illusies en Incidenten*, R. Bruin et al, 1988.
373   The *Fokker* T-V no. 856 escorted by two *Fokker* G-1 twin-engine fighters. Only one of the G-1's survived this mission. The other two aircraft were intercepted on the way back and shot down with all occupants KIA.
374   An para-trooper battle report by *Leutnant* C. Tietjen (7./FJR.1), the 'Pioneer Officer' who carried this out with a few men, indicates that all charges were removed on 10 and 11 May.
375   The RAF followed up many requests for air support in Holland and also initiated many recce sweeps along the coastal region. Particularly, they fol-

lowed up on strategic interest, such as airfields that fell into German hands which obviously threatened Britain too. Also strategic objects in Flushing, Rotterdam-Pernis, Hook of Holland, Ymuiden and Amsterdam were visited by demolition commando's (see also "*XD Operations - Secret British missions denying oil to the Nazis*", C.C.H. Brazier, 2004, pg. 14 ff). BAFF flights along the river Meuse were carried out on a number of occasions and the road Tilburg-Breda was attacked by the RAF, as well as many railway-stations in that sector, particularly after the Dutch capitulation though. The RAF did pay attention to strategic targets. It is therefore remarkable that the Moerdijk bridges were not counted among these targets, so that it is tempting to think that the lack of British help in this respect was a deliberate omission. However, as yet, there is no evidence of this.

376 There was an aligned air force command (British Air Forces in France, or BAFF, in France with the *l'Armee de l'Air),* in part a purely British command for all maritime and strategic elements. It mostly consisted of light assault and recce squadrons as well as *Hurricane* fighter squadrons. RAF Air Marshal Sir Arthur Barratt was Commander-in-Chief of BAFF and coordinated with the French Air Force and Georges' Headquarters. Thus operations of the BAFF were coordinated with the French, but those of the RAF usually were not. (See also "*Divided and Conquered*", pg 112, J.A. Gunsburg). The bulk of the RAF including all its modern formations and strategic forces remained based in Britain as part of homeland defence and strategic missions on the continent serving the former purpose.

377 It was remarkable that the French did not use the very capable 1.DLM – which on paper was considerably stronger than the 9th *Panzer-Division* – to attack the Germans in the flank in the Netherlands, especially when on 12 and 13 May heavy fighting occurred between Eindhoven and Turnhout. Here the fear of confrontation and the obvious losses came into play, while the chosen alternative – the retreat to the south – brought much greater losses, without much harm to the enemy. The DLMs (each of which included about 80-90 *Somua* S-35 medium battle tanks and about 80-90 *Hotchkiss* H-35/H-39 infantry tanks) were pre-eminently divisions intended for manoeuvring and counterattack but were seriously misused in poorly fought defensive battles within the French strategy.

378 PEC 2C, 7405.

379 PEC 2C, 7405.

380 With exception of the time needed to get the allied formations into their anticipated positions in Belgium and the Netherlands, which Gamelin considered very time-critical, he had constantly been under the impression that time was in his favour and things would progress gradually. His assessments and anticipation of German progress proved wrong on very crucial points, most profoundly in relation to the Ardennes. See also Frieser (p. 167) on the Prételat prediction that it could take only 60 hours to reach the Meuse at Sedan, which was mocked by Gamelin by saying that this prediction

was "*jouer le pire*" ("sounding apocalyptic"). Many older senior officers – including the Dutch – failed to adapt to modern times where manoeuvres developed very fast and the third dimension mattered significantly.

381 Maxime Weygand (1867-1965), already 73 years old in May 1940. He was an orphan from Brussels, who later took the name Weygand. He moved to France as a young child and raised as a Frenchman and had a flourishing military career during the First World War, largely under the wings of General Ferdinand Foch. In the final phase, Weygand was appointed to the Supreme War Council as the French representative. During the interwar period, Weygand was one of the prominent Generals in the French army and retired in 1935. In 1939 he was reactivated and appointed commander in the Levant (a post in which he would be succeeded by Mittelhauser after the latter had returned to France after fleeing from Holland). Weygand had already been recalled to France before Gamelin was actually dismissed on 19 May to succeed him directly. The general could no longer turn the tide and was to join Pétain's Vichy government after the armistice, as Minister of Defence. When Weygand did not accept full cooperation with Germany in 1942, he was interned in Germany.

382 PEC 2A/B, pp. 89-91, 97 et seq. Remarkably enough, these coordination processes required the personal input of the OLZ, often accompanied by the Chief-of-Staff. Those who analyse the interactions of the sheltering Cabinet with the OLZ will be surprised that the Supreme Commander of the Dutch armed forces took so much time to report to the Cabinet at its safe shelter – away from the GHQ. It calls into question the time management and priority setting of the OLZ. The Minister of Foreign Affairs E.N. van Kleffens and the Minister of Colonies C.J.I.M. Welter were already in London. Van Kleffens would work during the May Days for British support from the only just appointed Prime Minister Churchill. The only thing that came from this was a fighting unit of reservists consisting of *Welsh* and *Irish Guards* (under Lt. Col. Haydon), protected by about 200 British marines (of which about half were in fact non-combatants). They arrived on 12 May and were intended solely to get British civilians to the Hook of Holland under protection, and possibly to support them by helping control order in the Hague. The latter was not carried out. The British remained in the Hook and nearby 's Gravenzande and did not move. They would suffer 11 fatalities from German bombing and left Dutch soil in a hurry on 14 May, leaving behind almost everything they had brought with them.

383 She left on board of the Royal Navy destroyer HMS Hereward. For a while it was planned to go ashore again in Dutch Flanders (the port of Breskens), but in the end it was considered too dangerous there and so the ship set sail for England where at about 17:30 hrs it moored at Parkeston Quay in Harwich. Also on board were the personal entourage of the sovereign as well as three GS-III officers, Major Van de Plassche and the Captains Olifiers and Schoonenberg. They were on the German list of wanted persons that

was intercepted in the Adelheidsstraat when it was recovered in the crashed Ju-52 on the first day of the invasion. Queen Wilhelmina travelled on by special train to Liverpool Street Station in London where she was received by the British monarch. Her daughter (crown-princess) Juliana with Prince Bernhard, who had left the Netherlands the day before from Ymuiden seaport, were also there to meet her.

384 PEC 2A/B, 105.

385 Interestingly enough, the Germans themselves did not yet realise this and did not do so until around 20:00 in the evening. They had already decisively pushed through the stop-line but were repelled by the last Dutch defences along the railway embankment in Rhenen around noon. A tactical retreat by the attackers was ordered in anticipation of Ju-87 *Stuka* support, that came early in the afternoon. Later Dutch infantry presence in Rhenen was so deceptive that the Germans only discovered the line being deserted by sun set.

386 This counter-attack, to be carried out by four reserve battalions, was poorly designed and executed. It was carried out with troops that had been displacing for days before, who did not know the terrain and had no military maps of the operational theatre, who were squeezed into an open plain which made them visible and vulnerable to German observers (and therefore artillery and air power) and, moreover, had no coordinated fire support. The Dutch field regulations were peacetime manuals. Artillery was only allowed to give fire support with unreal margins of security, and artillery fire shortly before the advancing infantry (the so-called creeping barrage) was unacceptable. There was no 'danger close' procedure and field commanders were very reluctant to bend the rules and risk close support fire over the alternative of being overrun. All this while the Dutch artillery was technically possibly the best service branch, together with the engineers. These limitations led to two Dutch battalions advancing into the open plain north of the Grebbeberg without artillery support, without a smoke screen to at least temporarily hide them from view and without the front on their right flank (the Grebbeberg itself, up to the stop-line halfway the elevation, had fallen in the early morning) being in friendly hands. It was a recipe for ignominious loss, but it typified the Dutch Field Army which was not able to design offensive actions.

387 This observation deserves one nuance. The German air force lacked the quantity to be omnipresent in the Netherlands. The focal points were elsewhere and where they were within the Netherlands, it was over the southern front of the Fortress where KG.4 and other formations were active. For the battle on the airborne corridor, some tactical support was also available and fighter cover was relatively good. For the battle north of the Rhine river and to the east of the airborne sector, no *Luftwaffe* tactical support unit was available and even fighter-cover was often absent. This was also the reason that the Dutch air force itself had almost free play in this theatre on 12 and

13 May and could fly a relatively large number of sorties. If there would have been good *Luftwaffe coverage*, it would have been more likely that losses would have been taken by the retreating units, especially those of the 4th Division, which moved westward in large numbers by daylight (and were recognized as such by German reconnaissance planes).

388 The 227th *Infanterie Division* operated with little distinction in Holland. Not only did *Generalleutnant* Friedrich Zickwolff have by far the slowest movements of May 1940 to his credit, but his (first) attack on the Grebbe-line near Scherpenzeel on 13 May was a tactical failure. He directed his attack exactly into a rectangular corner of the Dutch defensive position, so that his most forward regiment was exposed not only in front but also on the left flank to fire of Dutch weapons. Moreover, here the cooperation of the Dutch infantry and artillery was excellent and on the German side very poor. The attack was repulsed with considerable German losses. During the night of 13/14 May, diversionary artillery fire from a few straggling batteries was enough to hold this German division in place. Zickwolff failed to send out probing patrols so he fell into the deception. More remarkable was the fact that 207.ID detected the evacuation of the Grebbe-line on 13 May at 20.00 hours and shortly afterwards began the pursuit. Because 227.ID, under command of the same 10.AC, heard nothing of this breakthrough, it did not move west until the morning of 14 May. The cross-unit communication of these German units was very weak, although one must not exclude the possibility that German high ranking officers competed with each other and preferred to take opportunities themselves rather than to give them to the adjacent unit. This is a well-known disadvantage of the "*Auftragstaktik*".

389 SS Regiment "*Der Führer*" had been taking the lead from the very first moment of the invasion. It had first forced a costly crossing of the Yssel river east of Arnhem (at Westervoort) and was subsequently used as an assault troop element ahead of the 207.ID to which it was attached to overrun the Dutch forward positions of the Grebbe-line, east of Rhenen, along the Rhine river. During the three-days' battle of the Grebbeberg this SS-regiment suffered heavy losses. Its third battalion as a unit was as good as wiped out. Of this, about one and a half companies remained and the battalion commander was seriously wounded. Other battalions also suffered considerable losses so that their fighting power was also affected. Moreover, the regiment had been in combat from the first hour. It had four days of fierce fighting behind it when the Grebbe-line was broken through.

390 Colonel of the Marines (and Commander of the Marine Corps) Von Frytag Drabbe was the Commander of Maritime Resources (all navy and naval forces) in Rotterdam. He commanded the naval resources in the port but also the depot of marine troops and the Marines, the latter at that time being the only professional corps of soldiers of the entire Dutch military beside the small corps of Police Troops. He was not under the army Staff

and not under the Cantonment Commander (Commander of all garrisoned troops in Rotterdam), a matter which the Cantonment Commander, Colonel P.W. Scharroo, had already reported before the war to the C-VH as an objection. Without success. During the May Days there appeared to be little coordination between the two Colonels and their respective staffs. The poorly prepared marines assault on the Willemsbrug on 13 May – celebrated by the Marine Corps to this day as a great saga (which it was in terms of bravery) – became a tactical fiasco because of it. Despite four days of fighting at the same point and attempts by the land forces to get the Germans out of the tall Bank office-building on the Boompjes (north side of the traffic bridge), they had not succeeded. However, the naval depot troops and marines, who launched an autonomous attack on 13 May to retake the Willemsbrug, had remained unaware of the German presence in that very building and ... found them suddenly in flank and rear as the attack progressed near the bridge. This would stall the attack and demand considerable casualties among the marines. Von Frytag Drabbe would write pejorative reports about his army colleague Colonel Scharroo and be responsible for his tarnished reputation. Moreover, a huge myth would be built around the marines who – as it were – would have saved Rotterdam. This myth only seems to be gaining momentum these days. The reality is that a few dozen marines in the first hours of the invasion, together with engineers, depot troops and the garrison battalion, managed to turn the German expansion north of the bridges and pushed them back into a very small perimeter. Afterwards, battles were fought along the Nieuwe Maas river which on 10 May saw quite a lot of action from again a few dozen marines, but the contribution of engineers and other army units was at least as great. The previously described action of 13 May was a naval affair, courageous, but tactically poorly prepared and executed and above all uncoordinated. For courage and fearlessness the marines of those days deserve respect, but their role was more modest than was remembered then and especially now.

391 Nevertheless, the army decided not to evacuate the civilian population from the inner city. They learned from that decision in Middelburg (capital of the Zeeland province), that would come under siege of German forces and was evacuated in time, and as a result there were hardly any casualties on 16 and 17 May despite French and German shelling of the town causing massive fires and much destruction.

392 The deployment of a fleet of surface bombers to destroy a large part of a city can hardly be called tactical, and certainly not when it is accompanied by the threat of total destruction of the same city and thus a decisive breakthrough of a front. It is therefore a complete mystery to the author of this book how even nowadays some military historians show so little insight that they still call the German bombardment of Rotterdam tactical, or dare not call it strategic. The presumed direct connection with Hitler's directive to rapidly end Dutch resistance makes it even more piquant that this act

393   was strategic. This is more than simply military semantics, but further elaboration is beyond the scope of this book.

393   Rotterdam is often referred to, nationally and internationally, as an act of terror bombing. The question is whether this is a correct title, especially since Rotterdam was a defended city that had been bitterly fought for during the five previous days. The allies would give the phenomenon of terror bombing a new momentum with the destruction of German and Japanese cities as a result and ending with the climax of the two atomic bombs on Japan. During the Normandy campaign, the allies used total destruction of cities as a systematic means. No historian would describe the destruction of cities such as St Lo, Caen or Falaise as terror-bombing, but they were, at least if one wants to refer to Rotterdam (which 'only' had to cope with 60 tonnes of explosive-bombs) as such.

394   No *Luftwaffe* unit was available for this attack. The only unit that was available, KG.54, was re-equipped for a second attack on Rotterdam after it returned to its airfields after the first attack on Rotterdam on 14 May. That second attack was launched and called off over the Betuwe (the region between the rivers Waal and Rhine) after a message had been received this time that the city had capitulated. It is almost certain that the threat to bomb Utrecht was a pure bluff. Other Dutch commanders also regularly received similar threats without it actually being an issue. In Willemstad, Flushing and at the Bathstelling and at various other locations, Dutch reports testify to similar threats.

395   Frieser, p. 108.

396   Remarkably enough, as discussed earlier, General Reijnders also held this opinion in 1935, when he referred in a memorandum to the then Minister of Defence Deckers to the possibility that perhaps in time, even a Franco-Belgian alliance could not offer sufficient counterweight to a powerful German military force.

397   Neutralism; a fundamentally neutral foreign policy, which in practice severely limits all the nuances that one might make of a neutral stance (such as anticipating 'if-then scenarios') and blindly and stoically carried through, making a pretence of ignoring all circumstances and developments.